# THE FAIRYTALE AS ART FORM AND PORTRAIT OF MAN

# THE
# FAIRYTALE
# AS ART FORM AND
# PORTRAIT OF MAN

## *Max Lüthi*

### TRANSLATED BY JON ERICKSON

INDIANA UNIVERSITY PRESS

*Bloomington*

The English language edition of this book was
made possible, in part, by a translation
subsidy from INTER NATIONES.

Translated from *Das Volksmärchen als Dichtung: Ästhetik und Anthropologie*
Copyright © 1975 by Eugen Diederichs Verlag
Copyright © 1984 by Indiana University Press

Manufactured in the United States of America

**Library of Congress Cataloging in Publication Data**

Lüthi, Max, 1909–
    The fairytale as art form and portrait of man.

    Translation of: Das Volksmärchen als Dichtung.
    Includes bibliographical references and index.
    1. Fairy tales—History and criticism.    I. Title.
PN3437.L79813  1984        398.2        83-48897
ISBN 0-253-32099-2
  1   2   3   4   5   88   87   86   85   84

# CONTENTS

# TRANSLATOR'S PREFACE

In making the present translation of Max Lüthi's *Das Volksmärchen als Dichtung: Ästhetik und Anthropologie* (Düsseldorf/Cologne, 1975), I have attempted so far as possible to approximate the style of the German original in the English. Where well-established English equivalents of the German technical terms exist, I have tried to make use of them. Against the advice of professional folklorists, however, I have translated the most significant term, the German *(Volks)märchen*, simply as "fairytale." Since the book can be read profitably and with enjoyment not only by the folklorist but also by the interested nonprofessional reader who has been brought up on such works as the Grimms' Fairytales, it seemed sensible to use the term current in general usage. Two other important terms, *Zaubermärchen* and *Sage*, have been translated as "fairytale of magic" and "local legend" respectively. Since these translations have been used with complete consistency, the reader who prefers other terms, e.g., *folktale, magic tale,* and *wandering legend* in the three instances, can feel free to make the corresponding substitutions. In the case of most technical vocabulary, the German has been supplied in parentheses the first time it appears in the discussion, so that the reader familiar with the German terminology can see how it has been rendered. Citations have been given in German with the English following in the case of short texts or examples in nonstandard German, where the point being made can best be seen in the original, and where short quotations appear from standard literary or philosophical works. Occasionally, a key German word or phrase has been supplied in parentheses where I felt it might be of interest to the reader.

A few minor additions and alterations have been made by the author where he felt they would be useful in the translation. The apparatus has also been adapted for the English reader. In some cases more extensive bibliographical information has been supplied. Works originally published in English have been so cited; and insofar as they were known and available to me, I have cited the English translations of scholarly works. No attempt, however, has been made to provide references to English translations of German literary and philosophical works that appear in the notes, since this would only have increased the length of the notes, and to no very obvious purpose. The glossary has been reworked to provide the English reader with an overview of names and terms used in the discussion, and the index of tale types and tales has been added on the model of Lüthi 1982. The above alterations were made with the author's cooperation and consent, and the last two paragraphs of the introduction have been modified to reflect them.

The translation could scarcely have been completed without the active and dedicated help of my two assistants at the University of Cologne, Gabriele Ammann-Voss and Andrea Grote. Mrs. Ammann-Voss read through and made corrections to the original draft of the translation, and Miss Grote spent countless hours working on the apparatus and crosschecking references for me. Dr. George Heffernan provided advice on the translation of philosophical terms, and Dr. Gottfried Krieger offered invaluable assistance in finding suitable translations for several difficult passages in the German. Various parts and versions of the manuscript were typed by Mrs. Ammann-Voss, Miss Gudrun Anhuth, and Mrs. Veronika Türcke. To each I owe my thanks. My special thanks go as well to the author, Max Lüthi, who originally encouraged me to make the translation and who, despite the burdens of a heavy schedule and serious illness, never lost interest in the project and managed to work through the whole manuscript and make innumerable corrections in both interpretation and style. These were always made with sensitivity, patience, and enormous tact, and they have contributed substantially to whatever accuracy and readability the final translation may lay claim to.

Much-Oberbruchhausen
Summer 1983

# INTRODUCTION

In the present book we will examine the traditional fairytale from two related points of view, from the point of view of *esthetics* and from that of *anthropology*. Esthetics is in the more limited sense the study of beauty, but in the broader sense it is also the study of the means of artistic expression and of the effects produced by art. Anthropology is the study of the nature of man. We will be concerned both with the fairytale as art form and with the question of whether the fairytale projects a particular image of man and his world.

Anyone who speaks of the special artistic character of the fairytale—of its style and construction—and of the portrait of man it projects cannot fail to have noted that various tellers show a certain uniformity in the way they construct their stories, that orally transmitted narratives tend to be similar to one another. They are similar in the way they are told, and they are also similar in the way their plots unfold. And while each story appears to offer its own version of the portrait of man, one is still left with the impression that the fairytale as a genre offers its hearers a representation of man which transcends the individual story, one which reappears time and again in countless narratives.

And anyone interested in the fairytale as art form is not in the first instance concerned with whether the sequence of events narrated reflects real social or—just as real—intrapsychological happenings, whether the narrative encourages revolutionary or conservative thinking, or with the role that the narratives have played and still play in society and in the individual groups of society—in the family, for example, in the kindergarten or the schools, on radio and television or in books, with respect to adults or to children. But he—and that means the writer of the present book and those who are willing to read it—is first and also last interested in the narratives themselves, not in their cultural or economic background, not in the historical circumstances out of which they developed, not in their circumstances of delivery, the "performance," their immediate narrative and broader cultural contexts, but in the fairytales themselves, stories which for hundreds and perhaps thousands of years have produced their own fascination. Fairytales have been told time and again not because they are so easy to tell, but because they have provided pleasure. An esthetics of the fairytale must be concerned with reasons why these narratives have been and still are a source of pleasure. But literature is more than just pleasing form. It presents scenes and suggests with them a particular way of looking at the world and at human existence. Thus in the present study we will explore not only the artistic qualities of the fairytale but also the portrait of man which it projects.

We will be concerned with the fairytale as traditional folktale. The designation "folktale" encompasses only such narratives as have over a period of time passed from teller to teller. When there are many and diverse renditions of a given story, we can be sure that it has been transmitted orally and, in the process, changed. The subject of variants offers an exciting field of study. One sees the most various possibilities materialize in the development of a narrative kernel; one can pursue the "adventure of narration"—the groping toward ideal and alternative forms, the development of latent narrative possibilities, the discovery of new narrative goals. The index provides relevant references to some of these phenomena under the key words *end form, teleology,* and *self-generation.*

The originality and representational talent of particular narrators stand in contrast to the sterility and failure of others. "Fairytales" *(Volksmärchen),* told for hundreds of years to gatherings of adult listeners, were not created by the "folk." It is possible to demonstrate influences on them from written literature. Nonetheless, they are properly called "folktales" because they have been modified by popular tellers, at times becoming shredded in the telling, spoiled, but at times being told better, polished, and further developed—by laymen and for laymen. The circle of listeners has played a role in the retention and shaping of these stories; narrators have always taken into consideration the needs and wishes, the inclinations and dislikes of their public. Petr Bogatyrew and Roman Jakobson, in their now-famous discussion of 1929, have rightly called attention to the forceful "correcting influence of the group" *(Präventivzensur der Gemeinschaft).*[1] Fairytales were—and partially still are—at home among the people, earlier among grownups, today among children, the latter still exercising a sort of correcting influence, which the adult teller does and must take into consideration.

The book will concentrate on the "fairytale proper," the fairytale of magic *(Zaubermärchen),* primarily of the European variety. But oriental tales will also be discussed, and other genres of the fairytale—e.g., the farce fairytale *(Schwankmärchen),* the novella fairytale *(Novellenmärchen),* and the religious fairytale *(Legendenmärchen)*—will be brought in. It will be important for us to maintain constant contact with the texts. We will primarily take into consideration faithfully recorded and faithfully reproduced narratives, on the one hand, since they show us especially clearly the features of stories shaped by oral transmission, and the Grimms' tales, on the other, since they are best known and one need only refer to them. Despite the fact that the Grimms' tales combine different versions of a single story in one, and despite the narrative embroidery which the Brothers Grimm allowed themselves in editing the stories, the collection offers in general a good selection of the various types of fairytale. And if we begin our discussion with an investigation of the role of the beautiful in the fairytale, it is because beauty has always been the subject of esthetics in the narrower sense and because its imprint on the fairytale of magic has been much greater than on other genres of folk literature. We will begin by examining—in much greater detail than in later chapters—one specific example, a story from French Canada, which was taken down verbatim. Using this story, we can illustrate general characteristics of the fairytale.

In previous publications I have examined extensively the basic style of the fairytale.[2] In what follows we will go only briefly into these basic stylistic characteristics and into the general structural principles worked out by Vladimir Propp.[3] Our discussion will center on those important and typical special features which are indicated in the table of contents and in the index. Such things as are obvious to every fairytale reader, like rhythm and play on sound, or humor and wit, will be mentioned only in passing. Our attention will be reserved for those features which are not at first obvious—for artistic economy; for the special forms of irony which are not immediately apparent on the surface but which emerge from an examination of the underlying structure; for the relationship between coordination and subordination, as, for example, that found where realistic elements have been slipped in amid the nonreal, the imperfect amid the perfect, or where polarity appears within patterns of three; and for the ways figures operate, as manipulators and scene managers or as unsuccessful imitators. Throughout the discussion, directly or indirectly, both the esthetic and the anthropological will be taken into consideration, the artistry of the genre and its anthropological message. Many narrative techniques lead in and of themselves to an artistic effect and at the same time are instrumental in calling forth a particular portrait of man.

Since they mainly contain only information about text sources and bibliographic references, the notes have been placed at the end of the book. It is intended that they should not distract the reader. When a note offers important supplementary information, however, its number is followed by an asterisk (*). There is also a short glossary of names and technical vocabulary used in the discussion.

The key words listed in the index have been chosen on the basis of the importance which individual notions and phenomena have in the book. Common items which appear time and again, like magic, fairytale, fairytale hero(ine), witch, motif, style, etc., have not been included. A separate index of tale types and of the individual Grimms' tales supplements the main index. Those key words which have particular significance in the book have been printed in italics in the index. In this way, the index supplements the table of contents and the glossary in making clear what the book is concerned with and where its priorities have been placed.

# THE FAIRYTALE
# AS ART FORM AND
# PORTRAIT OF MAN

# 1

## Beauty and Its Shock Effect

In an investigation of ten randomly selected French versions of the story of Cinderella, it was discovered that the little words *beau* and *belle* "beautiful" appear in each; *bon* "good," on the other hand, appears only in two.[4] Well-known titles of French fairytales suggest that such a preference for the esthetic might be a peculiarity of the French: "La Belle au bois dormant" [Sleeping beauty], *"La Belle et la bête"* [Beauty and the beast] *(animal bridegroom)*. Anyone turning to Italian fairytales, however, would soon come upon such expressions as *una bella ragazza* "a beautiful girl." And if a special "sense of beauty" *(Schönschau)* has been attributed to the ancient Greeks, one is easily able to find it as well in the Greek fairytales collected in the nineteenth and twentieth centuries. It could be that the French and the Greeks have a special talent for seeing beauty and casting it in relief, but receptivity to the beautiful, a tendency to see and evaluate on the basis of esthetic considerations, is a general characteristic of the fairytale. It seems therefore sensible—and especially in our age of "the separation of art and beauty" *(die nicht mehr schönen Künste)*—to begin the present book with an investigation of the role played by the beautiful in the fairytale.

### FIGURES

When one speaks of the sense of beauty of the ancient Greeks, one thinks primarily of the humanization of the gods, of the portrayal of the gods in human form, in a form whose lines were felt to be beautiful. Likewise, in the fairytale it is primarily figures with human form that receive the designation "beautiful." That both the European and the oriental fairytale happily reach for cosmic metaphors to designate human beauty, that a comparison with the sun or the moon, with gold or with silver, should be used to make clear the beauty of a person, not only demonstrates the

1

status and also something of the character of such beauty, it demonstrates in addition specific basic tendencies of the fairytale: its universalism, its propensity for antipodean values and extremes, for the bringing together of the human and the otherworldly.

We begin with an example in order to show the form beauty tends to take in the fairytale and what effects emanate from it. An example of the *Our Lady's child* type told in Canada in 1954, "Le Beau Magicien d'Afrique" [The handsome sorcerer from Africa],[5] has the words *beau* and *belle* running through it like a leitmotif. The only daughter of a certain widow is so beautiful that the mother gives her the name La Belle. When the seven-year-old child is in the king's forest collecting wood and is stumbled upon by some foresters, they address the child, whom they do not know, immediately as La Belle. "Hey, how come you call me La Belle?" "You're so beautiful that we couldn't call you anything other than La Belle." "But that's really my name—La Belle." Later the foresters ask about her mother: "Is she as beautiful as you?" "She is beautiful, but she is not as beautiful as I am." Then, when the girl lands in the house of a magician she does not know, a variation on this routine occurs: "Bonjour, La Belle." "How come you know my name?" "Oh, I've known your name for a long time. . . . I'm the handsome magician from Africa. I know everything that happens in the world." She remains in the service of the beau magicien d'Afrique for three years, and one evening he gives her a pair of golden shoes. Again after a period of years, when she is put on as kitchenmaid in the royal castle, the other girls find her so beautiful that they immediately stop their work. They have to keep looking at her, and thus the beautiful girl must also take care of the work of the others in addition to her own. One day when the prince happens to come down to the kitchen and gets a look at the beautiful girl, he stops in the middle of the staircase as if his shoes were nailed down. "He found her unbelievably beautiful; he stared at her. He could neither go back up nor continue descending." Finally, however, he does turn around and goes straight to his mother. "You have to know, the girl that you've just taken on—she'll be my wife." "Your wife!" "Yes." "You can't marry someone like that." "She's beautiful." "She is beautiful, but that's all she has—beauty. . . ." "I'll send her to school, I'll have her taught. . . ." And it goes according to the wishes of the son. Soon, as happens in so many fairytales, while he is away at the wars, his young wife bears him a handsome son ("un beau garçon"). But the magician comes and takes him away from her: "He is beautiful, La Belle, but not as beautiful as you. You must let me have him." The same thing occurs after the birth of the second son. The beautiful girl falls under suspicion of having eaten her children, and she is set adrift in a shiplike box, which her husband "has had made as beautiful as only he could do." Later, having been rescued—and disguised as a boy— she comes back to the royal city and becomes a clerk in a shop. The shop is quickly half sold out, since people come "solely to look at the clerk, so beautiful was he." The king's daughter seeks to seduce the supposed young man, but to no avail. So "he" is fastened down to an iron table and is to be hanged. The magician then returns. "Beautiful as the day," he says, as he looks upon her face ("belle comme le jour"). She now gets her sons back; the one is twenty, the other twenty-two years old, "the best looking boys anyone had ever seen" ("les plus jolis jeunes hommes qu'i'aviont pas vus"). That the mother in the meantime has grown older is not mentioned; it has had no adverse effect on her beauty. Fairytale figures do not grow old.

The word *beautiful* thus occurs time and again in various forms (*beau, belle, joli*), but the actual form the beauty takes, whether it is the beauty of the princess, her mother, her sons, or even the ship in which she is locked up, is not made explicit. The beauty is *abstract*. The listener must fall back on his own imagination; he can and must color in the outline to suit himself. "Beautiful as the day" is a conventional if also clearly meaningful formula; one finds it in fairytales of the most diverse regions of the francophone area. About the particular sort of beauty of the princess, it says nothing, and it should say nothing. For it is not a question of individual nuance; it is a question of *beauty*. But one thing is clear from the comparison with the day, just as in the case of a comparison with the sun or with gold: It is a radiant beauty.

The intensity of the beauty is shown still more strongly by its *effect* than by the comparisons, whether with the day, the less-beautiful mother, or the less-beautiful children. As soon as the mother instinctively names the child La Belle, when strangers naturally address her with this name although they do not know her, the listener or reader, it is true, is not told about the type of beauty involved, but he is about its degree. That the other kitchenmaids drop their work in order just to stare at her and that it is obvious to the girl so stared at that she must now do the work of those she has enchanted, points up the radiant power of this beauty the more clearly. And that the prince, when he sees the beautiful girl, is frozen in his tracks must be called a sort of shock effect. Similar things can also happen in non-European fairytales: "Prince Yangnyung stood motionless for a long time."[6] We will get to know still more pronounced forms of this shock effect of beauty in the fairytale.

Lessing observed in Homer and in other great epic poets that they do not describe beauty but rather indicate its effect, and he recommends this procedure to the epic poet in general. The fairytale observes Lessing's rule without knowing it. It describes not beauty but its effect, and in accord with its characteristic inclination to the extreme, represents this effect as a sort of magic. That the fairytale does not go into the special nature of the beauty intended in each case is, of course, not just because the epic, for various reasons, tends to be sparing with description. An individualization of the beauty observed would not be suitable for the fairytale, which aims for universal validity and the essence, not the particulars, of phenomena. The word *beautiful* is enough. When it wants to go further, it reaches for timeless values that are recognized worldwide: The princess is as beautiful as the day, the shoes are golden. The connection of gold with the sun and the symbolic worth of such a connection are well known.

It is noteworthy, and not really out of the ordinary, that the beauty of the heroine here, just as in the Grimms' "Snow White and the Seven Dwarfs," stands without having ugliness as a foil. Instead of an ugly stepsister, she has a beautiful mother—intensification instead of contrast also being a means of emphasizing the perfection of her beauty. Ugliness enters into the French Canadian story, though without really having the effect of a foil, at best in the magician's actions, which are observed by the girl, although she is forbidden to do so. The magician goes to the trouble of flogging the corpses *(cadavres)* of fifty hanged men and in so doing breaks out in a heavy sweat. She denies that she has observed him, whereupon he leads the beautiful girl, who in her hasty getaway after watching the flogging scene has lost one of her golden slippers and thus given herself away, into a room and shows her the bones of slain victims. But even then he does not get her to confess. Only in a very broad sense can one look upon these scenes as ugliness entering into the fairytale world. The word *ugly* never appears, not even in some paraphrase, and in view of this, the fact that beautiful *(beau, belle)* appears more than fifty times seems telling. The scenes mentioned—the strange, compulsive work of the magician and the showing of the piles of bones—do not appear to be demonstrations of obvious ugliness. They have other functions, similar to those of a third scene which one might mention in this context: The magician sees to it, each time he takes her children away, that the bedclothes of the beautiful girl are "full of blood," and on one occasion her mother-in-law remarks that she has "jaws covered with blood" ("la gueule pleine de sang"). The intent is not to diminish her beauty. In other versions of this fairytale type (named after the Grimms' story "Our Lady's Child"), the formulation moves further in the direction of the ugly: The mouth of the innocent young mother is "smeared" with blood.[7]

In the example we have chosen, the heroine is the central embodiment of beauty. The beautiful mother, the beautiful children, and beautiful flowers are peripheral; and the beau magicien belongs only to the title—there is no indication of how he looks. But even though beauty thus appears in feminine trappings, one notices scarcely a hint of the erotic. The undescribed, abstract beauty is compared with the day and with gold or is made impressive by what it results in: One must greet the beautiful girl as "Beautiful" or name her this; one must stare at her, forgetting everything else; one must take her as wife, thus raising her to the level of princess. Beauty spellbinds and attracts, and with magic power. But there is no talk of sensual vibration, either with respect to the beautiful girl herself or with respect to those affected by her. This is essentially true of all the beautiful figures in the fairytale. One can at most speak of "erotism" with respect to the important role played by courtship and marriage in the fairytale and specifically with respect to beauty's being manifested in female figures. But there is little trace of the actual erotic to be found in European fairytales; they tend to sublimate everything real. In the oriental tales, where the most important collections have been artistically reworked, the situation is different.

The heroine of our story is a mortal beauty. So also are the well-known beauties of the Grimms' tales: Snow White, Allerleirauh, Cinderella, and many fairytale heroines from other regions, whether princesses or daughters of poor families. With respect to the mother of Snow White, however, who has a magic mirror at her disposal, it is probably necessary to ask whether she does not belong to some other realm. Irish queens, and others who persecute their stepdaughters or daughters-in-law, clearly display—even when they possess matchless beauty—witchlike characteristics. And the fairytale differs from both the local legend and the so-called superstitions of the folk in that magicians and witches are no longer clearly denizens of our world. In addition to such beauties partially endowed with otherworldly features, there are those more clearly otherworldly—thus the daughters of monsters, who, like Medea, but luckier than she, stand by the hero and escape from the other world with him (AT 313; the fact that in many versions the princes whom they have aided when in need often later forget them does remind one, however, of Medea). In a modern Greek fairytale, "the beautiful girl" is the daughter of a female dragon,[8] in an Austrian one, the daughter of a witch from the underworld;[9] in another Greek fairytale, the nereid, who is so beautiful "that she radiates" and who weaves golden garments for herself, is even the daughter of the devil,[10] as is also true of the "beautiful white maiden" in a German fairytale from the Odenwald.[11]

The category of otherworldly beings also includes the beautiful swan-maidens (AT 465—the Indonesian sky-girls can serve as a non-European example of this widely spread fairytale type),[12] the beautiful maidens who emerge from oranges and lemons (AT 408), and many others. Among these only the modern Greek "beauty of the world" (ἡ ὄμορφη τοῦ κόσμου, ὥραια τοῦ κόσμου, or πεντάμορφη τοῦ κόσμου) may be an exception. In accord with Arabic usage, "beauty of the world" apparently means the most beautiful girl of this world. She has her counterparts in Italy (*la bella del mondo,* Sicilian *a bedda ti tuttu lu mundu*), Albania, and among the Turks, Kurds, Syrians, etc.[13] She is not always as readily identifiable as an otherworldly being as the swan-maidens or the nereids (nymphs); at times the otherworldly is indicated only by the distant, unknown land or the deadly castle. Often, however, either she or her father displays demonlike features. The Albanian "beauty of the earth" lives in the underworld. The hero of the story is successful in stealing a golden hair from her head and bringing it back to the king of the surface world: "It had the property that whoever took it in his hand shined like the sun."[14] A Greek "beauty of the world," like Brunhilde, defeats her suitors and turns them to stone.[15] Another must allow herself to be transformed by her father into a blackamoor and then do battle with her suitors, the heads of the defeated suitors being impaled on iron poles.[16] A third kills all her suitors and builds a tower out of their heads—"and one head was still missing for the tower." But the last, the rightful, suitor knows how to fulfill the condition set; and when he gets to see the "beauty of the world," her beauty overwhelms him. She also now finds it "a pity that so many young men have wrongly lost their lives." The father of the beautiful maiden crowns the pair with garlands, and the marriage is celebrated joyously for forty days.[17] Similarly, the hero of an Albanian fairytale finally lives "happy and contented together" with his "beauty of the world," who has time and again robbed, betrayed, and tortured him.[18] It is scarcely accidental that, among the beautiful maidens of the fairytale, it turns out to be the most beautiful, "the beauty of the world" ("la piu bella giovane del mondo"), who displays otherworldly features, who appears in conjunction with death and killing, with cruelty, falseness, and lack of constancy. This connection between beauty and harm is shown in another way in a Finnish fairytale, where the hero poisons his wife because he has heard sung of another still more beautiful, whom he seeks out on her island in the sea and marries.[19]

The "exquisitely beautiful Princess Truda" of the Russian fairytale has a love affair with a six-headed dragon. The dragon has to be killed. She herself must be beaten with switches, and then afterward still be cut in two. The worms that emerge from her are burnt, the two halves of her body put back together and sprinkled with the water of life. From then on the beautiful maiden is as sweet as she had earlier been bad.[20] This is a fairytale of the *grateful dead* type (AT 505–508), like the Norwegian one about the traveling companion, which has so many similarities to Andersen's well-known story. In the Norwegian story, the princess is the beloved of a mountain troll, whom she visits at night in the mountains. She has to be beaten with nine new birch rods, then bathed three times in milk and scraped in order to be freed from her troll's skin. The Old Testament story of Tobias, which belongs to the same fairytale type, shows the bride whom Tobias courts in the power of the evil demon Asmodeus; and the twelve beautiful princesses who gradually dance their shoes to pieces in an underground world (AT 306) are, like so many other beautiful maidens of the above-mentioned and other types of fairytales, likewise

under the spell of dark powers. The beautiful princesses who are kidnapped or supposed to be kidnapped by a dragon or some other monster
are innocent; they are afraid of the monsters and hope to be rescued, set
free, disenchanted. But from the point of view of the narrative, they are
still linked to dragons and man-eating giants. Anyone familiar with the
techniques of the fairytale, who knows how to analyze its complexes, to
set the individual components next to one another in order to make their
relationships clear, will see in the juxtaposition *(Nebeneinander)* of dragon
and princess a constellation *(Miteinander)*, a belonging together; and
against a background of countless stories showing beautiful maidens in
conjunction with beings from the underworld or as daughters of demonic
beings, the impression is intensified that even the beautiful maidens who
are kidnapped by monsters and held prisoner somehow really go together
with evil. As numerous popular versions of the *Rapunzel* type (AT 310)
show, it is not uncommon for them to learn the arts of sorcery from the
magicians or witches holding them prisoner. During their flight from
these otherworldly beings, these arts then turn out to be especially useful—the flight turns into a magical flight.[21] In the fairytale, beautiful
maidens of the otherworldly sort and those of the mortal sort are often not
clearly distinguishable. As a result, even those figures clearly belonging
to the mortal world, but whose overpowering beauty raises them into
another sphere, take on something of the radiance of the otherworldly
and also something of its gloom.

Even where no cruelty, evil, or direct threat comes into play, the shock
effect of beauty *(Schönheitsschock)* is characteristic of the fairytale. In the
Grimms' version of *Faithful John* (KHM 6, AT 516), the young prince is
not supposed to enter a certain room: "There is something in there . . .
which would *shock* you," namely, the "picture of the princess of the
golden roof." "And as soon as he looked upon the picture of the maiden,
which was so magnificent, sparkling with gold and precious stones, he fell
to the earth in a swoon." In a Pomeranian variant, as soon as the prince
comes face to face with the portrait of the "marvelously beautiful
princess," he falls "lifeless to the floor."[22] A religious fairytale from Transyl-
vania, probably of Magyar origin, develops this feature. God gives St.
Peter the following commission: "Go and scratch a picture of a beautiful
girl in the stone beside the street so that Alexander will see it when he
passes." Alexander, the son of a cook, who here plays the role of Faithful
John, experiences, upon seeing the picture, the shock effect of the beautiful. He comes to the "stone, where such a beautiful maiden was portrayed—as beautiful as the sun, the moon, and the stars put together. He
couldn't even move from the spot, so much did she please him." Here we
have the same spellbinding effect which we observed in the story from
French Canada; and, just as there, the immediate conclusion: "Oh, my

God, how this girl pleases me! I must go and seek her in order to make her my wife." He now fetches his friend and quasi foster brother, Prince Philipp, in order to get him to go along on the quest. When they begin to approach the stone with the marvelous drawing, Alexander warns, "'Don't look at it with both eyes at the same time, or the beauty will kill you.' But Philipp looked nonetheless and fell down as if dead. It took a long time for him to come round again." Here it is stated clearly: Beauty kills.

The unsuccessful preventive measure of the mentor has its parallel in Grimm: After "Faithful John . . . had opened the door, he went in first, thinking he would cover the picture so that the king would not see it before him. But what good did that do? The king stood on tiptoe and looked over his shoulder." Faithful John then carries the king, who might just as well have been struck by lightning, off to bed and doses him with wine so that he comes round again. "The first word that he said was 'Alas, who is in the beautiful picture? . . . I will give my life to win her.'" In our Transylvanian-Magyar story, the situation is made more complex, since both young men are smitten. The narrator unties the knot elegantly: "Philipp . . . needed a long time to come round again; then he began to weep, and wept until the stone became soft. Then Alexander said: 'Poor Philipp, if this girl pleases you so much, I'll let you have her. Perhaps God has also destined one for me. Come, let's go look for her.' Then Philipp stood up and didn't weep any more."

This is an elegant solution, because the central themes of stories of the *Faithful John* type are in any case renunciation, self-sacrifice, and voluntariness, so that the possibility of showing the Faithful John figure at this point as self-sacrificing fits in well with the overall thematic structure. This variation echoes the basic theme. The weeping of a hero is a feature which appears frequently in the world of the fairytale. Here it offers an opportunity to reactivate a faded metaphor, to actualize it. The set phrase "it could have softened a stone" is dramatized, just as indeed the fairytale, whenever possible, moves everything onto the level of action.[23] The narrator thus conforms not only to theme but also to style, and works, moreover, with artistic economy in that it is not some stone or other which is made soft, but the very one under discussion, the stone that set the whole pattern of events in motion. In addition, this softening mirrors that of the sympathizing Alexander, and it is at the same time a reaction caused by the picture scratched in the stone and thus a remote effect of the beautiful Russanda. It is indirectly the power of beauty which makes the stone dissolve. The father of Prince Philipp is called the "king of the whole world" or "from the whole world," and the names of several beautiful girls in this fairytale type are reminiscent of the "beauty of the world" discussed above. In the Slovakian versions she is called exactly that and must be fetched from some other world. In the Lower Engadine she is referred to, even in the title, as "la pü bela suot al sulai" ("the most beautiful under the sun"), in Denmark as "den skjøneste Jomfru, der er under Solen" ("the most beautiful maiden under the sun"); and in our Transylvanian version she is, as we have already heard, "as beautiful as the sun, the moon, and the stars put together." In this fairytale type, as well, we also see in numerous versions, including the Transylvanian, a dragon in the room of the beautiful girl, threatening her and her consort. She has not fallen into its clutches, as in other fairytales, but a constellation of the two features, beauty and the threat of death, is again established. The dragon would not have appeared had the prince not brought the marvelously beautiful girl home with him. In numerous versions there are serpents rather than dragons. In a Bulgarian-Macedonian version, the serpent appears not from outside but out of the mouth of the most beautiful of all princesses. The helper cuts the serpent's head off, just as in Serbo-Croatian, Slovakian, Russian, Gypsy, and other variants of the story of the grateful dead.[24]

In the story above and in many others, it is the picture of a beautiful maiden who is unknown and far away which produces the shock effect. It can also be a statue or a dream vision. The painting or drawing occurs most frequently, however; it best corresponds to the stylistic demands of the European fairytale. What is drawn or painted has sharper contours, is more clearly apprehended by the eye than a dream vision. Another possibility, one already used in the ancient Egyptian story of the two brothers, is the beautiful lock of hair (AT 516 B). The Egyptian writer—around 1200 B.C.—represents the situation as follows: The daughter of the sun god, Ra-Harachte, loses a lock of hair. The sea carries it to Egypt and "deposited it at the place where the pharaoh's washing is done. The scent of the lock of hair entered the pharoah's clothing." The pharaoh has the woman, "whose appearance was more beautiful than that of all the other women in the entire land, and in which every god was reflected," fetched and makes her his consort.[25] In South Arabia, three thousand years later, at the end of the nineteenth century, the story was told as follows: "The daughter of the sunrise," having been freed from the power of a man-eating demon, "was bathing in the river, combing her hair. Some of her hair came out, and she put . . . it into a leather bag. She forgot the bag on the river bank. A flood then came and carried the bag down to the royal city." The king has "the daughter of the sunrise" kidnapped.[26] Whether the two stories are connected does not have to be discussed within our context.[27] What interests us in all the various stories, whether they have been faithfully passed down or are independent developments, is the appearance everywhere of the constellation sun, beautiful woman, monster. In the South Arabian story, the beautiful woman is thus "daughter of the sunrise." The hero, who catches sight of her only from afar, takes her to be "a beautiful fire," but he is informed: "This fire is a woman." "If this fire is a woman, this woman is even more beautiful than you," he says to his consort on their wedding night. "How many days' journey is it to her?" "Five months'." The next morning he sets out to seek the "beautiful" fire. In the European fairytale, a lock of gold, just like a statue, a dream, or "what one reads in the book of days" (it is written of the prince that he is to fetch "the beautiful Rora, whom twelve fairies have made from dew"),[28]* is a good deal less frequent than a picture. The lock of gold is a bit of reality; the painting or drawing belongs to the world of artifice. *The fairytale delights in artifice.* Even a photograph can produce the shock effect of beauty. The emperor's son falls down in a swoon upon seeing one, and later, when he shows the photograph to others, they all fall "in a swoon, the four women and Haita-chin-Cîmp. When they again came round, they began to weep because of her beauty," and the emperor's son knows: "This is my destiny. I must seek her."[29]

Peter von Matt, under the title "The Portrayed Beloved," shows that for the writer Ernst Theodor Amadeus Hoffmann (1776–1822), the picture, the dream, the "phantasma" of the beloved is not something merely preliminary, not the final step before the immanent consummation of love. On the contrary, the actual person of the loved one must be cast aside in favor of the phantasma, if the hero is not to follow a false path like the painter in "Kater Murr," who goes mad. The phantasma is the picture of something absolute, a picture of the timeless and nameless "innermost core of the person" ("innerste Mitte des Menschen"). Over against the bringing of the picture to life stands the much more valid procedure of transforming the loved one back into the picture. The picture is "the concretized projection of the inner being" ("der konkretisierte Lichtwurf des Innern"). It is not the actual beloved but only the exterior, the picture, that is important. Von Matt also calls attention to "the frequent bringing together of the beautiful maiden and the ugly old crone in the works of Hoffmann," the confrontation of the ageless inner portrait with a reality subject to temporal decay, "of the eternally youthful picture within the artist with the woman grown old."[30]

The fairytale, especially that of the orient, also takes pleasure in juxtaposing the crone (often in the role of matchmaker) and the young girl. It is no accident that she is present in the South Arabian fairytale about the daughter of the sunrise. There is even to be found in the fairytale something corresponding to the double procedure of bringing the picture or imaginary vision to life and of retransforming its subject back into picture or vision. In the fairytale type of the *black and the white bride* (AT 403), the heroine is as "beautiful as . . . the sun" (KHM 135, edition of 1815, later expanded to "beautiful and pure . . . as the sun . . . , white and beautiful as the day"). Her brother paints her portrait. He "hung up the picture in his parlor, in the castle of the king whose coachman he was." As soon as the king gets sight of it, he wishes to take only her as his wife. But on the journey to the king, the stepmother pushes the bride out of the coach, into a deep body of water, and presents the king with her own coal black daughter (in beautiful garments of gold—but she is still "ugly as sin"). The king becomes "very angry," but must still make do with the witch's daughter—until the true bride, having suffered death and come back to life, stands before him. "She . . . looked just like the picture which the brother had made of her." Speaking in terms of popular psychology, this sequence of events may reflect the alternation of attraction and repulsion between the sexes, here reflecting specifically the emotional life of the man. In a Jungian interpretation, which sees in the fairytale above all an expression of intrapsychological *(innerseelisch)* processes, the two figures, the beautiful girl and her dark shadow, reflect two sides of or possibilities in the psyche *(Seele)* of the man, or they make visible his contrary relationship to his own inner being.[31] In yet another interpretation, cosmic phenomena are portrayed—here, the alternation between full moon and new.[32]

Fairytales are variously interpretable. One may put more stock in some interpretations than in others; still, they need not exclude one another. But they remain interpretations, hypotheses. What is shown directly, however, obvious to every eye, is the fascination with the beautiful, the longing for the ultimate degree in beauty, for the absolute. It is likewise indisputable that, in contrast to this absolute, this superlative beauty, there is something ugly, a distorted form which at times pushes the beautiful aside and takes its place. Moving over, ourselves, into interpretation, the king (in other versions, the prince), whom we can look upon as the representative of mankind in general, is confronted with the polarity between matchless value and absolute worthlessness. He strives for the one, but, at least temporarily, cannot get away from the other. But finally the true bride, having proved her identity through her beauty, assumes her rightful place. She "looks just like the picture." In light of Hoffmann's theory and practice, this formulation would be more correct than the one in the Grimms' version of *Faithful John* and in many other fairytales: "The king saw . . . that her beauty was still more beautiful than the picture had portrayed it." To the degree that one takes *beautiful* to be an absolute, the picture is always more beautiful than reality. In Shakespeare, one of course reads otherwise: The appearance of Cleopatra exceeds the beauty of the portrait of Venus, which in its turn eclipses nature, "o'er-picturing that Venus where we see the fancy outwork nature." And not only the picture, but also the word is unequal to representing the beauty of the queen. Her actual appearance "beggar'd all description." So avers Enobarbus, intoxicated by the sight of Cleopatra.[33] And yet the magic of Cleopatra is most beautifully and impressively attested to by this speech of the admiring Enobarbus, much more impressively than through the person of the actress. It is as if Shakespeare, without saying it, indeed while asserting the contrary, wished to demonstrate the magical power of the poetic word: Beauty is more perfect in the representation engendered by the word than in the actual world. It is telling that Enobarbus, in his attempt to characterize the superiority of reality over picture, finds no more suitable expression than "o'er-picturing." The picture, the representation in the imagination, and the fairytale are all more beautiful than reality. And that is nothing bad. It is in fact the task of the writer, according to Gottfried Keller (1819–1890), to invent beautiful pictures of women, such as are not brought forth by the bitter earth. In contrast to them in the fairytale are the pictures of the ugly old or even of the ugly young, in surrealistic intensification, of the dragon, the witch, or the monster, these also being static pictures, however, not, as von Matt has postulated for E. T. A. Hoffmann, indications of the possibility of growing old.[34]

The fairytale also has handsome *men*. The most striking example is the man made of semolina or marzipan. A princess, who is pleased by none of her many suitors, finally fashions a man for herself. She takes forty days and forty nights, and she uses three kilos of almonds, three kilos of sugar, and three kilos of semolina (or just sugar); and in answer to her prayers, God gives him life. "He was of marvelous beauty, and the entire world heard of him and his name" (Mr. Simigdali, Mr. Marzipan)—a parallel to the "beauty of the world." This fairytale is also found in the Greek area, and because of the number forty, it points as well to the orient. This particular beauty of the world, as one could call him, does not lack the supernatural element, but it is strangely transformed: The consort is not like Amor, in the classical story of Amor and Psyche, a mythical being, nor does he stem from some other world or appear in the form of an animal bridegroom; instead, he derives from completely worldly material as a result of the problematical cooperation of God. In Basile he is called Pintosmalto ("one who is enameled"), and the one who gives him breath is the goddess of love. Basile does not miss the opportunity to point out the symbolism of his material: "More than one among the listeners would have given a finger of his hand if he could have created a helpmate according to his own taste, especially the prince, who would much rather have seen a bit of pastry at his side than the poisonous portion which had fallen to him." The fairytale abstains from such commentary; instead, it shows the magic of beauty through its effect: A princess in a far-off kingdom, who hears of the marzipan man, who is handsomer than all others, thinks that she must die if she cannot have him as her husband. She has him kidnapped, and he remains her consort until he is won back by his creator after a strenuous wandering search—she needs three pairs of iron shoes for it, a well-known motif.[35]

Masculine beauty can also produce a shock effect, and not only in that faraway princesses hover on the verge of death as soon as they get word of such beauty. Where Faithful John seeks to cover up the portrait of the princess so that it does not endanger the prince, in the Turkish fairytale it is the other way round: There is a "man so handsome that he always keeps his face covered."[36] A girl falls in love with him as soon as she hears tell of him, just as in another Turkish story a (man-killing) maiden must not be looked upon because she is "too beautiful."[37] Other men are so handsome that they do not wish to marry any girl who is not as handsome as they;[38] thus they must undertake long journeys, but in the end, the narrator is able to say: "He now had beside him a girl who was just as handsome as he," a concluding statement which is equivalent to the well-known formula "They then lived happily ever after." The winning of the fair by the fair signifies that the very best has been achieved, everything has turned out well.

The attribution of beauty to male figures occurs less often than to female. In the Canadian fairytale which we have chosen as a representative model, the sons of the beautiful girl are referred to as *joli* ("good-looking"), not as beautiful. Most frequently, the stronger epithet occurs at the point when the animal bridegroom is disenchanted: He is transformed into a "handsome young man," "he was as radiant as an angel."[39] Here the designation comes in almost of its own accord as a contrastive expression. But mostly the handsomeness of the hero is indicated only indirectly: He has golden hair or perhaps only splendid clothing, silver armor, or a magnificent horse. The focus is always on the *actions* of the fairytale hero, and in this respect the fairytale, if only distantly, has something in common with the heroic epic. His handsomeness is only an accompanying characteristic, whereas in the case of the heroine it is often precisely the central consideration.

Beauty, however it may also be tied up with terror or danger and in the clutches of evil, for the fairytale—for its heroes, heroines, and noncentral figures just as for its narrators and listeners—is quite obviously a positive value. It is visible perfection. Theological esthetics would speak of the reflected glory of divinity. The fairytale differs from the myth in that God and the gods are always peripheral. But because the beautiful in it so often appears as gold or luster, especially as metallic luster, the fairytale takes on the shimmer of the perfect, the indestructible, the timeless, the absolute, and with it that of the transcending, even of the transcendent. Gold has probably always been a symbol of the sun, or at least been connected with the sun. And the journey to the sun and to other heavenly bodies which appears in so many fairytales is the journey into another world. The sun shines upon everything earthly but is itself unearthly. The important role which metals and metallic transpositions (golden hair; a golden finger, forests of gold, silver, or copper, etc.) play in the fairytale has led individual interpreters to conclude that the telling of fairytales is something which originally grew out of ecstatic experiences (e.g., those of the shamans).⁴⁰* Be that as it may, the luster of gold which projects from those figures and things in the fairytale which are looked upon as beautiful, shows, in any case, that in the fairytale the beautiful is something of the highest worth.

## OBJECTS AND NATURE

The fairytale is a story about people. Objects and nature never occur in the fairytale for their own sake. Objects stand in relationship to figures, mortal or otherworldly. Many stem from the otherworld, hence the magic objects which mortals receive from otherworldly beings. The hero receives from the ant one of its little legs, from the wolf a hair, from the eagle a feather, with the help of which he can summon these animals or even change himself into them in order to have access to their powers and abilities; the heroine receives from the sun, moon, and stars or other representatives of the otherworld a golden, a silver, and a star-studded gown, or a golden spinning wheel, a golden spindle, and a golden reel. Unlike the body parts donated by helpful animals, which serve as *pars pro toto,* the latter are not magical objects in the usual sense of the word, but they are in the extended sense: They can so enchant the heroine's rival, who is now the husband's consort, that, often just upon hearing of the beautiful objects or clothing, she must have them. This desire is analogous to that aroused in the fairytale hero who hears of a beautiful faraway princess or who has seen a picture of her. Just as with the magic of pictures, of ideas, or of dreams, one can, in the case of golden objects whose beauty can cause a woman to be compulsive, speak of the magic of things. These beautiful objects do not even have to stem from otherworldly beings. In many versions of *Faithful John,* hero and helper bring along with them from home lovely objects with which the beautiful girl (in a Slovakian version she is herself referred to as "the golden maiden"⁴¹) is supposed to fall in love. The Grimms' "princess of the golden roof" (whose servant girl draws "gold-flashing" [*goldblinkend*] water⁴² from the fountain with "two golden buckets") is so delighted by the "beautiful golden things" that she allows herself to be enticed onto the ship and is so engrossed in looking at the golden objects that she does not notice that the ship has pushed off and she has been kidnapped. For hours she is not aware that the ship is under way—such a fascination with the beautiful, here with golden objects, moves ultimately toward beauty shock. In the Grimms' Fairytales *(Kinder- und Hausmärchen),* it is often difficult to determine to what degree the Brothers Grimm themselves have embellished the stories. But when they report that everything the princess has around her is "of gold—tables, chairs, bowls, cups, vessels, and all other household goods," and on shipboard she then found "the most ingenious and exquisite pieces ever fashioned in gold," they deviate from the orally transmitted fairytale at most in specifying the individual golden objects. Elaboration is not characteristic of the orally transmitted fairytale, but gold is a sort of *summum bonum* in the fairytale. "Nach Golde drängt, am Golde hängt doch alles" ("To gold still tends,/On gold depends/All, all!")— not only do the figures in the fairytale, the girls, farmers, vicars, and sextons, stick to the golden goose, the fairytale itself displays a tendency toward the extreme, to the superlative in esthetic considerations just as in other things, and thus mentions, of all metals, gold most often and by preference.

Gold is for the fairytale the expression of the highest degree of beauty—so much is apparent. Whether it is also the sign of a higher, even of another, world is a question of interpretation and subject to debate. Its unmistakable connection with the sun, however, is suggestive of such an interpretation. The fascination with gold goes so far that the beautiful in the fairytale—male as well as female—often have golden hair, even in southern countries. The fairytale is permeated with the beautiful, and many of its props are, like the hair or the fingers of some of its heroes, likewise dipped in gold. The constant reappearance of the words *beautiful* and *golden* is an element which helps to give the fairytale its distinctive style.

The fairytale speaks less often of glass and crystal than of gold and silver, but these materials are also appropriate for the expression of the stylistic bent of the fairytale, with its striving toward the clear, the unambiguous, the extreme, and the distinct. The breakable and yet seldom broken glass in the fairytale is in its way as extreme an example of a material substance as gold. Glass coffins, coaches, and tools (axes with which unfortunate fairytale heroes must fell trees, etc.) belong just as much to the fairytale as glass mountains, glass castles, and glass slippers. The realistic nineteenth century believed that the glass slippers of Cinderella derived from a misunderstanding: It was supposed to be absurd that the beautiful girl should let fall a glass shoe without its breaking; instead of *pantoufles de verre* ("glass slippers"), one should read *pantoufles de vair* ("fur slippers," i.e., "slippers lined with fur"). Such was the opinion of Balzac and Littré. For a long time everyone accepted this "scientific" explanation without question. It was Marc Soriano who first rejected the argumentation of Balzac and Littré; he pointed out that in the fairytale the absurd is not avoided, but, in fact, in many cases is given preference. "A glass slipper—that is really a perfect absurdity. But isn't this detail selected precisely *because* of its absurdity?" Soriano's reasoning is not completely convincing. First, the emphasis with respect to the glass slipper is not directly on its absurdity (and thus on its charm), as, say, in the case of the "absurd paths" in "Little Red Riding Hood," about which Paul Delarue (whom Soriano cites) remarks that it is the absurdity of a

needle path and a straight-pin path (instead of a stony or a thorny path)
that puts (modern) adults off but delights children. Second, in other
fairytales the use of glass as a material is really meant to be absurd: A glass
ax is worthless for felling trees. Soriano is quite correct when he rejects
the fabrications of Balzac and Littré.[43]* Yet the fairytale provides Cinderella with glass slippers not because of its delight in the absurd, but
because of its delight in the bright material. Like gold, glass and crystal
are connected with light. In the fairytale, the beautiful is bright, radiant,
shining like the sun, "like the day." Hence the fairytale narrators' delight
not only in gold but also in glass, which also fits superbly well into the
sublimating style of the fairytale.

In the world of fairytale objects it is not just the shoe that is beautiful,
but clothing in general. There is much talk of the splendid clothing of the
rivals and partners of heroines and heroes, but as soon as the right moment arrives, their clothing is upstaged by the magnificent clothing or
armor of heroine and hero. Contrastive intensification is one means of
making beauty palpable. The fairytale prefers to speak of clothes rather
than of bodies. The former are artificial; they are nonplastic, nearer to the
abstract, to the geometrical, than is the body, and for this reason they are
especially in accord with the depthless, sublimating style of the fairytale.
The beauty of both mortals and otherworldly beings in the fairytale is
indicated above all through what is associated with them—clothes, castles, cities, marble palaces, gold and silver bridges along their way, etc. It
is unnecessary to pile up examples. We run into them in every fairytale,
and in the course of our presentation they will turn up frequently.

Even *nature* is frequently transposed into the metallic: The hero rides
through copper, silver, or golden forests and breaks himself off a copper,
silver, or golden twig. This rigid, metallic quality satisfies the sense of
beauty of the listener to fairytales more completely than the living breath
of actual nature, the disorderly profusion of shrubs, bushes, trees, flowers, grasses, and mosses in actual forests. It is not the beauty but rather
the danger and adventure potential of the forest which stand in the foreground in the fairytale. What is specifically singled out as beautiful in
nature is more likely to be the garden, thus again something artificial,
nature as organized and limited by man. In our Canadian *Our Lady's
child* fairytale (see pp. 2–5), the princess entices the heroine, who is
disguised as a boy, on to ever more beautiful flowers in the royal garden.
Especially memorable is the hero's role as gardener in the fairytale of the
scald-headed boy. It is in the middle of the garden which the boy tends
that his handsomeness is revealed to the princess, who suddenly sees the
golden hair instead of the scurfy scalp.

Nature is happily incorporated into clothing. The very fact that the beautiful gold- and silver-colored clothing is the gift of the heavenly bodies shows this merging of beautiful nature and beautiful clothes. But especially characteristic of the fairytale are those pieces of clothing on which—as, for example, in Greek and Italian fairytales—"all the flowers of the earth" or "all the waves of the sea" are to be seen, garments on which are embroidered "the sky with its stars," "the earth with its herbs," "the sea with its fish and its ships" (a nice example of the concurrent mentioning of animals *and* things for their own sake, although even here the human reference point is not lacking), or "the earth with its mountains and trees."[44] This is the way the fairytale brings man and nature together. Man incorporates nature into his clothing; he wears it on his garments—a picture of his possibility of establishing a relationship with everything. The fairytale says very little about the inner life, the feelings and moods, of its figures. They are just figures, carriers of the action. Their depth of character is mostly not even hinted at, and therefore their feeling for nature, the mood and atmosphere tied to season and time of day, to the play of the sun, the clouds, or the mist in various forest, sea, or meadow landscapes, also never becomes apparent. The fairytale looks at nature completely unsentimentally. But the heroes and heroines of the fairytale receive its gifts, and with these something of its beauty and luster. They incorporate it into their clothing or also into their gardens. In a Sicilian story of the *black and the white bride* type (AT 403 A), the hero must, in a single night, "lay out a garden in which all the trees and all the flowers of the earth are to be seen." In a second night he is to gather together in this garden "all the birds which exist on earth." And he carries out the task while sleeping—that is, his sister, who was pushed into the water by the false bride and who now, as a direct result, has magic powers, lays out this all-encompassing, "marvelously beautiful garden" for him. The universalism and "estheticism" in the fairytale come together in such gardens and pieces of clothing.[45] Its tendency to transform what is living into something rigid comes into play where a Greek girl picks poppies and (with the needle she has with her) sews them onto her skirt. A passing moira (one of the fates) is forced to laugh at this and thus wishes her good fortune: "The flowers you're wearing will become brilliants and diamonds." And these flowers, which are first sewn onto the skirt—and thus already abstracted from life—and which then become precious stones, dazzle the eyes of the king. He stands "nonplussed in the presence of her beauty": "Are you a person or a mirage?" And she becomes queen. Air and glass, gold and silver, metal in general, precious stones, and clothing or gardens which incorporate the diversity of nature—the fairytale is full of such things. In clothing and gardens, but also in brilliants and diamonds, nature is united with the artificial, and the fairytale, itself an artificial form, is attracted by the artificial. It is not a tangled, disorderly waxing and waning nature which the fairytale finds beautiful, but a shaped, limited, unchanging one; not a nature of scents and sounds, but one clearly visible to the eye.

The connection between man and the beauty of nature is not as close when during the magic flight a girl or a boy changes into a beautiful flower, for the accent here is not on beauty—the persons fleeing could also turn into a pond and a duck or even into a church with a sexton, where the world of nature is completely left behind, without as a result the beauty of architecture coming into play. But the esthetic sense is still called upon with the flower. Even though the function of the motif segment is exactly the same, it makes a difference to the listener whether a girl transforms herself into a duck or into a flower. Also in the case of the swan-maidens, it is no accident that the swan was chosen. Beauty is connected with the swan, just as with the flower. The idea of beauty plays no role, however, when animal hair, scales, or feathers give the fairytale hero not only the power to invoke the respective animals, as occurs in many instances, but even the power to turn himself into them; the ant can be involved just as easily as the wolf or the eagle. It is only the completely unsentimental yet close and effective contact with nature—here with the animal kingdom—that is expressed especially strongly, more strongly still than with the animal helpers in general that are associated with heroes in so many fairytale types (see pp. 138–139).

It is not only persons that can be the source of the shock effect of beauty, but nature and artifacts as well. Where it is reported of a certain princess: "She was so beautiful that she could not at all be looked upon" (Greek); of another: "Because of her beauty her father had her locked up," after many suitors had fought with one another to win her (Rhaetoromance); and of the daughter of a dragon: "She transformed herself into a beautiful girl, who was so beautiful that you could have looked into the holy sun more readily than you could have looked at her" (Rumanian)[46]—it is correspondingly reported of a meadow: "The meadow was so beautiful that one could have looked into the sun more readily than upon the meadow" (Hungarian); and of a horse: "It was so marvelous that you could have looked into the holy sun more readily than upon that horse" (Rumanian). And in the world of things, "One might have looked into the sun without being blinded more readily than upon that ship, it was so beautiful." "You might have looked at the sun, but not at this staircase!" "You might have looked at the sun, but not downward, so many precious objects were there, shining and glittering" (Rumanian).[47] Glittering treasure which dazzles the eye seems still more or less realistic; staircases that are so dreadfully beautiful that they cannot be looked upon are more fairytale-like. Also fairytale-like are the beautiful flowers that "the poor girl combs from her hair." These too are "so beautiful that one might more readily have looked into the sun than at these flowers." Her eyes, which had been poked out, are restored to her: "In her happiness two flowers sprang up in her footsteps, and these two flowers were still seven times more beautiful than the others which she had combed from her hair."[48] Despite such intensification, everything dreadful has vanished. The joyous appearance of flowers in her footsteps bears witness not only to the beauty and, in clear symbolism, to the purity of heart of the girl, but also indirectly to her contact with nature: Girls who produce flowers when walking or laughing, girls—or even men—who produce roses when speaking or smiling, attest in their way to the successful interaction of man and nature.

However many flowers and beautiful things appear in the fairytale, from roses, rings, combs, and girdles to gardens, castles, palaces, and cities, the designation "beautiful" is applied, directly or indirectly, preeminently to humans and to otherworldly beings having human form. In oriental tales of the Arabian Nights sort, palaces and cities are described with zest in all their magnificence. But these stories appear in written redactions; they have been edited. Of the famous "City of Brass" it is reported in the Arabian Nights: "Its walls are of black stone, and it has two towers of Andalucian brass; they appear to the observer like two fires lying opposite one another. For this reason it is called the City of Brass." "The walls looked like a bank of cliffs or like iron that had been cast in a mold." "Lofty palaces beckoned and shiny domes flashed . . . the gardens stood in full magnificence, . . . and the trees were laden with fruits." The city has "gates of gold," statues of brass, "ample rooms . . . painted in gold and silver and every imaginable bright color"; over the spouting marble fountains stretch canopies of brocade; in the halls stand "benches of ivory decorated with glittering gold and hung with silk coverlets." "Golden trees with fruits of costly gems, rubies, chrysolite, pearls, and coral. . . ."[49] Such magnificence is foreign not just to the European fairytale. In the Arabian fairytales which Enno Littmann partially took down himself during oral presentation and partially had taken down, it says of the City of Brass only: "In the entire expanse of this city, everything was of brass." Then it moves on immediately: "When Prince 'Alî came to this city, he heard that the daughter of the king of the City of Brass was beautiful and a famous woman warrior. Then in his heart he longed to do battle with her. . . ."[50] It is characteristic not only that the orally transmitted story does not allow itself to go into description, immediately getting on with the story, but also that the city is now really a city of brass, not a city put together from the most diverse materials with two brass towers, as in the Arabian Nights. "Truly, that was no ordinary city," it says in one of the stories of the Swedish Gypsy Taikon. "Everything was of copper—the houses, the streets, the trees."[51] The fairytale passed on from teller to teller, and without literary editing, offers us a city of what one might call abstract uniformity. It is entirely of brass, or, for the Gypsy, of copper (the City of Silver being respectively of silver and the City of Gold, of gold). The Arab says nothing of its beauty; the adjective *beautiful* is reserved for the princess. The Yemenite Jefet Schwili narrates in a corresponding style, though even more laconically: "He rode and came to a city. There he ran into an old woman on the street. She had a beautiful daughter. She dressed up the daughter beautifully [and] showed her to the prince."[52] It is not the City of Brass, but still a foreign city. The narrator has not a single descriptive word left over for it. It is obvious that the effect emanating from this sort of narrative style, even when one reads the stories instead of listening to them, is a completely different one from that of the tales from the Arabian Nights. The delight in description characteristic of the Arabian Nights and related collections tempts us on from detail to detail; the outline of the whole becomes obscured; the plot gets bogged down. The oral narration, however, offers us simple, clear pictures and a smoothly flowing plot line. A city or a bridge (see pp. 22–23) of metal— whether it is of brass, copper, silver, or gold—is in the context of the fairytale not a curiosity but rather, with its abstract uniformity and timelessness, in its way a perfect creation. The undescribed beauty in the fairytale is one of nonreal perfection. Metal cities, bridges, and forests, in their luster, in their rigidity and uniformity, are the epitome of fairytale beauty.

## MODE OF REPRESENTATION

The fascination with metallic objects, precious stones, and exquisite materials which we find in the Arabian Nights and other literarily edited oriental stories is shared by the orally transmitted fairytale. But the fairytale is simpler, more understated—not baroque like the former, we are tempted to say, but close to classical simplicity. The compulsion to describe is alien to it. It has its own mode of representation. Whether this mode of representation is entirely the result of the demands of oral presentation and/or oral transmission is something we will look into.

The most noticeable feature of the representation of beauty in the European fairytale (and to a large extent in the oral tale from the orient) is *generality.* Beauty is almost never made specific. We learn nothing about eye color or complexion, about stature or type of build; we hear nothing about the characteristic beauty of the nose, the lips, or the breast of hero or heroine, nothing about the lines of the beautiful ship or the type of the beautiful flowers. In the Canadian fairytale with which we began our observations, one hears time and again of "belles fleurs" ("beautiful flowers"). Whether they are roses or carnations or in one case asters and in another dahlias or chrysanthemums, we never learn. This assessment is already an answer to the question of whether the lack of individualization is only the result of the lack of sophistication of the narrator, on the one hand, and of the laws of oral transmission, on the other. In the folksong, for example, even in the narrative song, in the ballad, various types of flowers are mentioned by name. Even for the simplest, most primitive narrator it would be possible to say "beautiful lilies," "beautiful roses," or "white lilies," "red roses," if he only chose to, just as he could vary "beautiful girl" with "pretty girl," "pretty child," "sweet girl," etc. But time and again he prefers to formulate in the same way: "beautiful flowers," "beautiful girl," not—or not only—because it is easier, and better allows him to think about the progress of the story, but apparently also because the general formulation and the repetition of this general formulation satisfy his feeling for style and that of his listeners. Just as the city of plain brass produces a sharply drawn, nonambiguous mental picture—clearer and purer than the city made partially of gold, marble, and brass (see pp. 19–20)—the unvaried use of the same formula, "beautiful flowers" or "beautiful girl," results in another way in a firm and certain impression. It is still more general and less individualized than "City of Brass." It does not, of course, call forth the same picture for every listener, but it will always call forth one appropriate for him. As we have already emphasized, a further advantage of this quasi-abstract generality is that the listener is not tied to one particular special picture; his imagination is free to create and visualize in its own way. Not only each listener, but each epoch and region, as well, possesses this freedom. Anyone who hears the expression "beautiful flowers" is not bound to any particular favorite flower of any particular time or country, and the "beautiful girl" is not unacceptable to some other century or people because of an ideal of beauty tied to some particular time. In this sense, the fairytale possesses something timeless or ahistorical—and completely without the narrator's striving for such timeless validity. It comes of its own accord.[53]* Differing from written literature, from ancient up to modern times, the fairytale tells us nothing of the beauty of individual parts of the body. Even saying that the hair is golden is not a specific description but only an indication of the importance of the character having it. Not that one can pedantically limit the fairytale to a constantly uniform style—naturally, there are deviations, a limited range of varying possibilities. Hair can also be black—but then it is as black as ebony or as coal, where, just as in the case of gold, an extreme degree is indicated. And the skin is white as snow, the cheek red as blood. There is no attempt at nuance, but just the opposite, the unmistakable extreme. The fairytale tells us nothing of the softness of the skin or the individual type of complexion. It strives, and not just because of the narrator's lack of skill, for the *beauty of the extreme.*

One of the means of achieving this goal is the *comparison.* Such comparisons have already appeared in the material discussed up to this point—for example, the formula used for hero or heroine, "beautiful as the day," found especially in French fairytales but encountered other places as well (see pp. 3–4); and the universalistic superlative "as beautiful as sun, moon, and stars put together" (see p. 7). Both comparisons are based on light and luster. "Beautiful as the daylight," it says in one Gascon story; "more beautiful than the day," in another.[54] Comparisons with the sun and moon are especially popular in the orient. Within the sphere of influence of the Arabian Nights, boys and girls are time and again compared with the two heavenly bodies. One boy is "more beautiful than the moon"; another exceeds "the sun in beauty and grace"; a third is already at birth "beautiful as a sliver of moon," a fourth "as the rising sun."[55] Girls are as beautiful "as the shining moon" or "as the moon the night it becomes full."[56] The same formula can be used for a bird.[57] Boys as well as girls can look "as if they emerged from the mold of beauty and grace,"[58] a comparison more abstract than that with sun or moon, but just as perfectionistic. In Hungarian, one reads, less emphatic: "A boy as beautiful as a poppy,"[59] where, however, the reference made is surely not to the complexion of the boy, but rather only to the perfection of his beauty. In the Bulgarian, a saddle is "as beautiful as the sun" (just as in the case of a boy);[60] in the Czech, a newborn baby boy is as "beautiful as a blossom."[61] The comparative "more beautiful than" is made use of quite happily, not only in comparisons with heavenly bodies but also in comparing beautiful things with one another: "If the City of Copper was beautiful, then the City of Silver was . . . still more beautiful" (Gypsy).[62]

Instead of comparing, whether positively or through intensification, many stories emphasize that one cannot say how beautiful the beautiful is. "Everything was constructed of flashing silver, so wondrous and shiny that one cannot describe it." "And yet if the City of Silver was beautiful, then the City of Gold was so beautiful that one cannot even dream of anything so beautiful, much less describe it." The same illiterate Swedish Gypsy tells of "a park that is so beautiful that one cannot describe it. . . . Never have you seen the like, never heard tell of it, never—not even in a dream—seen anything similar." And in the same fairytale it is said of the silver bridge: "Its luster was like sunshine. Its railing was such as I cannot convey, cannot describe. No, not even in a dream can I see something similar." "Below, the silver bridge was mirrored in the water. Ah, my friends, not even in a dream can I call it back, because it was more beautiful than everything beautiful in the entire world. I wept, as I am weeping now, my children. But I rode on." Somewhat later: "If the silver bridge was beautiful, the golden bridge was yet a hundred times more beautiful. I looked at it. It was more beautiful than everything beautiful. Who can describe the most beautiful of the beautiful? My friends, now I am silent. Now I can no longer speak your language." "Below, I saw the reflection of the golden bridge in the clear water." "That was a picture—so beautiful that I cannot describe it, cannot tell of it, cannot describe in words how beautiful it was."[63] Despite all these disavowals, however, it is still words which bring the beauty of the much-praised bridges and cities home to us. In the vortex of the repetitions, the beauty of things is suggested to the listener with almost magical force, much more vividly than minute descriptions could do it. Like Shakespeare, the Gypsy demonstrates the magic power of words in the same breath in which he denies it. And when he says that not even in a dream could one see such beauty, his fairytale is indeed nothing other than a dream, among other things of unspeakable, indescribable, unnarratable beauty that cannot even be looked upon. The fairytale avoids descriptions not just for technical reasons—because epic narrative literature, as Lessing observed, must observe normal chronology, or because the "average man of the people" is not up to description—but because, as the famous Johan Dimitri-Taikon, who died in 1950 as the leader of the perhaps 550 Gypsies living in Sweden, has given us to understand, the beautiful is just not describable. However it may be that the absence of description frequently arises from the narrator's lack of ability, in the context of the fairytale its result is similar to the speechlessness of the mystic who wishes to speak of God. That beauty leaves the narrator speechless is its highest praise.

In his study of the Laocoön, Lessing explains that the narrator represents the degree of beauty most impressively when he shows its *effect*. The fairytale uses this "trick" frequently and happily; we have often run into it in the course of our discussion. The effect of the beautiful is expressed most sharply where it produces a shock, where it strikes the onlooker dumb or paralyzes him, where it knocks him unconscious or even brings him near death's door. In the Greek narrative area, a sleeping girl is "so beautiful that the monk stood frozen in place when he saw her. The whole room was alight with her beauty." A "beautiful princess" is "so beautiful that the sun stands still; the morning star shines with reflected light."[64] Here the effect of the beautiful reaches so far that not only are heavenly bodies halted in their course or made to shine more brightly, but the narrator is motivated to move from prose over into verse, one of the effects of the beautiful reaching outside the narrative. And here again one thinks of Shakespeare: Viola, when she stands before Olivia and sees her beauty—not only with her own eyes but also with those of her lord, who adores Olivia—switches over, taken with Olivia's beauty, directly from prose into poetry (*Twelfth Night* I.v). If beauty can stop others in their tracks or cause them to become unconscious or die (see pp. 3f., 5, 7–10, on the shock effect of beauty), it can also protect its possessor from death. In the notes to their first edition (1812), the Brothers Grimm report a version of "Snow White" in which the dwarfs, just as in many other variants, are not particularly benevolent: "In a cave in the forest live seven dwarfs, who kill every girl that comes near them. The queen knows this." She sends Snow White into this cave: "The dwarfs come and at first want to kill her, but because she is so beautiful they let her live." In a Korean story it says of a beautiful girl: "She was too beautiful to be cast into the sea."[65] The Grimms' 1812 version of "Cinderella" shows a nice touch. The sisters tell Cinderella about the appearance of the unidentified princess at the ball and about her disappearance: "The prince danced only with her, and when she was gone, he no longer wished to remain, and the whole affair came to an end. . . . It was really as if all the lights had suddenly been blown out." Here, for once, it is the absence of beauty whose effect is described. Beauty is thus presented indirectly. Even if the formulation, in which one seems to hear the cadences of German Biedermeier, stems from one of the Brothers Grimm, it is in accord with the tendency of the fairytale not to describe beauty but to capture it in terms of its effect: "It was really as if all the lights had suddenly been blown out." The appearance of flowers in one's footsteps (see pp. 18–19) is undoubtedly of popular origin and in character for the fairtale: The beauty of the girl is made visible in that it is projected outward and at the same time is translated into another medium. Factoring (*Ausfaltung*) and juxtaposition are two of the most effective means of representation in the fairytale. The fairytale travels many paths in order to characterize beauty. It is especially ingenious, for example, to make beauty transparent: "Two children, beautiful as the sun" are "so beautiful . . . that one saw through the flesh to the bones and through the bones to the marrow. So beautiful were they" (Southeastern Europe, Gypsy).[66] There is no doubt that this turn of phrase, which appears here and there, was current among the "folk." It is possible that it goes back to the Mohammedan conception of the beautiful in paradise, through whose bodies and through seventy veils one sees the marrow of their thighs.[67] But that the body becomes transparent, to a certain degree glasslike, corresponds entirely to the stylistic tendency of the fairytale toward sublimation. This representation thus slips effortlessly into the fairytale.

The simple word *beautiful*, however, without comparison or contrast, without any further embellishment, is the most valid way of representing beauty in the fairytale. It is expected by the listener, and with its constant reappearance it brings evenness into the narration. It is the best indicator of beauty, for the beautiful can in the end be represented only by itself. Every attempt at particularization limits it.

Still, the question again arises: Is it art or just lack of imagination when the narrator of the fairytale lets the simple word *beautiful* suffice? In the case of individual narrators, this sparseness of expression may in fact stem from a shortage of talent. But it is not the poor but rather the good narrators that have been the real agents of transmission. The listeners crowded around them, and the talented among the listeners, not the untalented, then themselves became narrators much in demand, who continued to tell the old stories and to renew them. Once he let himself go, a man like the Gypsy Taikon was at no loss for words: The boy "plowed and harrowed and planted the earth. He toiled away, the sweat dripped, the tears ran. . . ." "Now the princess spoke in an entirely different voice, so soft and sweet that her words warmed him like the summer sun. Happy and with a light heart, the boy went off to the emperor."[68] As soon as it is a question of beauty, however, Taikon knows that no variations in expression are in order—the radiance of the beautiful suffices. He knows, even when he says it playfully, that he must remain silent. In the end, there is only one thing that is appropriate to beauty—the abstract word *beautiful.* Doubt has often been expressed as to whether one can describe the style of the fairytale as "abstract." This designation is, of course, a simplification. But that the style of the fairytale moves toward the abstract reveals itself to us time and again.

## MUSIC

To the degree that the beautiful actually appears in the fairytale, it is essentially something for the eye. In the oriental fairytale, music and fragrance play a more important esthetic role than in Europe. In the midst of a veritable concert of "golden tablets and bowls of porcelain and crystal," "gold and silver chandeliers," the scents of musk, camphor, and ambergris, and "sweetmeats, juices, and candies," it also comes to an *actual* concert with flutes, lutes, harps, and singing. "Then the girls raised up their voices in the unity of song, so that I thought the castle was revolving in a circle about me. At the same time, I observed the beauty of the queen and her castle and marveled over the magnificence of the enormous wealth." Esthetic sight, taste, smell, and sound perceptions are the backdrop for the beauty of the queen in this Arabian novella fairytale written down in the thirteenth century.[69] It is indicative that the magic of the singing is also largely perceptible through its effect, and again one can speak of something approaching the phenomenon of beauty shock: "I thought the castle was revolving in a circle about me." Such opulence is not found in oral literature. In a Japanese story of the *animal bridegroom* type, it says: "He sang the song of a stableboy in a beautiful voice. The horses moved in time to it and made the little bells on their necks jingle."[70] Korean girls of "radiant beauty" speak in a "soft voice"; the princess "with carmine cheeks" whispers sweet nothings in the ear of the monk. When "grandiose music" is spoken of, it must really be attributed to literary editing or to translation. Fragrances are also mentioned. The heroine of the "most famous and most widely attested Korean story" is called "Fragrant Spring"; the lotus blossom exudes a beguiling fragrance; and the tiger, smelling human flesh, cries, "Oh, lovely smell!"[71]

In the European fairytale, sound and fragrance as esthetic values are also found most readily in literary reworkings. In the magic castle of the invisible white cat the intruder hears "two charming voices" ("deux voix ravissantes") singing consolingly seductive verses (Mme d'Aulnoy, "La Chatte blanche"). The beautiful girl in Mme Leprince de Beaumont's famous version of the *animal bridegroom* fairytale ("La Belle et la bête") listens during the midday meal to "un excellent concert," without seeing anyone. Later, an effective contrast, the whole palace echoes with the terrible whistling into which the sobbing of the beast is distorted. The oral fairytale, on the other hand, is reticent in its esthetic interpretation of sound perceptions, and more so of those of smell and taste. With respect to these last-mentioned sensual impressions, narrators are in complete agreement with St. Thomas Aquinas, who called attention to the fact that we may well speak of beautiful things and beautiful tones, but not of beautiful tastes or smells ("non dicimus pulchros sapores et odores.")[72] Nonetheless, if one does not demand the use specifically of the accompanying word *beautiful,* one can indeed find esthetic references to the areas of taste and smell. In the English *animal bridegroom* fairytale about the dog with the little teeth, the heroine finally refers to the dog no longer as "foul" but as "Sweet-as-a-honeycomb."[73] Wormy figs, in the sense of *captatio benevolentiae* or *euphemism* (see pp. 32–33), are praised as tasty. Taikon extolls the aroma of the magnificent fruits that the hero is not allowed to pick (see pp. 22–23). Still, auditory impressions are more frequent with him, as well. When his prince—or he himself, for Taikon suddenly begins narrating in the first person—rides over the glittering copper bridge, there rises suddenly "a loud noise up to the heavens . . . : Ök-doj-trin-schtar-panch!" When the hooves of the horse come in contact with the silver bridge, it resounds "like music . . . , ök-doj-trin-schtar-panch!" Of the golden bridge it is again reported: "Like music it resounded in the golden arch: Ök-doj-trin-schtar-panch!" In individual versions of the ride through the copper, silver, or golden forest, when the male or female rider tears off a leaf, each time there is either a loud noise or a soft rustle. Even the beautiful sound of the human voice is sometimes mentioned: "Indeed how beautifully Dolores can sing!" "I have never before heard anything so beautiful." "What a pretty voice!" Karlinger: "Whatever is not reachable in the normal context *(im realen Bereich)* is achieved on the level of singing."[74]

In general, however, impressions of smell, taste, and touch, as well as acoustic phenomena, are far less common in the fairytale than those involving sight. The eye is "the sharpest organ of sense," that conjoined to reason. For it, above all, is St. Thomas's observation true: "sensus ratio quaedam est" ("sense is a kind of reason, an organ of knowledge").[75]* The ear—and this is even more the case with the other sense organs—is dimmer, leading into the interior of man, i.e., into the invisible, into the depths. What is seen is something which clearly stands "in front of the eyes," out there in the real world. Moreover, everything visible can be described more clearly. Colors and forms are easier and more clearly indicated in words than are sounds. *Red* or *small*—that is a more clearly understood language than *G sharp* or *minor key*. The fairytale is committed to clarity, tangibility—and beauty. Among the sounds and scents, it is the pleasant ones that primarily stand in the foreground, just as is the case of the beautiful among the colors and forms, the buildings and objects.

Magic flutes, pipes, and fiddles indicate nothing about or attest only indirectly to the beauty of music, but they indicate the direct power of its effect, forcing all who hear them to dance or come running—whether it be humans (KHM 110, AT 592) or animals (sheep, goats, hares: AT 570, *The rabbit-herd*). Not infrequently mention is made of minstrels. In individual versions of *Faithful John*, it is believed that a story devised by a minstrel can be identified in the background. But even narrators who are themselves minstrels take very limited advantage of the opportunity to portray fairytale heroes or a supporting figure as minstrels. Jachen Filli from Guarda, an enthusiastic singer and clarinet player and the leader of a dance band, does indeed tell of the fiddler who plays and sings so beautifully before the statue of St. Cecilia that she tosses him one of her golden slippers (*St. Kümmernis* type, KHM 157 A), and he quite happily mentions the music and dancing at the festival closing the fairytale—but, unlike in the Grimms' version, he does not have Faithful John make music during the sea voyage.[76] These purely mood-setting touches are alien to the oral tradition of fairytale narration. Music and musical instruments are as a rule only mentioned when they have some function in advancing the plot. In the Finnish story in which the hero is supposed to fetch the emperor a "living kantele," a sort of self-playing zither, both the expedition to the far-off country and the (continually interrupted) making of the instrument by otherworldly figures are painstakingly described— but whether the kantele then actually plays and how, we never learn.[77] Local legends and saint's legends show much more interest in things acoustic than the fairytale. The Kümmernis-Cecilia story is a religious fairytale; the *singing bone*, whose numerous versions almost all contain verses to be sung (the tunes have been noted down here and there),[78] is a local legend fairytale. The real local legend tells not only with zest of things heard, but also of when otherworldly beings have bestowed on humans the art of singing, yodeling, or alphorn blowing (see p. 99). The saint's legend also has a sensitivity to smells—the corpses of saints give off a marvelous, pleasant scent. The Zurzach Book of Miracles tries to make the effect of music palpable using a taste simile: The singing of the angels "was as sweet in the ears of the listeners as is honey between the teeth of those dining" (". . . vox psallentium angelorum . . . tam dulcis in auribus audentium, velud mel est in dentibus manducantium").[79]

The power and beauty of sound naturally come into their own in another way in the fairytale insofar as a narration is an acoustic reality. The rhythm and melody of the voice of the male or female narrator are just as much a musical element as the imitations of the sounds of nature, alliterations, assonances, and verses. Leopold Schmidt correctly observes that musical instruments in the fairytale are "played not for artistic reasons and not for entertainment," that they serve more "to foster a magical, conjuring effect in a story."[80] This is also largely true of recited and sung verses in the fairytale; they are not "lyrical interludes" but have "a very direct function" (Karlinger),[81] one often magical: Otherworldly beings speak in another language, e.g., in verse ("The Frog King," KHM 1; "The Singing Bone," KHM 28; "The Juniper Tree," KHM 47, etc.), and the sung verses are there to bring something about—in the *singing bone* fairytale type (AT 780), for example, it is the revenge of the murdered boy. The bone flute is a transformation of the boy; through it he comes back again—it is his epiphany. Nonetheless, although both the musical instruments and the verses almost always have an important plot function in the fairytale—especially in the European—a basic difference exists between them: One does not hear the musical instrument—perhaps it may not even be indicated whether it is actually played (see p. 27)—but the melody of the sung verse is realized; the narrator sings it. To this degree the verses to be sung in the fairytale have an actual esthetic function, not only of a higher degree, but of a quite different sort from that of the instruments mentioned in the narratives. Above the level of the bare plot rises the level of speech (dialogs, monologs); above that, the level of spoken verse; and this last level is still transcended, exceeded by the verses sung.[82]*

## THE OPPOSITES OF BEAUTY

The direct opposite of the beautiful, the *ugly,* is in the fairytale first and foremost the foil of the beautiful. Though it may also be the case that genetically the ugly has temporal precedence over the beautiful in the same way that misshapen giants and demons may be older and more primitive than gods (Adorno: "If at all, it is more likely that the beautiful originates in the ugly than the other way around"),[83]* in the fairytale the beautiful is dominant. It is primary, the ugly secondary. Through the effect of contrast, the beautiful becomes still more prominent, more clearly visible. The idea of the beautiful contains the idea of its polar opposite; the narrative only concretizes what is already provided for in the conception of the beautiful. The beautiful engenders its opposite just as good, poor, and success call forth the opposite ideas of wicked, rich, and failure. In this sense, as well, one might say that the fairytale is self-creating.

"A widow had two daughters, one of them beautiful and industrious, the other ugly and lazy." So begins the Grimms' fairytale "Frau Holle."

This sentence remains unchanged from the first to the last edition of the famous book. *The kind and the unkind girls* is the international designation for this fairytale type (AT 480, KHM 24). The Grimms' passage cited, in bourgeois Biedermeier manner, reduces *good* to *industrious*, but still *beautiful* is put first. Here, as throughout the entire story, beauty appears to be the outward manifestation of the good, of the morally proper. Appearance and reality coincide, otherwise than in the case of the riddle-posing princesses and other female task setters, who—or whose fathers—decorate the city wall with the heads of suitors or build towers out of them. In the case of each of these far-distant beauties, both the distance and the cruelty are apparently indications of the otherworldly. The fairytale hero and heroine, who almost always clearly belong to this world, the world of man, are as a rule beautiful and good at the same time, even when their beauty is for a time not visible. Since it is on the whole the goal of the fairytale to portray a world which, despite a few things being out of kilter, is largely in order, it is the norm for the beautiful and the good to occur together, both being specifications of the "proper." Cruel beauties are somehow not in order—but they can be healed, whether simply because, after ninety-nine unsuccessful suitors, finally the right one comes along, or because the helper of the hero in an artful operation draws the snakes out of the body of the beautiful girl so that subsequently she is just as good as she is beautiful, or because the traces of her connection with evil are flogged and washed away through a determined purification process (see p. 6).

The fairytale, in more than one sense an art form of juxtaposition, prefers to assign good and evil, beauty and ugliness, to two different figures rather than, as in the instances described above, to unite them in one. Juxtaposed against the girl who combs flowers from her hair or produces roses when laughing, or out of whose mouth falls a gold piece at each word, is another who combs lice from her hair or out of whose mouth come toads, who stands there covered not with gold but with pitch: She is "frightfully ugly" ("laide à faire peur").[84] The means used to portray the ugly correspond to those we have observed used with the beautiful. In the many and various stories about the false and the true bride, the ugly and the beautiful are likewise played off against one another, especially pointedly in the fairytale type *The three oranges* (AT 408, see p. 5). First, the principle of intensification: Out of the three cut-up or cut-into oranges, lemons, or apples spring, one after the other—the sequence *(Nacheinander)* being merely juxtaposition shifted to the time dimension—three girls, each more beautiful than the former, the last to be the bride of the prince. Before he brings her into the city, however, he wishes to provide her with clothes. For this or some other reason, she has to wait for him, and in order to be safe, she climbs up into a tree. Below is a fountain or a well. A young Moorish or Gypsy girl comes to draw water.

"When she sees the reflection of the maiden in the water, she believes that it is herself and cries: 'Ah, how beautiful I am, and still my mother sends me to fetch water.' When the maiden heard this, she could not help herself and broke out laughing. Then the Moorish girl looked up. . . ." She throws the beautiful girl into the well and passes herself off as her with the prince: "Tell me, my love, why have you stayed away so long that out of pure longing for you I have become black and wrinkled?" (Greek, from Asia Minor).[85] The Macedonian Gypsy girl answers the question of the czar's son, "Alas, girl, how is it that in so short a time you have become so black in the face?" still more cleverly: "From the sun, Lord, it has burned me . . . ; for in the apple up to now the sun could not reach me, even though I am the sister of the sun."[86] What is bright, light, and like unto the sun is considered beautiful and good; dark complexion, the Moor, the Moorish girl, and the Gypsy girl are the opposite. Having similar qualities to those of the sun has at all times and among many peoples been found to be beautiful; it is not something merely limited to one particular time or race. That is why golden hair plays such an important role in the fairytale.

In most cases, ugliness is as little particularized as beauty. Its degree, the character of its extreme value, or lack of value, is at times brought out through comparisons. Beside the humorless "ugly as sin," one can run across a jocular "uglier than debts."[87] Fundamentally, it is as true of ugliness as it is of beauty that the imagination of the listener is given great freedom to picture it in accordance with his own tastes, which does not at all imply vagueness in the wishy-washy sense. The unadorned word *ugly* is suggestive and calls forth according to the nature and experience of the listener a correspondingly precise picture, while every attempt at description remains just an attempt, something open-ended and incomplete. Where in the first edition of the Grimms' Fairytales the witch is a "small, very old woman" ("kleine steinalte Frau"), whose "head shook," in the later editions she is a "very old woman, who was leaning on a crutch." And we learn here not only that her head shook; Wilhelm Grimm lectures us further: "Witches have red eyes and cannot see very far, but, like animals, they have a keen sense of smell, and they sense it when people approach." What is left when the story is then transmitted orally? Only "Then out came an ugly old woman. She was a witch" ("Do kümmt dor ne oll häßliche Fruu herut. Dat wir ne Hex"), or "Then out came an old woman on crutches" ("Dann kümmt ein oll Fruu up Krücken dor ruut"). That she is a witch is only then stated in this Mecklenburg version when one is told of her intention to eat up the two children. In the rest of the story, she is consistently referred to as "the old woman" ("dei Ollsch"),[88] which corresponds fully to the habit of other fairytale narrators: "An old woman," "an ugly old woman" are common formulas.

A contrast to the beautiful which is related to the contrast based on ugliness is offered by the unpromising or unprepossessing *(unscheinbar)*. The prince with the golden hair appears to be scald-headed—he has drawn an animal skin or bladder or a piece of cloth over his hair—and he thus becomes, according to individual accentuation, either ugly to look at or simply unpromising *(scald-headed/golden-haired,* AT 314, 502, KHM 136). Unpromising also are the Cinderellas, ash-sitters, lazybones, numskulls, underestimated youngest children, and, in a special sense, also the animal children, animal brides, animal husbands, and, of course, the beggars and thrushbeards to whom princesses are given in marriage—that is, a large part in fact of all the fairytale heroes and heroines. In the end, however, they all show themselves to be superior in some way. Those in whose shadow they stood sink into nothingness. The toad is in the end not only the most beautiful but also the cleverest bride (KHM 63, AT 402); the despised son-in-law who sets out dressed in rags and riding on an old nag achieves victory in the battle now mounted on a magnificent steed and dressed in shining armor. Just as beautiful, cruel princesses finally set aside their cruelty, so also the misjudged fairytale heroes and otherworldly beings let fall the trappings of their lack of promise and show themselves for what they are. It is the same with the many unpromising objects and animals. The worthless-appearing nut contains the most precious things, and indeed exactly those which the heroine needs in order to gain back her husband. It is often recommended to the hero that he choose as his reward from everything offered to him that which is most unpromising: the three-legged or the bony, tubercular, or mangy horse—for this is the magic horse which will help him further. "When your lord then pays you your wages, you dare take from all the gold and silver only three kreutzers, and then go backwards out of hell" (Upper Palatinate).[89] "There are two birds in the bushes, an ugly one in a dirty wooden cage and a pretty one in a golden cage. But don't take the pretty one. It's the dirty one you are to take!" There "is a musical tree. If they offer to give you the whole thing, take only one small twig from it" (West Prussia).[90] "There you will see a fortune—silver, gold, paper money, and enough of everything. . . . But see to it that you don't snatch the money up when you get there! You dare not take any of the money. There behind the door is a pile of stones, each the size of a fist. Take yourself some of those!" (Moravia-Walachia).[91] "In our stable there are three thousand stallions. When you are taken there so that you can choose one for yourself, choose the one that is standing at the far end of the stable—the one that is injured" (Greek, from Northern Euboea).[92]

Of all the fish that are asked, none knows anything about the ring of the princess that was cast into the sea—except the last; the one coming too late, the drunken La Chique, has found the ring.[93] In the same fairytale from Lorraine, among the ravens that are called together, it is only the late-arriving and drunken "old soldier" La Chique who knows where the water of life is to be found. The feature that only the apparently least able (here the dead drunk) helper really can help appears in other stories in less farcical form: Among all the birds called together by the eagle, none has any information; finally a lame hawk that has not come to the "meeting" is called, and he is able to provide the information (Greek). In another Greek fairytale, of all the birds it is only a limping crow that is able to fetch the water of life.[94] In the above story from Lorraine, we find evidence of another variety of the unpromising: The hero considers gifts received from thankful animals—the ant's leg, the hair from the rat's mustache, the raven's feather, the whisker of the giant—to be worthless. "What am I supposed to do with this?" he asks, following the stereotype; and time and again in other fairytales we hear the same question, always in similar form. But the unpromising animals or old women and old men who are in this way underestimated provide the decisive bits of advice or magic help.

The unpromising in the fairytale takes many forms. It is represented by hero and heroine—the American *ash boy* as well as the European Cinderella, the numskull, the lazybones, the scald-head—by their male and female helpers, and, above all, time and again, by animals and objects. The hero is not given cake and wine for the road like his older brothers, but only bread or ashcake and water. These provide him, however, with the indispensable help of an otherworldly being—of course, only because he is friendly, sympathetic, and generous—but the gift which he can hand over to the asker is specifically, and tellingly, nothing special, just as the clothes of the chosen hero are very often hand-me-down, torn, and soiled. In place of these—they are only a sort of mask—sooner or later appear exquisite clothes, just as the limping nag is replaced by a magnificent steed, whereas the once well-equipped older brothers, on the other hand, after they have squandered everything, are in "hand-me-downs," "dirty and all black" (Czech—Walachia and central Bohemia).[95]

Much can be said about the significance in the fairytale of the unpromising figures and things that so often appear. In our last example a bit of reality has been made visible. The spendthrifts are impoverished and come down in the world; the ragged clothing is suitable for them; there is no cleft between inner reality and outer appearance. The ragged or soiled clothes of the hero or heroine are, however, only appearance; and just as in the case of helpers, whether they are in human or animal form, and of unpromising magical objects and other manifestations of the unpromising, we see in this motif one of the most important carriers of the theme of the contrast between *reality and appearance* (see pp. 125–128). The unpromising serves further as a way of testing the hero, his modesty and humility, his willingness to be of help. In an especially pointed borderline example, one leaning toward the motif of ugliness, he must overcome his disgust: He must eat wormy figs, drink from a dirty, foul, or even festering spring, and at the same time enthusiastically praise them: "Oh, how good these figs taste to me! If only the king could have some of them to eat!" "Ah, what good water this is, how crystal clear!" (Greek).[96]* Here the demand of the neglected—and, by extension, the downtrodden and insulted—to be taken seriously comes into play. And even when the clever pretense, carried out on the advice of the helper, serves the hero's own ends, an attitude of affectionate inclination to the disgusting, the ugly, and the unpromising becomes evident.

The theme of affectionate inclination to the unpromising or monstrous also echoes through many animal husband/wife stories. Not only in the "La Belle et la bête" (1758) of Mme Leprince de Beaumont is it what disenchants the beast and transforms it into a prince "more handsome than the day" ("plus beau que le jour"); also in the English fairytale the ugly dog transforms into an attractive young man when the merchant's daughter no longer addresses him as "big, ugly dog with small teeth" but, out of pure pity and no longer under compulsion, as "Sweet-as-a-honeycomb."[97] (Nonesthetic parallels: When the witch or the man-eating giant is addressed as "Mother" or "Father," he or she ceases to be dangerous and becomes a helper. See pp. 47–48). In other places, the notion of an inverted world comes out: In the other world everything is different, and the gray garment indicates that one belongs to the underworld—or to the fireplace (Cinderella!), to the earth, or to those beings sprung from the earth. Gods disguise themselves as beggars; the unpromising or the ugly is a sign of the completely different *(Ganz Anderes)*, of the numinous. Christ and Peter wander unrecognized in simple clothing from house to house, for example. In other contexts shabby clothing or animal masks serve the purpose of fooling demons. Lévi-Strauss sees Cinderella-type figures, who appear sometimes in soiled, other times in magnificent, clothing, as mediators between poor and rich, or phallic figures that mediate between the sexes.[98] For Bruno Jöckel, "poor clothing" is a sign of "the immature, the still childlike," whereas "rich, magnificent . . ., golden clothing" is a sign of the mature person who has reached the "kingdom of life," that is, adulthood.[99] These are interpretations and attempts at interpretation, some plausible, others far-fetched. Esthetically, however, all the various forms of the unpromising operate as a counterweight to the beautiful and glamorous. And they have, like the ugly—which at times invites similar interpretation and at times nonsimilar—the power of quantity contrast (see pp. 105–107). The transitions are fluid. The soiled work dress or the wooden cage in comparison to the magnificent dress or the golden cage can just as well be designated ugly as unpromising, and yet the two phenomena—the unpromising and the ugly—clearly differ from one another in terms of ideal type. Both belong to the fairytale—the witch and the unpromising and misjudged youngest child *(unpromising hero)*; the otherworldly being as unpromising old man or old woman and the man-eater, the clumsy giant, or the ugly dragon; the animal partner as something unpromising (a donkey) or as something ugly and repulsive (frog or toad as bridegroom or bride). The two spheres—the unpromising and the ugly—are separate expressions of the opposition to the beautiful. In any given fairytale neither is indispensable. For the fairytale as a genre, however, an important element would be missing if either the ugly or the unpromising were not represented, not just because of the loss of differentiation in symbolism, but also for esthetic reasons: The beautiful, which dominates the fairytale, would decrease in significance if it were not in contrast to two different forms of opposition, the markedly unpromising and the ugly. That the daily humdrum, moreover, also has its place and its effect from both the esthetic and the anthropological points of view, will be discussed later (see pp. 145–149). Esthetically effective, however, are above all the contrasts beautiful/ugly and magnificent/unpromising. It is therefore not surprising that they appear in countless fairytales. In the fairytale—in contrast to the popular novel (*Trivialroman*), which pretends to be realistic—they are a part of its total style. The use of extreme forms is one of its basic tendencies.

## THE BEAUTIFUL AS *MOVENS* AND AS *ABSOLUTUM*

Like almost everything else in the fairytale, the beautiful—and to a lesser degree the ugly, as well—is a moving force in the plot. This is less true of the ugly not only because it appears less often and is from the point of view of the presentation less strongly accentuated, but because, almost paradoxically, it lacks a similar shock effect to that of the beautiful. One could not with like justification speak of the shock effect of the ugly as one can of the shock effect of beauty. Of course the prince is horrified when, instead of the beautiful girl of the orange, he sees an ugly creature standing before him, as is the king who, instead of the beautiful girl praised by her brother and portrayed in the picture, is presented with the ugly daughter of the witch, but he marries her anyway ("he wished," like Brentano's King Haltewort, "not to break his royal word").[100] An ungrateful prince spits twice in the face of his rescuer, who has for his sake "exposed herself to storm and burning sun" without eating, drinking, or speaking "for seven years, seven days, seven hours, and seven minutes," and whose skin has become blackened in the process, her face ugly and her limbs stiff, and then he abandons her ("all men are like that").[101] But scarcely any figure is motivated by pure ugliness to commit criminal deeds, as in the case of the Finnish hero who kills his beautiful wife in order to win one still more beautiful.[102] And none falls in a swoon or even lifeless to the ground upon looking at the ugly, as happens when one looks upon a painting or drawing of the beautiful (see pp. 7–10). Only as a farcical twist can an ugly boy who has been promoted to court jester maintain that he himself is indeed ugly, but his mother is ten times uglier, that he fears if someone looked her in the face he would fall over dead from fright. (In reality, the mother is "a marvelously beautiful woman, all colors, all colors!")[103] Ugliness can, as we have seen, put a young man to flight, but not spellbind him or freeze him in his tracks, as the myth says of Medusa and as the beautiful princesses or their portraits can do in the fairytale. The ugly figures and objects in the fairytale are of course also relevant to the plot, but many fewer are actual plot movers than is the case with the beautiful figures, pictures, and objects, the beautiful girl in the picture, the beautiful girl to be rescued, the golden jewelry, the golden spinning wheel, or the magnificent garment.

In many instances beauty sets the entire plot in motion, as is the case in the stories of the beautiful girl in the picture, or where one sets out to seek someone as beautiful as he or she is ("Is there one in the world who is as beautiful as I am?"—Greek),[104] or where a mother wishes a beautiful child for herself ("Snow White"). Often it also operates as *movens* within a story that is already underway, as advancer of the plot. Such is the case in the *Cinderella* type, where the beauty of the girl dancing or the girl in church sets the prince in motion; in the *Snow-White* type, where the beauty of the girl is instrumental in her salvation—non-European parallels to this motif: "She was too beautiful to be cast into the sea" (Korea);[105] and where beautiful golden objects entice a princess onto a ship or motivate the second wife to allow the former bride or wife, who has wandered from afar, to spend three nights with the (actually or—on the third night—only supposedly) sleeping husband.

Beauty, however, operates not *only* as a moving force in the plot; it has a radiance of its own. As instigator of the action it of course is functional, but even as *movens* it is, because of its nature, not to be set on a par with other instigators of the action. It is not the same thing when one sets out, like the Grimms' Thumbling, because he has "courage in his heart," as it is when one is set in motion by the picture of a beautiful princess. The fairytale, which likes to show its heroes and to some degree its heroines as wanderers (see pp. 136–137), employs the most diverse pretexts for having them set off—the simple desire to see the world or the necessity to go abroad in order to earn money; the fear of an incestuously inclined father or, conversely, a commission to fetch an ailing father the water of life; the duty to keep a promise or a summons from a faraway king—and still many others. Each of these possibilities has its own properties, its own coloring; it is not just some means of mechanically setting a particular train of events in motion. Each of the many possibilities points up a different aspect of man or of human existence; each of them displays different overtones and undertones, another symbolic value. Beauty, whether it is instigator or advancer of the action or just setting and context, as in the case of the faultlessly perfect castles, palaces, and cities, or the metal bridges whose luster makes narrators (really or just supposedly) ecstatic and leaves them speechless, has a value of its own in the fairytale—it fascinates. Its precise nature, as we have seen, is mostly left unspecified. But when it is specified, more is likely to be said about color and material (gold, a precious gem, or a garment) than about contour and shape.

Even where indicated solely by contrast, by juxtaposition against what is for the fairytale—or more precisely for the narrator in his capacity as teller of the fairytale—something ugly, the beautiful is identified in terms not of form but of material and color. As ugly appear the blackamoor, skin which is burned brown or black, pitch and dirt, hair from which lice fall, or the mouth out of which toads appear. But real contortion, the grotesque, and disharmony in form are rarely presented, unless it involves an addition by a collector, editor, or illustrator; at most one finds a slightly accented representation ("a dirty, torn dress"). Even villains and giants, dwarfs, and demonic otherworldly beings have normal proportions in the fairytale, a different situation from that in the local legend, where there frequently occur otherworldly beings with heads on backwards, smirking mouths, and quaking voices and mortals with swollen cheeks or unnaturally puffed–up chests. What is labeled as beautiful in the fairytale—partially explicitly, partially through the stigmatization of its opposite—is thus not, or at least not prominently, harmony, symmetry, and order, but rather the lustrous, the golden, and the bright. And these are the properties not only of wealth and power, but also of the divine as it appears in the religious legends of the most diverse peoples and in the visions of numerous mystics.

When "beautiful" is not more precisely specified, listeners of all epochs and regions are free to bring their own notions of beauty into play. To this extent, the beautiful in the fairytale is timeless, ahistorical—something relevant to the presently much-debated question of the timelessness of the fairytale and of the work of art in general.[106] The fairytale contains components which are of timeless relevance. Expressions like "castle," "beautiful maiden," "king," and "princess," just as others like "a tiny little man," "an ugly old woman," or "a sick king," are understood everywhere, even in countries where there are no more kings. Their generality is the prerequisite for the most diverse individualization. Each sees the not-more-closely-specified figures and objects just as seems right to him. In this sense the most general is also the most individual, the most abstract at the same time the most concrete.

The definition of the beautiful in terms of material and color is in any case of broader validity than that in terms of form. The ideal of harmony is more strongly time-bound than the idea of light, day, or sun (and along with it of gold, luster, or luminosity) as an esthetic value, an esthetic value which apparently rests on the beneficent character of the day, the light, and the sun. The esthetic has its roots in the nonesthetic. Luster and magnificence are attributes of the rich and powerful, of kings and princesses; and it is not just the fisherman's wife who sees the progressive stepping up to farmer's wife, mistress of the castle, queen, empress, and pope as stages upward in the direction of divinity. Wealth and power, united in the kingship, are the reflection of divine being. And when at the end of so many fairytales it is said that the hero or the heroine and her partner lived happily ever after, be it as princes, kings, or simply rich people, it has in the context of the stylizing, sublimating fairytale a completely different effect from that in the context of a story which attempts to be realistic. Within the world of the fairytale one can observe that even in stories with a comparatively strong realistic strain, the happy ending will most likely be felt to be simply a state of being rich and free of care. The marriage to the princess and the winning of half or all of the kingdom will be taken without question as being symbolic.

The beauty of the fairytale is a perfect one, one conceived to be perfect and thus one that is absolute, just as is the case with the divine in the imagining of many. It is absolute in two senses: of highest validity, highest value, an extreme, a superlative, and to this degree incomparable, independent—but independent also in the sense of being set apart, of *absolutum*. Even though the beautiful, like almost every important element in the fairytale, is also a plot factor, a carrier of function, it still shines forth out of the whole and leaves an impression because of what it is, which is similarly the case with the ugly. It is no accident that upon hearing the word *fairytale (Märchen)* one thinks instinctively of prince, princess, castle, and witch. The beautiful and the ugly, especially the beautiful, and under this rubric above all the beautiful in human form are in the fairytale representatives of the numinous, just as is the case with everything golden. Only representatives, however—for the numinous to its full degree is not present in the fairytale. An encounter with the otherworldly is cause for neither surprise nor fear. The terror which experiencing the numinous calls forth in the local legend is absent in the fairytale, because its actors are not complete humans, whose psychological reactions could be wholly captured or suggested in their subtlety and depth, but figures without nonsurface characteristics. Whatever would happen within them—if they were individual humans—is projected outward and thus made visible. The falling down lifeless before the fascinatingly beautiful portrait (or, in some fairytales taken down in our own time, a photograph) is already such a translation of an inner emotion into action. One is reminded of figures in the stories of Heinrich von Kleist (1777–1811), whose agitation or consternation is often expressed as an abrupt marionette-like sitting down on a chair. Even though the numinous to its full degree is absent in the fairytale, it is somehow still there in translated form. The extremely beautiful and the extremely ugly are such translations. They are place holders for the numinous or for aspects of the numinous, where the *fascinosum* is more strongly represented than the *tremendum,* the latter expressing itself almost always only indirectly, as, for example, in beauty shock. The *mysterium* is still more weakly represented: Neither in the dragon nor in the helpers who, for unknown reasons, possess magical powers do fairytale figures see anything secret or mysterious.[107]

If the notions of beauty and ugliness in the fairytale are, on the one hand, grounded in the nonesthetic, in the needs of life, on the other hand they still reach up into the spiritual, the religious. Perfect beauty, like perfection in general, is a demand or creation of the spirit. To this extent one can speak of an esthetic of the extreme, an esthetic of evil, even of an esthetic of the ugly and of the extremely unpromising. The fairytale is permeated with a fascination with the extreme—in its style, in its representations, just as in the selection of its building blocks: swine-herd and princess, pitch and gold, silken sail and soiled dress, poverty and riches, ugliness and beauty. Perfection, beauty, and luster are attributes of the divine, a projection of religious longing, but at the same time they are a projection of erotic longing, which, like the religious in the fairytale, is only indirectly expressed. The real erotic is missing for the same reasons as is the real numinous. The dangerous character of beauty—the room with the picture of the beautiful princess is not to be entered, the existence of a taboo—indicates not just a tranquil state of completion but something which tempts or forces in the direction of transcendence. This characteristic of beauty establishes a connection with the sphere of the erotic just as it does with that of the numinous—both lead man to go beyond himself; both offer danger and opportunity at the same time. The shock effect which in the fairytale so often emanates from the beautiful shows it to be both of great value and a danger to life. Among the countless fairytales which have been recorded since the collection of the Brothers Grimm offered the original impetus, there are many which, like Shakespeare's fairytale drama *The Tempest,* demonstrate that the promise which the beautiful vision represents will not, or at least not immediately, be fulfilled: The beautiful creature is cruel, heartless, under the control of a demon, or full of serpents and worms. In a fairytale from Patmos, the princess, "a beautiful little girl," even as a babe in arms, an infant, sucks the blood out of horses: "If we don't kill her, she will destroy all of the animals around here, and finally us all."[108] Beauty, like so many other things in the fairytale, can also be used as a carrier of the theme of appearance versus reality (see pp. 125–128). But even as appearance it has radiance and exercises power: Ninety-nine suitors for the hand of the beautiful princess are beheaded because they do not solve the problem posed.

Beauty as *movens* and as *absolutum* is not really two separate things, however.[109] As *movens* the beautiful demonstrates its elevated fascination. If we chose to believe Lessing's rule, the plot of many a fairytale would be nothing other than the making visible of the power and nature of beauty. Structuralist analysis of fairytales, on the other hand, could partially seduce us into seeing in the figures—thus also in the beautiful figures and objects in the fairytale—only arbitrarily interchangeable carriers of the action. In reality, the plot of the fairytale is both—something in its own right and at the same time the translation of the values represented by the figures into observable action. And the figures are also both— representatives of values and contrastive or antivalues, of attitudes, and of modes of existence, *and* carriers of the action.

This chapter, "Beauty and Its Shock Effect," has been concerned with objectified beauty in the fairytale. One might also ask whether the style of the fairytale, its structure, and its method of narration can also lay claim to the designation "beautiful." In the following chapter, which focuses on the style and composition of the fairytale in general, this question will be of interest.

# 2

## Style and Composition

### LINEARITY AND ISOLATION

Style and composition can also be looked at from the point of view of beauty. The style of the fairytale has the beauty of the clear, the definite, the orderly—the beauty of precision. Much of this has already been discussed in our first chapter, which was concerned with beauty from the point of view of content and material, hence the inclination to the abstract, the tendency to make use of juxtaposition and sequencing. Other features have been discussed in my previous writings on the fairytale, so that we need here only refer to them: depthlessness *(Flächenhaftigkeit)*, one-dimensionality *(Eindimensionalität)*, the tendency to isolate *(Isolationstendenz)*, the use of metallic and mineral transpositions *(Metallisierungen, Mineralisierungen)*, sublimation *(Sublimierung)*, and the abstract style.[110*]

Both the representational and narrative techniques of the European fairytale, in particular, tend to be linear. Objects and figures are seen as linear shapes, and the development of the plot and the ordering of episodes, sentences, and words can also be called linear.

Without letting itself in for descriptions, the fairytale manages to achieve linear clarity through the choice of the props which it uses and through the technique of simple naming. When it speaks of nuts, eggs, or tiny boxes (in which talismans, clothing, spinning wheels, or even whole castles and cities may be contained), the listener or reader is able to see their sharp outlines. The preference for castle and city moves in the same direction. Differing from the open village and crumbling ruin of the local legend, castles and cities are closed constructs. Anyone who hears the word *city* or the word *castle*—and how often the fairytale has its heroes enter a city or a castle!—sees instinctively before him straight lines, the verticals and horizontals of the towers, walls, windows, doors, and stair-

40

cases. The picture which is evoked by the words *castle* and *city* is then made concrete through the mentioning of particulars. There is, for example, mention of the city wall (upon which the heads of the unsuccessful suitors have been put on display), the door to the forbidden room, the window high above in Rapunzel's tower, or the castle stairs upon which Cinderella loses her golden or glass (or perhaps also not further specified) shoe. A golden shoe, a glass shoe—in addition to the predilection for the linear, there is a preference for inflexible materials. Objects of iron, stone, or glass have sharper contours and are clearer in form than organic materials, and the same is true of copper and silver forests in comparison with real forests. Even clothing, especially the magnificent garments of which the fairytale delights to speak, is linear, flatter than the body of the male or female wearer, as is metal armor. The fairytale prefers to speak of clothing and (golden or silver) armor rather than of bodies, not just because they are made of exquisite, shining materials, but because clothing and armor are artificial creations, because the structure, the geometry, of the raiment is further from nature, nearer the spirit, more abstract than the plasticity of the body. A golden spinning wheel is certainly already clear enough in its lines, but the egg or the nut that contains it is even closer to the perfect circle or oval. This is also true of the hazelnut out of which, as Cendrouse (Cinderella) opens it, come coach, horses, and coachman.[111] The fairytale delights not just in the line as such, but above all in the simple, clearly drawn line. It is here again worth considering whether such simplicity does not derive in part from the simplicity of the narrator and the demands of oral presentation and oral transmission. But the result of such demands is not listened to and further narrated because it is easy to remember and easy to tell, but because one takes pleasure in telling it. The clarity and purity of line, even if they were only a result of the lack of ability of the narrator—which is certainly not the case—would still satisfy the esthetic sense of both the narrators and the listeners.[112*]

The simple sequencing of words, sentences, and episodes is also a result of the predisposition of the tellers and of the demands of oral delivery. The teller of fairytales narrates primarily incrementally rather than by using subordination, which results in a linear, not a three-dimensional, narrative structure. To this degree the structure of sentences and of narrative periods and the unfolding of the plot are comparable to the presentation of the props and figures. One can speak of a linear style on both levels, that of the figures and objects that are significant in the plot and that of composition. As much as possible, words and sentences are not subordinated to others, but stand on the same level with them: We see this linearity with words in "Er ging und ging" ("He walked and walked") and "Se weent un weent" ("She cried and cried") and with sentences in the following passage:

Dar is mal'n Burn weß, de hett'n Knech hadd, de will so gern dat Gruseln lehrn un dat kan he nich. De Bur hett'n Koppel (eine Wiese) hadd, dar spökelt (spukt) dat, dar hebbt de Peer (Pferde) gahn, un de schall de Knech mal abends in'n Düstern haln. Den Burn sin beiden Bröder hebbt sik Bettlaken ümnahmen, un de een stellt sik in't Hecklock (Tor der Umzäunung) hen un de anner bind sik en Ked (Kette) an't Been un steht op de Koppel. De Knecht kümmt je an, en Knüppel hett he in de Hand hadd. . . .

There once was a farmer. He had a farmhand. He (the farmhand) wants so much to learn how to get the creeps, and he just can't. The farmer had a meadow. There it is haunted. The horses have gone there, and the farmhand is to fetch them in the evening after dark. The two brothers of the farmer draped themselves in bedsheets, and the one places himself in the gate opening, and the other hangs a chain on his leg and stands in the meadow. The farmhand gets there. He had a club in his hand. . . .[113]

It is not the case that there are no subordinate clauses, no modifiers, but nonsubordination is dominant. It is still more apparent with figures and episodes than in the grammatical context. "Nu is dar'n Bur, de hett drê Söhns: Dumm Hans, Klôk Hans un Middel Hans" ("Now there was once a farmer who had three sons—Dumb Hans, Clever Hans, and Middle Hans").[114] As usual, each of the three sons is assigned a task, and thus an episode. The two older boys behave equally clumsily; the youngest, Dumb Hans, is sly and wins the king's daughter. No exchange of experiences takes place; each episode stands on its own. This situation appears in countless stories. In others, plot figures do report what they have experienced, but the actor in the next episode nevertheless behaves autonomously. Pechmarie in the fairytale "Frau Holle" does not imitate the modesty and industriousness of her stepsister, but is lazy and saucy. The middle brother or wander comrade also does not draw any benefit from the failure of the first—he behaves just like him. The episodes are all on the same level; they are to this degree independent, encapsulated, isolated. The success of the youngest is generally not the result of his knowledge of the fate of his brothers; he naturally behaves differently, because he is different from his brothers, and pleasantly shares his wretched bit of cake with the little man that he meets.

• *Isolation* is one of the governing principles in the fairytale. It is not just the case that each individual adventure constitutes a unit of its own—so that in the extreme of the ideal case, even when the same thing happens again, everything is narrated anew, and completely, without any reference to the earlier episode—but the figures are also isolated; they wander individually out into the world. Their psychological processes are not illuminated; only their line of progress is in focus, only that which is relevant to the action—everything else is faded out. They are bound neither to their surroundings nor to their past, and no depth of character or psychological peculiarity is indicated. They are cut off from all that—isolated. In the extreme case, they are just carriers of the action, figures.

• The simplicity and clarity of this linear style have their own fascination, their own beauty. The tendency to the extreme, which is at work in every nook and cranny of the fairytale, not just in the contrastive juxtaposition of beautiful and ugly, contributes to this clarity and sharpness: great riches, half a kingdom, the hand of the princess, or rule over the whole empire as reward if the tasks set are fulfilled, death if they are not. Luster and magnificence, on the one hand; cruel punishments or dirt and rags, on the other. One brother or neighbor is poor, the other rich. One is good, the other bad. The one couple has no children, the other has twelve. The hero or heroine is an only child, a stepchild, or the last, the youngest, of a group. The hero is thought to be a numskull or is underrated as an animal child, but comes out ahead of everyone else. He appears to be scald-headed, but really has golden hair. In the midst of hell shine the three golden hairs of the devil. The representations are everywhere sharp and straightforward, the relationships unmistakable. The cruel punishments are just one of the elements in this totality held together by a uniform style.

• And yet this totality is not without its secrets. The glassy or metallic clarity and surface simplicity are paired with a nontransparent world structure: It is seldom clear what the source of the power of the other-worldly helpers is and who has sent them, what sort of framework they belong to. It is of no interest to the hero, to whom their help is welcome; and, very much in contrast to the local legend, the eye of the teller and of the listener to the fairytale is not focused on the otherworldly as such but rather on the hero and his path, on the heroine and her fate. The long paths which the hero, and often also the heroine, has to travel, the mobility of the figures traveling great distances, and the reachability of goals—there being no unbridgeable gulf between this world and the other (which mostly does not really appear as such, but rather just as a far-off realm)—all makes its contributions to the achievement of clarity in the fairytale. But the far-off realm itself remains unexplored. Likewise, the fairytale also tolerates blind spots in its structure, blind and blunted motifs and features, that is, motifs and individual features which are either completely without function or whose relevance to the whole somehow remains obscure. In this sense, the strange behavior of the great magician in the fairytale used as a model in the first chapter is a blunted motif; one does not know why he, mobilizing all his strenth—he regularly comes home evenings covered with sweat—must flog corpses. Regardless of how these blunted motifs come into being (it happens that in the course of oral transmission unity is lost, a connecting link is left out), the fairytale is scarcely conceivable without them; it would have a different character without them. Sublimation, depthlessness, one-dimensionality (the otherworldly not perceived as another dimension), linearity, isolation, juxtaposition and sequencing, and the abstract style all bring about optical clarity; blind and blunted motifs, unexplained connections, and inexplicable powers provide a counterbalance. And the tendency toward isolation, which on the one hand produces the clarity of figures and plot line, is on the other hand also partially responsible for the appearance of the unexplained. Because it clearly brings figures, events, and episodes out in relief, it leaves much in the darkness—light also gives both the shadow and the mysterious their due.

## FORMULAS

The many formulas that are put to use in the fairytale are also an element lending clarity of form. The preference of the European fairytale for the number three, and of the oriental for the number four (forty thieves, forty maidens, forty days, etc.), is well known. The listener to fairytales can rely on the fact that these numbers will keep turning up; they are one of the many constants in the fairytale. They give security not only to the narrator, who relies on them and takes pleasure in making use of them, but to the listener, as well. The forces which determine the production of a work of art or which help to determine it are also important for its reception. The esthetics of production and the esthetics of reception are parallel, just as mnemetic technique, the technical basis of oral narration in general, and esthetic effect are connected to one another. That which has some technical purpose can, in the sense of an esthetics of the functional, be pleasing at the same time. Formulas are memory props and transition aids for the narrator. They are useful to him and comfortable, but they are additionally agreeable to him—just as the hearer is also delighted—when they turn up time and again, because he feels the organizing effect they have, and also simply because they are familiar to him. This mixing of the familiar and unfamiliar, which, according to Charlotte Bühler, brings the fairytale close to the child, is also advantageous for the adult.[115]

Tripling *(Dreizahl)* occurs not only in conjunction with figures and props—three dragons, three brothers, three princesses, three magical agents—but also with episodes. It is at the same time both a stylistic and a structural formula. The teller knows that he has three adventures to relate one after the other, and the listener expects three adventures. In the western world the number three is woven in many ways into the general cultural structure. It is a mythic number, it has a central place in higher religion (the Trinity), it is a magical number ("Thrice must the words be spoken!"), and it occurs in children's games ("One, two, three, who's got the ball?") just as in serious art (the triptych). Its governing of the presentation of figures and objects in the fairytale and also of the unfolding of the plot gives the listener, who is used to it, a similar feeling of security to that of the narrator, for whom it is an aid to memory and a means of organizing, and therefore a means to artistic effect. The three stands between singularity and amorphous multiplicity. Coming after the one, which represents the individual, and the two, which represents at the same time the pair and the possibility of polarity, the three is the first representative of real plurality. The fact that in Indo-Germanic the singular, dual, and plural were distinct attests to the fundamental character of such a differentiation. Thus it is no accident when these three numbers are dominant in the fairytale: the one in the person of the hero or heroine; the two in the many polarities and in the tendency to divide into halves, into sequences of two; and the three in the structuring of groups and in the ordering of episodes. Only one, two, and three are relevant to the building of episodes. The higher numbers which often occur in the fairytale and thus are likewise to be considered formulaic—7, 12, 40, 99, 100—are used only to designate groups; a narrative of seven, twelve, or even forty episodes would be too complicated, would not satisfy the European demand for an overview, for simplicity, and for clarity. The three is not only the first but also the most impressive representative of plurality. It is optically still directly graspable, but, in conjunction with differentiation, intensification, and contrast, it can offer a clear basis for organization. In contrast to the symmetrical and equally balanced numbers two and four, the number three also has a certain dynamism. It is no accident that in our fairytales it controls the structuring of groups and the development of the plot.[116]

Sentences used for placing emphasis operate as a sort of stylistic formula, like the simple "So war gut," "Also war gut," "So ist denn gut," and "Also gut" of the West Prussian Karl Restin.[117] This formula has its parallels in other narrators and in other languages—in Rumanian, for example, where in individual narratives the interjections "Good!" and less often "So!" occur periodically,[118] and in the French "Ben i dit" or the still shorter "il dit," "elle dit," which one frequently also hears in the French conversation of unsophisticated people (it corresponds to the Bavarian "hot er gsogt"). The French examples again stem from our French Canadian model narrative; in other variants recorded verbatim of the same narrative type, something corresponding to Restin's "Also war gut" is found still more frequently. The tale "La Mangeuse d'enfants" [The child-eating woman], for example, begins, "Bon une fois c'etait bon vous dire c'etait une vieille." On the first page of the printed text, *ben* and *bon* used in the sense relevant here (e.g., "Bon ben i dit") are repeated ten times, *i dit* ("he said") and *a dit* ("she said"), eighteen times; in addition, one finds *pis* (= *puis* "then") eight times.[119] This sort of thing is no longer art, but rather artlessness, letting oneself go, so close do the two stand to one another.

With other narrators, along with the above-mentioned turns of phrase ("Ben, c'est all right," "Ben, i dit. . . ."), one other is prominent: "Ça fait que," literally "That makes that . . ." in the sense of "Thus it was so that. . . . " These sorts of common fillers—in most book fairytales *(Buchmärchen)* they are cut out by the editors—when used with discretion, mark pauses and accentuation. After almost twenty years, I can still hear the continually recurring "je dis" ("I said") of the report from memory of events which a young French woman gave in a train to her husband, who was returning from the hospital—I happened to be sitting in the same compartment. The "je dis" did not just indicate thought pauses, but was at the same time also a naively natural and undemanding means of emphasizing the young woman's own role in the family gathering about which she was reporting. After many years, only the melodic "je dis," which recurred with pleasant regularity, has remained in the memory of the uninvolved listener. With pleasant regularity. Such expressions which recur time and again like a musical motif are already an element of style in the simple everyday narrative, and the more so in the fairytale. Even when they are empty set phrases, they are not only a result of the clumsiness of the oral teller and an answer to his needs, but habits which have become agreeable and have a certain esthetic value.

More artistic—and thus not suppressed by editors and revisers—are connective formulas such as "But let's now leave the girl and see what the boy is doing" (Sardinian), "Now let's leave the boys in the garden, and let's go back to Rosamunda and see what's going on there" (Lotharingian, in German dialect), "Let's put that aside now and come back to Vienna to the king with the long nose" (Rhaeto-romance), "Let's leave the villain and see what our three boys are doing" (Majorcan), "Now back to the life of the family of the ruler of Heavenland" (Indonesian), and "Let's leave her now and turn back to the robbers" (Arabian Nights).[120] It has been assumed that such expressions have gone over from dime novel literature *(Kolportageliteratur)* into oral narration.[121] In individual instances this possibility is not out of the question, but the usage is so obvious for two-strand narrations and is found in so many places[122] that in principle polygenesis may be assumed. Fairytales normally make use of single-strand narration, but when two strands are used, it becomes necessary to have a connective formula. Formulations such as those we have cited lie close at hand; even simple tellers can stumble on them independently of one another. The passage of common oral formulas into dime novel literature is just as possible as the reverse. Because the influence of written literature on the oral narrative was so long underestimated, there is a tendency today to overemphasize it. From an esthetic standpoint it is unimportant where the formula originates. Whether it is improvised or taken over from an earlier teller or taken from something read, what is decisive is that it is accepted, that it is used time and again. It fulfills the narrative demands of both the performers and the listeners.

In likewise constantly similar form, one hears the famous words "Ich rieche, rieche Menschenfleisch" ("I smell, I smell human flesh"). Greece: "Scarcely had the first dragon arrived than he began to sniff about and to call out: 'Ooh! It smells of human flesh. It smells of human flesh.' And whichever one of them came in called out the same thing: 'It smells of human flesh.'" The Greek formulation ("sniff about") indicates a beastlike nature similar to that attributed to witches by the Brothers Grimm (see p. 30)—like the dragons here, witches are man-eaters. In the English farce fairytale about Jack the Giantkiller it says: "Fee-fi-fo-fum, I smell the blood of an Englishman." In Berber: "I smell humans."[123] The formulaic words said by someone who has been brought back to life are also found throughout the world: "My, how deeply (or, how long) I've slept!" Hungarian: "Oh, how sweetly I've slept." Rumanian: "Oh, my brother, how heavily I've slept." Gypsy: "Mother, I have slept heavily." The answer: "You might have slept on into eternity had I not come." Greek: "Ah, how deeply I have slept." The answer: "You weren't asleep, you were dead." Indian (from Central Brazil): "I have slept well." Answer: "No . . . , you have . . . not slept! A jahu ate you up."[124] In whatever contexts this formula may have its roots—it may be connected to awakening from the magical sleep of the trance—from an esthetic point of view it operates in the fairytale like a phrase expected by the listener, who indeed, in the times when fairytales were told among adults, was always an expert on the genre. One still recognizes in it something of the weight of the reality (or spiritual reality) which perhaps lies behind it; what sort of reality it was, however, the listener scarcely inquires into. The formula operates primarily as a formula; it belongs at this particular point in the narration, which is not to say that it must appear every time someone is called back to life, whether with the water of life or by some other method, but anyone who knows it would be disappointed if from time to time it did not return to its designated place. It is similar with the mode of address with which one can win over demonic beings. When the fairytale hero addresses the "iron-toothed witch" as "Mother" or as "Grandmother," she answers: "Lucky for you that you have called me 'Mother'; otherwise your bones would soon have been tinier than poppy seeds."[125] Instead of the plain word, elsewhere one finds symbolic action, which is indeed more primitive; it possibly goes back to adoption practices in the Mediterranean area. In an Algerian-Kabylian story, the man-eating witch (teriel) has slung her long breasts back over her shoulders (a very common feature) so that they will not disturb her at work. "The boy crept up very carefully from behind. He took the right breast of the teriel and drank of her milk. The teriel turned round and saw the human. She said: 'Now that you have been nurtured at my breast, I will treat you like my son and do only good to you . . . .'" In place of a witch one may have a wild beast. Someone who has broken his arms and legs creeps into a cave and comes upon some lion cubs. When the lioness comes back, the cubs push and shove to get at her breast.

> "I also pushed into the midst. I also drank from the breast of the lioness. By and by, the lioness turned her head around. She roared and cried out: 'A human. If you hadn't drunk of my milk, I would eat you up. But since you have drunk of my milk, I will protect you.' The lioness brought me food every day. The lioness doctored my broken limbs."[126]*

Superstitions and the local legend show precise rules for interaction with spirits (one must be sure to have the first and the last word; instead of one's hand, one offers the dead a wooden handle, which then begins to burn or turn to charcoal). The fairytale also knows such rules, but although they originally may have belonged to the world of belief, they have become in the stylistic framework of the fairytale fantastic and playful, and often they are revealed to the fairytale hero by otherworldly beings (in the local legend people usually already know how one deals with wretched souls, or they learn this from fellow humans): Dragons are asleep when they have their eyes open, but they are awake and dangerous when their eyes are closed. Monsters must be killed with their own sword; the sword is to be used with the left hand, and a second blow must not be given—it would restore the fatally wounded monster instead of finishing it off. Behind such rules stands the idea of a reversed world. Different laws apply to otherworldly beings than to mortals; everything is turned around. But in the framework of the fairytale, justifications of this sort are seldom, if at all, offered, and they also need not be apparent to the listener. It has become obvious through our examples that gesture and conduct formulas play a similar role to that of word formulas. The fairytale plays with both. Thus one can also run into the above-mentioned saving mode of address as an earthy, humorous embedding: "After three days the dragon woke up, turned over onto his other side, and let . . . a fart fly, which like a cannonshot . . . caused the place to quake. Then Diamantas called out, 'What do you wish, little father?' 'Huh?' said the dragon, surprised, 'did I give birth to you with my fart?'" The hero, Diamantas, well-equipped with advice, is able to convince the dragon that that is really the case. In another fairytale, likewise Greek, almost word for word the same: "The boy sprang forward . . . and said to the dragon: 'At your service, Father, what do you wish?' 'Who are you? And how did you get here?' 'Father, you produced me this very hour. I was born with the fart which emitted from your belly.' This seemed to the dragon a very happy event. 'Come closer . . . , so that I can touch you, my dear child. . . .'"[127]

Only a few more of the other prose formulas within the narrative will be mentioned. "Was willst du armer Teufel geben?" ("Canst thou, poor Devil, give me whatsoever?") we read in *Faust I* (Study Scene III, verse 1675). It is as if Goethe had in his ear the words of so many a fairytale hero who underestimates the abilities of potential helpers. "So what will you ever be able to do for me?" asks the Gascon lad of respectively the pike, the ant, and the bee, whom he has aided and who wish to reward him for doing so. In a Greek analog involving the same helpers the hero asks, "What can possibly come from you ants?"[128] Besides such remarks from the fairytale figures there are the stereotyped remarks of the narrators, as has already been brought out in the case of two-strand narratives (see pp. 46–47). The Gypsy Taikon excuses the absence of precise details as follows: "He rode for a day and he rode for two. How long he rode, I don't know, so I can't tell about it. But whether it was this way or whether it was not, they reached a land which was so full of houses. . . ." Beautifully concise is his "And what was said, was done,"[129] which occurs almost word for word in French: "Ce qui fut dit fut fait." [130] A fully artless formula, however, is "In order to make it short" (Greek), "In order to make a long story short" (Scottish), "Par favala pju kurta, kapite" (Italian).[131] If one can scarcely agree to call such set phrases formulas, one hestitates for another reason to designate spoken and sung *verses* as such: These are verses fitted to the particular situation and to this degree not formulaic, not directly insertable into other fairytale types. But as starkly structured speech elements, they still fit into the formulaic overall style of the fairytale.

Many fairytale openings and closings are truly formulaic. "Once upon a time" and "They still live thus today" are the most widely distributed. "Once upon a time" especially is current in almost all European languages. The formula immediately sets the beginning narrative off from the present, from the everyday world of teller and listener (or reader). To this degree, the use of the past has a specific narrative function, not just in the sense that it fictionalizes, as in the theory of Käte Hamburger,[132] but also in that it clearly indicates that henceforth a closed and thus easily surveyable train of events is to be described.[133] The opening words "Once upon a time," "Una volta era," "Μιά φορά ήτα" establish distance. They create distance from the present and, along with it, from reality, and offer an invitation to enter another world, a world past, thus one that does not exist. At the same time, the teller distances himself from his own narrative with the formula "Once upon a time": "Once there was, there never was," "There was and there wasn't." The taking back is not even necessary; the simple "Once upon a time," because it is a familiar fairytale opening, is indeed already the signal that one is entering into a nonreal realm, the realm of literature. The well-known ironic closing formulas also create distance, just as clearly as do the openings. "And if they haven't died, they're still living this way today" says the opposite from what it appears to say. The narrative is closed; the persons that were spoken of are no longer living, have really never lived, and exactly for this reason they live every place and always and thus also today. The irony of the closing formula is doubly indicated—one seems to see the twinkling eye that specifically goes along with verbal irony. Other closing formulas are completely unequivocal. Such is the case with the famous Russian one which follows the wedding ceremony crowning the fairytale:

> I also was there,
> Mead and wine I drank,
> Over my mustache it flowed,
> Into my mouth it didn't come.[134]

The irony is clear. The story told is projected into the realm of the unreal. At the end, the narrator conducts himself and the listeners back into the real world. The Rumanian folklorist Mihai Pop emphasizes that in many fairytales the opening and closing formulas correspond with mirrorlike symmetry—the opening formula leads from reality into the nonreal; the closing formula snatches the listeners out of the fantastic fairytale world and sets them, gently or not so gently, back in the everyday world.[135] "The conclusion," as Roman Jakobson expresses it with regard to the Russian formulas, using "rhymed patter, shifts the attention from the tale to the teller . . . the still-thirsty teller awaits his refreshment. Sometimes the allusions are more transparent: 'This is the end of my tale, and now I would not mind having a glass of vodka.' "[136] This last statement can again only with reservation be called a formula; in its drastic and unpoetic directness it is almost just a statement of fact ("The fairytale is ended") and a demand ("Vodka!"). But it also still marks the end of the narrative and leads, less refined, less gentle than the other closing statements, out of the sphere of dream and magic into the everyday world. This effect is characteristic of closing formulas in general. "They celebrated . . . forty days and forty nights long, and ate and drank and enjoyed themselves. Neither we nor you were there, so you don't have to believe it" (Greek).[137] One can also say this more nicely:

> I also was there
> In my red trousers
> And ate a lentil on a spit
> And if that lentil fits on the spit
> Then you also have to believe my tale.[138]

The most popular Greek closing formula, however, goes: "Then they lived well, and we better still." Is that meant ironically? In light of countless other closing formulas, like the Russian one cited, it seems probable. But Georgios A. Megas, who has often been present when a male or female teller has concluded a story in such a manner, writes me: "I have never had the impression that these concluding words . . . were uttered ironically. I am more of the opinion that the narrator, in tune with the optimistic tendency of the fairytale, addresses to himself and the listener . . . the wish: 'May it go still better with us!' "[139] This theory accords with the conclusion of the story of the girl from the lemon (AT 408): "Then the prince had the Moorish woman torn to pieces by four horses, took the maiden as his wife, and put on a huge wedding. And I wish that yours would also soon come to pass, and that I would be there."[140] In Sicily it is stated differently. There, countless fairytales end "And they lived happy and content, but we have come away empty-handed," "They remained rich and comforted, but we remain sitting here," and "They remained content and happy, and we like a bundle of roots."[141] Thus pleasant and perhaps also at times resigned irony and self-irony, fun and earnestness, are mixed together according to the humor of the narrators and listeners and indeed also of the readers and interpreters. The Sicilian closing formulas need not be altogether so sarcastic and by everyone so sarcastically intended as they are formulated; the Greek closings can be spoken by some in complete cheerfulness, but by others so as to have an ironic touch of social criticism. With still other narrators it is primarily a matter of comic contrast. All these formulas, however, have one thing in common: They provide a point of termination. This task can also be fulfilled by statements which, in terms of content, have nothing at all to do with the corresponding fairytales. The formula "I climbed up onto a mole hill and came out again by Labouheyre" closes completely different fairytales in French.[142] In Japanese, the most frequent closing formulas are "He prospered all his life" and "The market prospered." Since the closing formulas often do not fit with the end of the fairytale, however, the Japanese fairytale scholar Toshio Ozawa has chosen to translate freely: "That's all,"[143] an ending that fully accords with oral tradition. The Tadzhiks say "That's the end of it,"[144] the French "C'est tout."[145] The etiological closing, popular in other narrative genres, especially in the animal tales of primitive peoples *(Naturvölker)*, is also to be found in the fairytale. Thus a Greek narrative of the *brother and sister* type concludes with the words: "Since that time there are two new constellations in the heavens, . . . the Pleiades and the morning star."[146] An etiological coda is also a sort of terminal point.

The most important thing about a concluding formula is not its actual content or its tone (whether ironic or not), but its function as a formula. It brings the narrative to a close. Still, many tellers and listeners value the possibility of individual variation. Such freedom within the bounds set by a particular formula or by the pressure toward formulaic representation in general is part of the esthetic appeal of the fairytale. Knowledge of the formula "And if they haven't died, they are still living like this today" allows variations like "If he hasn't died, then he's still sitting there to this day" or "And if she hasn't died in the meantime, she is still lying about like this to this day."[147] Jokes of this sort are quite amusing against the background of the generally known formula, but they presuppose the formula. If in every instance an individual version were to appear in place of the basic formula, the effect would be lost. Just as in the existence of man, one observes a certain relationship between constraint and freedom in many places in the fairytale, as is the case here in the application of closing formulas.[148] And just as in the existence of man, constraint predominates, but a flexible area of freedom remains. Within this area not only irony and the desire to criticize turn up, but also pure playfulness, unintentional humor, wit, and comic contrast for its own sake. It is a nice individual touch when, at the end, the prince brings his foster parents, the miller and his wife, along with their children into the castle, and then it says "For a long time they soiled the black velvet of the chairs with their white clothing."[149] Other variations are traditional—one runs into them frequently—as in the case of the previously cited formulas indicating disillusionment. Instead of receiving something at the wedding feast, the teller is thrown out with such a good swift kick that he flies a long way through the air and lands on the chair on which he is sitting and telling his story.[150]* "To me they gave nothing, except a large bone, which they flung and hit me on the elbow with, and my arm still hurts." One can picture the accompanying gestures. This is a fake etiological ending.[151]

Frequently, the opening formulas are more extensively developed than the closing phrases. With many narrators, the need for setting the proper scene makes itself felt. The Greek can preface the "Once upon a time" with "I now want to begin the beautiful fairytale and wish our fine company a lovely evening."[152] The Gypsy can begin with "There was and there wasn't. If it hadn't happened, one wouldn't tell about it. I want to tell you the fairytale of the firebird. But don't interrupt me. Drink and smoke, but I'll do the talking. I will narrate for our happiness and well-being."[153] Hungarian narrators move their stories drastically and verbosely into a nonreal realm: "Where was it, where wasn't it? Somewhere, seven times seven lands distant and still further away, on the far side of the Operenzer Sea, behind an old stove in a crack in the wall, in the seventy-seventh fold of Auntie's skirt, there was a white flea, and in its middle, a magnificent royal city,"[154] or "Where was it, where wasn't it—right here on Kopovitsch Mountain there was a willow tree. It had ninety-nine branches, and on those ninety-nine branches sat ninety-nine crows. They're there to peck out the eyes of anyone who doesn't pay attention to my story."[155] The Turks, similarly and yet with a difference, lead one into the other, the inverted world of the fairytale: "In olden times, when the fly was still imam, when my mother was rocking my cradle, she tipped it over. My father reached for the firetongs; my mother grabbed the cradle and went round the four corners. When the camel was still the town crier, the donkey still barber, and I rocked my father's cradle, then a poor woman once had three daughters. . . ."[156]

Should one speak of cliché or of formula? If the term *cliché* is applied pejoratively, then it is appropriate where, instead of the cliché, a more original turn of phrase would be in order. There is a tendency to speak of "cliché" in criticizing the popular novel *(Trivialroman)*. With respect to the fairytale, however, just as with the Homeric epics or those of the South Slavs, the term *formula* seems more apt. For here the cliché—insofar as one can accept this word as a neutral cover term—forms part of the overall style. The fairytale is as a whole stylized, starkly structured, in contrast to the local legend and to popular literature *(Trivialliteratur)*, with its lack of concern for form. The formula is appropriate to the fairytale; it fits in well with the overall style. And if the formula is not always transparent—indeed, sometimes, as in the case of the Irish *ranns* (formulaic descriptions of battles, landings, and other happenings), it is not really understandable—it reflects the nature of the fairytale, which has a crystal-clear narrative technique, but, at the same time, fantastic or mysterious content. That the Hungarian is not (or no longer) really so sure what the "Operenzer Sea" is causes no difficulty, but, on the contrary, is precisely right, for it is not a question of some place that is geographically localizable but of a nonreal sea. And does every listener know what significance the "spoonful of beans" has which the woman narrator carries over the meadow? It is indeed not the case that in every fairytale a marriage celebration has been previously described, and yet the narrative can conclude:

> And crickcrick,
> My tale is through,
> And crickcrack,
> My tale is done.
> I walk over my meadow
> With the spoonful of beans
> I received. [157]

This little verse can be tacked onto any fairytale. It represents nothing other than the closing frame; and if it is not completely understandable, it will be just as readily accepted as blind or blunted motifs and features or the archaic *ranns*, which, in and of themselves partially incomprehensible, are spoken so rapidly that they cannot be understood at all. Like the fairytale in general, the formula has two faces: It has clarity of outer form, but taken as a whole it is in many ways not, or not fully, transparent.

## STRUCTURE

Like the style, the structure of the fairytale is one of great precision. Where the manner of representation is characterized by formulas, metallic and mineral transpositions, the expression of extremes and polarities, the absence of distracting description, and the tendency to clarity of line, the structure of the fairytale is likewise characterized by clarity, compactness, and exactitude. The Russian scholar Vladimir Propp speaks of "iron rules" of composition.[158] Despite realistic intrusions, a stable form of almost abstract precision results from the interaction of representation style and composition style.

The polarity minus/plus is the framework and basis of the structure of the fairytale, in its entirety just as in individual details. The normal situation is to advance from minus to plus, but what one can designate an anti-fairytale *(Antimärchen)* also occurs as contrast, whether it takes the form of a fairytale with an unhappy ending or appears as a contrastive episode within a normal fairytale: the failure of an antihero (e.g., the elder brothers, or the stepsisters who lose their originally better position) or of the hero himself, who disregards a prohibition, a bit of advice, or a condition and as a result temporarily loses a relatively advantageous position and lands in one that is disadvantageous.[159]* The most famous Grimms' "anti-fairytale," the Runge narrative "The Fisherman and his Wife" (KMH 19, AT 555), moves in the opposite direction—in its early episodes extremely positively, and only in the last negatively. Just as the fairytale incorporates features of the anti-fairytale, the anti-fairytale reciprocates by incorporating features of the fairytale. One can virtually speak of a tendency of both the fairytale and the anti-fairytale to integrate their opposites.[160] The appearance of such subordination contrasts itself constitutes a sort of subordination contrast to the predominant juxtaposition and sequencing. The very popular fairytale model of unsuccessful imitation (see pp. 97–104) also has some of its roots in the need for contrast subordinations.

A lack (or a villainy which causes a lack) and its liquidation provide, according to Propp, the basic structural pattern of the fairytale. Alan Dundes has coined the abbreviation L-LL: Lack/Lack liquidated for this pattern.[161] Examples of situations of lack are, according to Propp: The hero has no bride, so he sets out to seek one; the king is ailing, and in order to restore his health, medicinal water or a magic bird must be fetched; the parents are poor.[162] Examples of villainies are the kidnapping of the czar's daughter; the doing away with of a magical helper by the antagonist (the stepmother in many versions of the *Cinderella* type—e.g., "Little Earth Cow,"[163] "One-eye, Two-eyes, and Three-eyes" [KMH 130, AT 511]— destroys the magic cow or goat which helps the heroine, or she has it destroyed); parents' or stepparents' casting their children out; and an unknown being's stealing golden apples or laying waste the crops.[164] One sees that lack (e.g., poverty) can result in a villainy (the setting out of the children); a villainy (e.g., robbery) for its part leads automatically to a lack (loss of a daughter or of fruit from a garden). It is not necessary to single out the villainy for special attention, as Propp does; the villainy just brings about the essential factor, the lack, the missing element. Dundes speaks of "a move from disequilibrium to equilibrium." Behind this movement stands something more general, the general human pattern Need/ Fulfillment of need. This Lack/Remedy is in fact the basic pattern of the fairytale and, moreover, of countless stories and things that occur in life in general. It is reflected in various component sequences of the fairytale, especially in the constantly recurring plot sequences Task/Fulfillment and Interdiction/Violation. Even the interdiction is a sort of task, namely, an invitation to violation; it produces a lack which is "removed" through the violation, even when this violation can have unpleasant consequences, leading to a new condition of lack, which in turn must be overcome. This relating of all important fairytale happenings to the basic sequence Lack/ Lack liquidated (L-LL) makes apparent the clarity of the fairytale struc-ture—the clarity and, of course, also the generality, for lack, villainy, missing elements, and the corresponding need and striving for remedy dominate not only the fairytale narrative but life in general. Humans. animals, and even plants seek compensation for harm they have suffered, to heal an injury or relieve a lack which they feel. To this degree the happenings in the fairytale mirror in sharply drawn pictures general hap-penings in life. That the same basic pairing, Lack/Striving for remedy, also plays an important role in the myth in no way justifies the conclusion that the fairytale stems from the myth.[165]* It is much more something completely natural that such a central phenomenon of existence should find expression in the most diverse literary genres.

Just as the fairytale often contains a sort of anti-fairytale, and conversely the anti-fairytale a sort of fairytale, this tendency to countermovement is inherent in the fairytale. Propp has established that a state of happiness often exists at the beginning: The czar owns a garden with golden apples; the parents love their children. Only later does the mischief enter in.[166] This situation brings to mind the drama theory of Donatus and Diomedes (both fourth century), which was influential right into the baroque period and according to which a tragedy normally begins with an actual or appar-ent state of happiness, whereas a comedy begins with an adverse initial constellation.[167]* In the fairytale, such an initial ideal state is usually at best just hinted at. Still, it is apparent that the more comprehensive model Order/Disorder/Order stands behind the dominant pattern Disor-der/Order or Lack/Lack liquidated—even the fact that something can be felt to be a lack necessarily presupposes the idea of a nondeficient condi-tion. The myth of the lost paradise arises as of itself out of a condition felt to be lacking in something, likewise the projection of a new paradise lying in the future. The fairytale puts the emphasis on the goal, not on the starting; it is much more interested in the disenchantment than in the enchanting. The interest in the fairytale—beginning with its "Once upon a time"—is clearly directed forward, while the local legend often and willingly delves into the past, and it is the past, too, that the myth mythicizes. The fairytale—although it employs at times two-strand narration—makes no actual use of flashback. There are, of course, bends in the plotline, setbacks which, for example, result from violating prohibitions, but immediately thereafter the line straightens again in the direction of the goal. The blunt initial situation and the decisive conclusion (reward for the positive figures, punishment for the negative, and often a general concluding formula, as well) in conjunction with the slim, goal-oriented plotline and the basic pattern—Lack/Lack liquidated, Mishap/Rescue, Task/Fulfillment—which is manifoldly represented, provide an important contribution to the compactness also observed to be the characteristic result of the representation style. The fairytale not only draws with a sharp pen, it also has clarity of organization. The numerous repetitions and variations, which *also* belong to its characteristic structure (see pp. 76–94), cause nothing to be unclear; they not only are internally organized for their own part, but, like the repetitions and variations in a piece of music, serve the purposes of the whole. The reappearance of the same thing and the turning up of the similar contribute to the structuring of the narrative and lend unity to its continuity. A preestablished blueprint, foreshadowings, and positive and negative anticipations of later happenings (see pp. 103–104) are in the fairytale, which makes no use of retrospection, of flashback, an important means of linking and organization; and, moreover, they are the factor expressing its forward-directed goal orientation.

The structure of the fairytale is characterized by the basic *framing tension (Rahmen-Spannung)* Lack/Striving for remedy, behind which stands the pattern Happiness/Disturbance/Happiness restored (see p. 55), and by the *linking tensions (Binnenspannungen)* Prohibition/ Violation, Need/Help, Task/Fulfillment, Battle/Victory, Persecution/ Rescue, Kidnap/Rescue, Death/Resuscitation, and Loss of power/ Restoration, which follow one another in the development of the plot, depending on its structure and its content. At the end there is usually a reward, elevation in rank or power: marriage to a bride (identified as a princess or in some other way shown as special), riches, or rule. With two-part fairytales, whose second part is characterized by the formula Loss of power/Restoration and which can take the concrete form of loss of husband or bride, or loss of the water of life and being pushed aside by evil brothers, the final concluding signal is placed at the end of the second sequence. Contrastive tensions like Failure/Punishment or Crime/

Punishment fall ultimately under the basic pattern Lack/Lack liquidated, while Test/Failure and Battle/Defeat/Death present real contrasts. The former are "anti-fairytales," but they have no independent existence, since failure and crime are mostly assigned to antiheroes or antagonists, who are finally eliminated as exercisers of power; if the hero himself fails, this lack will be removed as a result of proper behavior later. In the course of the action in the fairytale, everything works out, basically, at least, in the ideal form—shortcomings, errors, slips, and other weaknesses are not fully out of the question with any narrator. In principle, however, fairytale narrators sense and accept the fact that everything must be neatly constructed, that everything has to be right: "Because it's a story, and everything in it has to fit," Karl Haiding heard one of his Upper Austrian narrators say.[168] The fairytale is in this way not a direct picture but rather one contrasting with reality, the prototype of a "story": In it everything has to be right. In this framework it is not the happy ending that is important but the exactness of composition. The Austrian was scarcely completely conscious of the importance of his principle; he was applying it to a concrete situation. Taken as a principle, however, it expresses the fact that literature in itself tends toward being consistently shaped—the main postulate of so many a learned esthetic theory. In this sense, the fairytale strives toward beauty not only in terms of content but also in its entire narrative form, stylistically and structurally. Our first chapter has shown that in terms of content it avoids commitment to any special ideal of beauty; it emphasizes much more its high *degree*, its perfection. The seemingly self-creating beauty in the manner of narration, the beauty of the style and the structure, the beauty of clear line and of clear construction, is also a beauty of completion.

## PERFECTION AND IMPERFECTION

The fairytale is perfectionistic. It seeks the extreme, the high degrees, the antipodean values. There are extremes in figures, preferably kings and queens, princes and princesses—or goose-girl, swine-herd, dragon, man-eater, or witch. There are correspondingly extreme fates, whether temporary or permanent, right up to death and resuscitation; extreme dangers (wild beasts guard the precious thing to be obtained or the princess); and extremely difficult—when realistically seen, unaccomplishable—tasks, for which the linguistically and logically incorrect but suggestive expression "impossible tasks" has become almost customary in fairytale research: to carry a mountain away or build a castle or cause a grain field or orchard to come into being in a single night. The miraculous is the intensification of the extraordinary. For the fairytale of magic, which, moreover, is regarded as the "fairytale proper," such an intensification of the unusual into the nonreal is a matter of course, for it carries things in general to extremes. The ultimate in formal completion, reaching the highest conceivable degree with respect to appearance or happening, is among the vital properties of the genre.

Another favorite form of perfectionism in the fairytale is the "just barely" (Gerade noch). The task set is completed at the last moment or fulfilled by the very last contestant, the hundredth one; ninety-nine have failed and have died as a result. A shortened form of this model is the pattern-of-threes: Two figures fail, the third accomplishes the task. And as a still more concentrated pattern, the hero or heroine just barely succeeds in reaching the goal. The woman, who after a long period of wandering ends up where her lost husband now lives, watches by his side for two nights to no avail; he does not wake up from his sleep. Only on the third, the last night that she has been able to negotiate for herself, is the reunion successful (AT 425, KHM 88). In a Pomeranian fairytale, the boy who must herd the witch's foals and who evenings must bring them back into the stable at the stroke of eight (or else his head will be lopped off and put up on the picket fence), falls under the influence of a sleeping potion and wakes up so late that even with the aid of the helpful lion he is just barely able to round up the runaway foals and drive them in; he arrives with them at the gateway just exactly "as the bell strikes eight," and the gates, which the old woman slams shut, almost shear off his heels.[169] The "just barely" is a way for the fairytale to demonstrate perfection; the grace period is taken advantage of right to the last second. The closing of the gates ultimately goes back to the myth about journeying to the otherworld, where, unlike the situation in our Pomeranian fairytale, the coming together of the cliffs can lead to actual peripheral damage: The Symplegades damage the stern of the Argo, which has successfully sailed through. But the fairytale listener has as little need to have this myth in mind, or even know about it, as does the narrator. In the farce fairytale the rabbit-herd deliberately waits until the very last second to use magic to call back the hare that has been bought or coaxed away from him: when the triumphant princess in her castle already has the hare on her lap and is holding fast onto it, or when it has already been cut up into pieces and is frying in the pan, thus even beyond the really possible last minute. This situation, however, is farcical; here the fairytale is not taking itself seriously.[170]

The disenchantment fairytale (Erlösungsmärchen), on the other hand—despite all the ironical opening and closing formulas—takes itself very seriously. It is no longer only a question of the "just barely," no longer just one of esthetic precision, when the sister of the seven ravens or the twelve swans, or whatever form the enchantment of the brothers happens to take, must make shirts for them, which may well be of nettles and have to be spun over a period of years, during which she must remain silent; and when she, further, in order to rescue the brothers, must allow her children to be stolen away and herself to be maligned, and what is required of her then is completed at that moment when the pyre upon which she is to be burned at the stake is already in flames. Here it is a question of the graphic representation of the greatest suffering and patient endurance, of something anthropologically significant. Only just barely does she accomplish what she has to do: In individual variants, the sleeve of the last shirt is missing—the arm of the youngest brother remains enchanted; in its place hangs a wing. This "tiny flaw" *(kleiner Fehl)* is, from the point of view of esthetics, another way of making the "just barely" apparent. It is an effective visual signal. This signal has more than just esthetic significance, however: In a human context there is no perfection. In such variants of the *seven ravens* (AT 451), perfection turns as if by itself into imperfection. Here imperfection is an indication of the well-nigh and thus, of course, still an indication of the theoretical possibility of perfection, just as, looked at the other way round, the hard slamming of the gates on the heels of the foal-herd or rabbit-herd suggests the idea that the heels could also have been sheared off. The deadline set is just barely missed in those versions of the *Amor and Psyche* type (AT 425 G) where, instead of an animal bridegroom, a prince lying in a magical death sleep must be disenchanted, and where, in order to do so, the girl, who ends up in an uninhabited castle (cf. pp. 119–121), must watch beside the "dead man" without falling asleep for forty days, forty nights, forty hours, and forty minutes or three months, three weeks, three days, three hours, and three half-hours—in a Sicilian (and similarly in a Turkish) variant, even seven years, seven months, and seven days.[171] On the last day she is overcome with sleepiness; a female slave watches the last half-hour (when the time period is more than seven years, the last three days) in her place and gets the prince, even when, as in Sicily, she is black and as "ugly as debts" ("brutta come i debiti"). Because of the missing half-hour, the superhuman accomplishment of resisting falling asleep for thirty-nine days or even for more than seven years is in vain; the tiny flaw, in the sense of a quantity contrast and at the same time something in accord with the principle of emphasis on the last element *(Achtergewicht)*, weighs more heavily. It is only the second part of the fairytale which then sets things right; the one truly responsible for the disenchantment, who has been reduced to the status of goose-, duck-, turkey-, or swine-girl, comes into her own, and the usurper is punished.

The tiny flaw, the tiny imperfection in the midst of a perfect world, appears in many forms in the fairytale. It is also to be found in other narrative genres, above all in the myth and the local legend; nowhere, however, does the tiny imperfection stand in such clear contrast to perfection as in the fairytale, for no place else is perfection pushed so far, made so clearly visible, striven for with such various means as in the fairytale. In the myth of Pelops, we run into the tiny flaw in a double form: Of all

the gods, it is only Demeter who does not notice that Tantalus has set as
food before them his cut-up and cooked son; she alone eats one of the
pieces of meat, a bit of shoulder. The resuscitated Pelops lacks this bit; it
has to be replaced with ivory. Thus out of a whole group, only a single
member commits an error: a tiny flaw in the group, and on the body of the
one resuscitated a small piece is lacking (since then all Pelopideans have a
small spot on the shoulder). Despite such impressive doubling (one can
speak of artistic economy—one and the same feature, here the tiny flaw, is
presented in two different forms), the effect of contrast to a world stylized
in the direction of the perfect is missing in the myth, which in comparison
to the fairytale is more realistic. Yet more realistic—still speaking comparatively—are the alpine local legends about the "hazel witch," who, at
the gathering of witches, is cooked and eaten by the other witches (she is
missing a rib, which was pocketed by a watching farmhand; a piece of
hazel substitutes for it),[172] and about the alpine herdsman, who has to look
on as the cow left behind at the alpine hut is gobbled up by ghost
herdsmen: The next morning the animal is again alive and whole, but it
limps because one of its upper legs lacks the tiny bit of flesh which the
ghosts compelled the herder to eat.[173] What is in myth and local legend
already in and of itself an impressive feature takes on in the fairytale
additional interest as a quantity contrast to the perfect world of castles, to
the perfectly beautiful or perfectly ugly figures, things, and scenery, and
to the precision in plot development. At the same time, since the fairytale
is a narrative in several parts, the "tiny flaw" as narrative element can be
more extensively varied than in a short myth or myth segment, as in the
story of Pelops mentioned above. The Grimms' "Sleeping Beauty," which
appears to be derived from Perrault but which is much less ornamented in
mode of narration, as early as the first transcript of Jacob Grimm
(Ölenberg Manuscript) is set in a castle, and before the twelve fairies are
set twelve golden plates. This is the perfectionistic framework: royal castle, the number twelve, gold; later come the one hundred (hundred-year
sleep), the fifteen (the main story begins when Sleeping Beauty is fifteen
years old—in Perrault less precise: "After fifteen or sixteen years"), the
order that "all spindles in the whole kingdom" are to be disposed of, the
sudden falling asleep of the entire castle (lacking in Perrault), and the
subsequently weakened extremely unpleasant gift of the thirteenth fairy:
Sleeping Beauty is to "prick her finger on a spindle and *die as a result*"—
in the formulation of the first edition of the Brothers Grimm (1812),
already sharpened to "prick herself on a spindle and *fall down dead.*" This
rudimentary comparison shows that the Grimms' informant—according
to Heinz Rölleke's discovery, not the "Old Marie" in the Wild household,
but Young Marie Hassenpflug, who stemmed from a Huguenot family—
despite her (direct or indirect) dependence on Perrault, not only
simplified the narrative but properly stylized it completely in tune with

the characteristic precision and perfection of the fairytale. Even the simple "twelve golden plates" is much more concise than Perrault's "couvert manifique, avec un étui d'or massif où il y avait une cuiller, une fourchette et un couteau de fin or, garnis de diamants et de rubis," which he assigned to each of his seven fairies, without again mentioning their number (which was earlier mentioned only in passing). Basile's version (1636), which historically preceded that of Perrault (1697), is still more diffuse: in place of the king, only a distinguished gentleman, "un gran signore"; instead of the seven or twelve fairies, "all the wisemen and soothsayers of the kingdom"; the prophesying, very vague, namely, "that great danger threatens her through a strand of flax"; and, correspondingly realistic, the orders of the nobleman "that neither flax nor hemp nor anything at all similar should be brought into his palace"—hence not the universalistic banning of these things from the whole kingdom, which here would not at all have been possible for the nobleman. Later (still nonspecific), one finds "when Talia had grown up" ("essendo Talia grandicella"), then the sudden falling to the ground dead, which the Brothers Grimm apparently picked up: "cadette morta'n terra."[174]* The Grimms' version, following an oral narrative, is thus clearly more perfectionistic than those of Basile and Perrault; the Brothers Grimm have retained and in places even extended the stylization characteristic of the fairytale, which they apparently took over from their woman informant. There are four flaw elements within this highly stylized framework. First, the king has only twelve golden plates; thus he cannot invite the thirteenth fairy (in Perrault he has no knowledge at all of the existence of the eighth fairy). Second, of the thirteen fairies, only twelve are friendly; the thirteenth is hostile, and she is able to cause deadly harm (quantity contrast). Here again is the flaw element within a group, as noted earlier (p. 59). Third, the absoluteness of death is modified to a hundred-year sleep: the weakening of the extreme. And fourth, all the spindles are banned from the entire kingdom, but one still remains in action, and that in the royal castle; and it—again a quantity contrast—is the decisive one.

What can be demonstrated in this one story—perfection with consciously worked-in tiny but virulent imperfections—is true for the fairytale world as a whole. Of the many forms in which the color spot of the "tiny flaw" turns up in the framework of the fairytale, a few may be mentioned.

The loss of the heels, which we said in our discussion of the Pomeranian foal-herd episode was an obvious possibility in terms of what one might think of or imagine, does actually occur in some fairytales.[175] "Fetch some of the water of life before it strikes twelve, or else the gate will slam again and you'll be locked in." But the tired prince falls asleep in the magic castle and wakes up again only as it strikes quarter to twelve: He passes through the gate just at the stroke of twelve, and it slams shut "so hard that it even took off a bit of his heel" (KHM 97, "The Water of Life"). Whereas after similar experiences in local legend narratives there is talk of the treatment and troublesome healing process of the painful wound, in the fairytale there is no further mention of the injured foot, the sheared-off heel, or of the bit of his shank which the Russian fairytale hero finally has to feed to the giant bird carrying him out of the underworld in order to keep its strength up. Such a narrative procedure is possible only because of the isolating tendency of the fairytale, which tends to take each episode as a separate entity, to a certain degree to encapsulate it. The artistic result is exactly that definiteness, that conciseness, which is appropriate to the fairytale style. The hero has a bit too little in the way of provisions along with him (the tiny flaw), and the result is the "tiny loss" on his calf—this feature, like so many things in the fairytale, appears only at some particular point and has no consequences. We find a form intermediate between local legend and fairytale in the Caucasian-Udian Rustam saga: The hero limps, and the great bird, which has noticed that recently it has received sweet human flesh instead of a hundredweight of animal flesh, regurgitates the human flesh and lays it on Rustam's shank, where it heals instantly to his leg—the appearance of the same sorts of instant wonders is a point of similarity between the heroic saga and the fairytale. Karl v. Spieß sees in the fairytales about glass mountains or glass bridges which can only be mounted with the help of chicken bones a transformation of the motif where a huge bird carries someone up out of the underworld. In the end, the climber of the glass mountain, since he has lost one of the little bones, must cut off his little finger. The one little bone which the sister of the seven ravens (KHM 25) receives and loses, so that she has to cut off "her tiny little finger," would then be a faded and deformed variation of the model just described[176]—instead of the great bird as helper, the skeleton of a chicken, and finally only just a single chicken bone, which first gets lost and is then replaced by a little finger! Whatever may be the genesis and history of this motif, the earlier stages are no longer much in evidence. But what every fairytale listener notices immediately in all the various narratives is the phenomenon of the tiny loss—even when it is not picked up again in the next scene, as is the case with many bird riders and the sister of the seven ravens.

The loss of a heel occurs also in another famous Grimms' story (KHM 21, AT 510) and in many of its variants: The first sister of Cinderella chops off a bit of her own heel (the other sister "a large bit of her toes," 1812). Cinderella herself loses a slipper or shoe—like the heroines of the Canadian fairytale about the handsome magician (pp. 2–5) and the related Greek story about the cannibalistic schoolmaster (AT 894).[177] The fact that this one shoe or slipper is lacking turns out to be significant in all three cases—the weight of the plot, the logic of the sequence of development, pushes the isolating tendency, just as in other cases, into the background.

Cinderella's lost shoe leads to her being identified and thus to happiness; in both of the other cases the lost shoe is a sign to the demonic antagonist that the heroine has eavesdropped on him, and leads to the suffering of the eavesdropper. At the same time, however, the condition of having only one shoe, like the loss of the heel and other partial forfeitures—the branded (gilded!) finger in "Our Lady's Child" (KHM 3) and in "Iron Hans" (KHM 136)—is an indication that something is not in order. The tiny flaw is here the transgression made concrete, material; a secret, once-only offense of the transitory past is made visible and stabilized, made permanent in this visual sign; the fugitive past has merged into the picture of the continuing present.

And Snow White? With all her perfection, she also has a tiny flaw—a moral one. Snow White violates the prohibition of the dwarfs, not, as in the case of the heroine of some other versions of the same and related fairytale types, out of pity for the woman who wishes to come in, but because she gives in to the desire for beautiful things. "Snow White looked greedily at the beautiful apple . . . [she could] resist no longer, she reached out her hand and took the poisoned half," we read in the final edition; and as early as the Ölenberg Manuscript we find:"Because the same comb now pleased her only too well, she let herself be led astray. . . ." In a Corsican version, on the other hand, Anghjulina opens up only because the old woman at the door whines: "Descendez, mademoiselle, descendez m'ouvrir, car je suis morte de froid!" ("Do come down, Miss, and open the door for me; I am dying of the cold!"). Anghjulina refuses resolutely to accept anything as reward. So the old woman asks to be allowed to do her hostess's hair: "Mettez vous donc sur ce fauteuil, que je frise vos cheveux!" Now Anghjulina finally gives in: "Et là, Anghjulina s'est mise sur le fauteuil, et s'est fait friser les cheveux." The editor, Geneviève Massignon, speaks of the "appeal to vanity (a weakness of young people)." The narrator, however (Widow Camilli, who had heard the fairytale from her father, a herdsman, and who told it to Miss Massignon in April of 1959), offers absolutely no indication of this possibility.[178] If one wishes to speak of a tiny flaw here, it is, in comparison to the Grimms' version, truly the tiniest flaw. The fairytale teems with commandments, conditions, and prohibitions. Each violation of a prohibition is a lapse. Thus the motif of the tiny flaw is in this sense, as well, embedded in the whole, in the style universally characterizing the European fairytale.

A few examples of the occurrence of the tiny flaw in the fairytale may be sketched briefly. When the hero has need of information about the person he is seeking or an object to be obtained, of the great number of animals asked, none has any information, but one is still missing (the tiny flaw in the group); it is only the little animal arriving late that brings the much-desired message. The coming late, however, is not the only imperfection; the little bird or little bee, apparently because it had to fly so far, has "become lame along the way."[179] The one coming late, the lame one, is the bringer of salvation—from afar the picture of one born in a stable and nailed on the cross shimmers through, one who specifically and only as sufferer becomes the Savior. The fairytale motif, in and of itself already playfully stylized, slips over into farce where, instead of the late-coming bee, a drunken raven or fish is the bringer of good news.[180] The motif of the household goods that speak is also handled as farce: Before they leave the lodgings of the witch, the lovers feed macaroni to all the household goods so that they will not reveal anything; they forget, however—the tiny imperfection—a saucepan hidden behind a pitcher, which then blabs everything.[181] But as serious as the climbing of the glass mountain or the mounting of the glass bridge with the help of bird bones, from which then one is lacking (see p. 62), is a related motif, the springing of the firehorse up to the tower balcony of the beautiful princess ("beautiful as the moon, and her ring sparkled like the sun"). On the first try the horse springs three steps too short, on the second, two steps, and on the third, its rider gives it such a hefty crack with the whip that "a whole piece of skin" comes loose from its upper leg, and finally it reaches the balcony. The episode thus contains the "tiny flaw" in several variations: First the goal is barely missed by three steps, then by two; only the lightly injured horse accomplishes the spring. And there is also the mirror image of the tiny flaw, the barely successful: Of three attempts, only the last is successful, and also "just barely."[182] So closely woven can the fairytale narration be; in so many and various permutations can one and the same element turn up in a single episode.

The tiny flaw is a willful imperfection, one of material, of content; *blunted* and *blind motifs* and *elements* are defects of composition— defects which can still have their specific qualities. They are often the result of what has been called narrative degeneration (*Zerzählen*); they arise from faulty performances in the course of oral transmission. Thus the shortened form of "Ali Baba," which the Corsican woman mentioned above (p. 63) took over from her father and which at some time must have come from the Arabian Nights, contains the well-known feature where the wife of the hero borrows a measuring vessel from her sister-in-law, who, becoming curious, smears the bottom of it with wax, in which a gold piece becomes stuck—but all that results is that the sister-in-law now knows what Cassin, the brother-in-law, has measured.[183] The wax on the bottom of the vessel and the twenty-franc piece that sticks there thus remain largely blunted; they have lost their real function. The person of the brother, another structural element which plays a large role in the Arabian Nights, and also in the Grimms' "Simeli Mountain," is completely blind. The Corsican story mentions him, to be sure, but he never makes an appearance—the entire important act of unsuccessful imitation is left out; this brother is not even a contrast figure, since both brothers are as poor as church mice. In a Rhaeto-romance Allerleirauh/Cinderella fairytale, the lost slipper remains without significance for the plot, because another sign of identification, a ring, brings the heroine and the prince together.[184] The expressions "blind motif" *(blindes Motiv)* and "blunted motif" *(stumpfes Motiv)* are mostly used indiscriminately for the same phenomenon. For me, a blind motif is only an element which is not made use of once it is introduced—for example, two older brothers to whom no role is assigned but who, because they are part of a pattern-of-threes formula, are still not deleted by the narrator; I refer to those elements as blunted which do have a particular function but are not fully developed. Completely blind motifs and features do not occur frequently with good narrators. Still, occasionally one runs into a magical gift which, protected by a pattern-of-threes formula, is also held onto even when it has no function in the plot. In the very deficient Corsican Ali Baba story, in addition to the functionless brother and his almost equally functionless wife, one could also call the gold piece which sticks fast a blind or almost blind feature, because it does not have any significance for the plot. The cutting off of a finger, on the other hand, when the glass mountain can be opened with it, is in no way a blind element; it remains, however, somehow blunted when the absence of the finger is never noted by anyone in what follows. The mutilation of the shank is also a blunted element when, as a result of the encapsulating of individual scenes, it later leads to no complaints at all, not even to limping (cf. p. 62). In a Gascon *animal bridegroom* fairytale (AT 425), the role of the second daughter of the gardener consists entirely in that, like her older sister, she says no when her father asks her if she would marry the giant lizard in order to save his life.[185] The youngest then does so, and the eldest is also later still active; the middle one, however, receives no further mention. Still, she has a rudimentary role: The difference between the refusal to make the self-sacrifice for the father and the contrastive attitude of the youngest daughter would come through less sharply if only one daughter said no. The double *no* shows that it is no accidental or capricious reaction, but a normal one characteristic of the average person. Even the lost slipper of the Rhaeto-romance Cinderella from Swiss Grisons, although robbed of significance, is not retained just by chance: It belongs to the framework or the narrative type; it has to be mentioned, for the listener expects it to appear. Whether it retains its original role or abdicates it to another prop is less important; the idea of the slipper, thus of the tiny loss, must still be there.

In a Bulgarian-Gypsy *animal bridegroom* fairytale (AT 552), the first brother cuts off both ears of the monster he has killed and sticks them "in his sack"; the second proceeds likewise with a two-headed, the third with a three-headed, monster, but the twelve ears cut off and carefully preserved are never mentioned again in the further course of the narration.[186] In the *dragon-slayer* fairytale, the tongues cut out of the heads of the dragon must later prove the hero to be the real rescuer of the princess and unmask the usurper. And in a glass mountain fairytale from Swiss Grisons, the earlobe of the numskull, which the princess, on orders from her father, bites off when he kisses her, serves as a means of identification ("The king sent two men with the piece of ear into each house").[187] Is the lack of plot relevance of the ears of the three "monsters" in the Gypsy fairytale the result of absentmindedness? Scarcely. For in the course of the story no place can be discovered where the ears could sensibly have played a meaningful role. But the operation provides a succinct termination to the victorious battle. Probably the narrator or one of his predecessors purposely slipped in the feature by analogy with the *dragon-slayer* fairytale and similar stories. The mutilation of the monster, a sort of castration, puts the seal on its defeat. Like a scalp, the ears are the trophy of the victor. Thus it is quite understandable here that a blunted feature might not just be retained but even grafted on. The element, which is irrelevant for the plot, has a visual esthetic valence and a symbolic significance.

Much of what one refers to as a blind or blunted motif is in reality only a partial motif: an element, a prop, a figure—a simple carrier of the motif. There are also real blunted motifs, however, even very important ones— hence the persistent denial of the heroine in many of the *Our Lady's child* versions, whereas in the related fairytale type involving the cannibalistic schoolmaster (AT 894), in which the heroine observes the teacher as he eats up one of her schoolgirl friends, it is completely clear why she steadfastly keeps quiet about it: out of fear of the teacher, who asks her threateningly, "Have you told anyone what you saw?" and beats her.[188] It does not become clear in many versions of *Our Lady's child* that the girl must remain silent because she does not dare betray the numinous, whether it is a saintly being, as in the Grimms' version, or a demonic one, as in our Canadian model narrative "The Handsome Sorcerer from Africa" (see pp. 3–4). The scene she observes in the French Canadian fairytale, the flogging of the fifty hanged men, is not explained—and it is not self-explanatory like the cannibalistic or vampiric activities of the *ghoulish schoolmaster*, who, in gratitude for the heroine's not having revealed his compulsion to eat corpses, expressly says at the end of one Irish version that he will now do anything for her.[189] The meaning of and reason for the strange behavior of the magician in our model narrative remain cloudy: a blunted motif. But this sort of secret, which is unexplained and apparently unexplainable, has its own fascination. Why the "handsome sorcerer" finally gives in and brings the stolen children back does not become clear—while in other variations, the *homme mystérieux* is freed, through the persistent silence and lying of the heroine, from a spell which he was under.[190] That so much remains open in our narrative, that it contains several blunted features, is felt to be more a part of its charm than a defect—imperfection as an integral part of the work of art. The blind elements in the Corsican version of "Ali Baba" are simply errors in execution; the phenomena which remain unexplained in "The Handsome Sorcerer"—it is not even explained why he is called the "handsome" sorcerer—operate as legitimate parts of the work of art. Something similar is the case with the self-opening and -closing of the magic mountain, which is left unexplained in the otherwise novella-like "Ali Baba" versions. How do the robbers come to know what they know, where did they get the magic word, and where does its magic power come from? That all this is not explained is what is really fairytale-like, not just the miracle itself.

Motivations are not obligatory in the fairytale. They may be there: The hero's going out into the unknown is almost always somehow justified. But the very diversity of the reasons given in the various stories—desire for adventure or to see the world; the necessity of accomplishing a task; to win a princess; to take up a post; the need to learn fear; being set out by the parents; flight from an incestuously inclined father, etc.—shows that the real reason is not revealed. Other things are not given any justification, not motivated, not explained. "I can only lend you this barque, because I still need it myself," says the donor of the self-propelling boat in a Provençal fairytale[191]—but in the overwhelming number of fairytales not the slightest attempt is made to explain why the hero does not also make use of such a wondrous boat or any other magical gift for his own pleasure and that of his family. The isolating style and commitment to plot in the fairytale are perfectly sufficient; for the listener it goes without saying that the self-propelling boat is to be used only for the accomplishment of a task or in an emergency situation, and not for holiday cruises. It follows from the extremism of the fairytale that the listener assumes that the task setter will threaten the hero with death if the task is not accomplished. From time to time, however, individual psychological justifications turn up. In a fairytale from the Provence of the *Ferdinand the faithful* type (AT 531, KHM 126), the intriguer whispers to the king: "You have to threaten the boy, or else he won't do anything. For he can do it, but he doesn't want to." Whereupon the king says to the hero, who has said to him that he does not have the slightest idea where he should look for the princess, "I'll give you three days to think it over. If you are then not ready to free my daughter, I'll have you executed."[192] Prohibitions, commandments, and conditions are in some cases respected, in others not. The listener requires justification for neither, for both are according to common convention. In the Grimms' "Simeli Mountain," it is neatly explained why the rich brother can no longer come up with the magic word: "He wanted to bring out his booty, but because his heart and mind were full up with treasures, he had meanwhile forgotten the name of the mountain" (KHM 142, AT 676). As early as Galland we find "L' esprit rempli de toute autre idée que de ce qui lui emportait davantage, il se trouve qu'il oublie le mot nécessaire" (Night 365). In the Arabic manuscript that became known in 1910, however, it says only: "He was almost beside himself with joy, and he would have liked to have taken the whole lot of the treasures with him. . . . Then he wanted to speak the magic words for opening the door; that is, he wanted to say: 'Sesame, open your door!' But they would not leave his tongue; they had completely slipped his mind."[193] Still more terse is a story from Holstein taken down by Wilhelm Wisser: "Un naher, as he sin'n Sack al füll't hett, do hett he de Nam vergeten" ("And later, when he had his sack all full, then he had forgotten the name").[194] Other narratives transcribed from oral tradition are similar. A fairytale fully motivated throughout would no longer be a fairytale—not only because oral renditions are less fussy than written ones, but because nonmotivation in one form or another simply belongs to the notion *fairytale*. The myth inclines to system, to a hierarchy of otherworldly beings, from the gods down to the spirits of forest and field. The fairytale is not concerned with what systems its otherworldly beings belong to, with why the unprepossessing old men and little old women happen to have their knowledge and power. The heroine can receive magical charms and arts from some intermediary, but she can just as well know them herself, without our being told why.[195] One heroine patterns her actions according to some set condition; another behaves exactly the same way although no condition, no commandment or prohibition, has been stated.[196] Volker Roloff, citing Gustav Ehrismann and other scholars, connects the nonmotivation of, for example, the commandment to be silent with taboo, which as such requires no justification.[197*] Nonmotivation, "leaving the question of the motivation open,"[198] however, is characteristic of the fairytale as such, well beyond reasons of content. It is one aspect of the lack of perfection which makes up the counterbalance to the prevailing perfectionism of the fairytale—a counterbalance of thoroughly esthetic significance: A hint of imperfection within the perfect creates esthetic tension. And at the same time, such nonmotivation, bluntedness, incongruence, and imperfection lend the fairytale the shimmer of the mysterious.

## STABILITY AND DYNAMISM

The fairytale is an art form marked by a union and simultaneity of compactness and lightness, of rest and motion. Stasis and dynamism, constraint and freedom, and stability and variability come together in it and give it its character. That is true in any case of the fairytale of magic, which in the scholarship has time and again been designated "the fairytale proper." The farce fairytale, with its tendency toward chain technique, and the novella fairytale, specifically of the oriental type, show less strictness, allow themselves free rein. And the so-called animal fairytale is often limited to a single episode, so that the interaction of stability and dynamism is not realized in it in such a variety of ways as in the fairytale of magic.

Propp speaks of iron structural laws, referring to a regular sequence of basic plot segments, the "functions of the dramatis personae" in the various narratives or narrative sequences. Whether this sequence is really as uniform as Propp believes, is the subject of controversy. But a certain regularity, even rigidity, in the development of the action is clearly inherent in the fairytale. And it is not just today's child that wishes each time to hear a fairytale that he knows in the "authentic" form, that is, in the form in which he heard it the first time—the adult audience of former times also tended to call to order any narrator making use of unrestricted variation. The relatively passive collectivity is more conservative than the (relatively creative) individual.[199] The stability of fairytale transmission over centuries, which constantly provides grounds for amazement, is only partially ascribable to literary influence (which was for a long time underestimated but presently tends to be overestimated). The listener's demand for the familiar, for what was felt to be valid, was also a factor; and the demands imposed by narrative and mnemonic technique on narrators, as well as their artistic sense, conspired to maintain what was successful in terms of rhythm and sound.[200] The narrator commits himself voluntarily to a formulation which seems to him to be optimal.[201] Such is the case with the modicum of freedom associated with the repetition that occurs in so many forms in the fairytale. It is not, or is only partially, a question of the necessity of repetition; a delight in repetition is also at work. The individual narrator would be free to make use of just a single episode instead of the three episodes passed on to him (see example, p. 94), but most are happy to retain the tripartite organization.

Within a given stable framework, the talented narrator has an appreciable latitude. He does not just vary externals, in that he modernizes props, replacing the sword with the musket, the inn with the hotel— Leopold Schmidt has coined the term "prop shift" (*Requisitenverschiebung*) for this procedure—and occasionally has his figures smoke cigarettes or use the telephone; he does not just add humorous, at times ironical, touches. He also mixes, combines, various types of narrative, sometimes cleverly, sometimes not, and he has above all the freedom to pursue and develop potentialities which are anchored in the inner logic of the plot. I have a number of times pointed out this tendency for narrative possibilities (*Erzählziele*) to develop on their own which follow logically from features, motifs, and motif constellations already present, but which are not recognized by every narrator,[202] so that here a few examples may provide illustration enough. When a severed head is to be put back on, there is always the possibility that it will be put on backwards. It is certainly to be expected that time and again there will be narrators who will take advantage of this suggestion. When Snow White is taken in, not by dwarfs but by robbers, there is the possibility that one of them may wish to have her as his wife, indeed that such a marriage should come to pass, and there are, in fact, Norwegian, Albanian, and Basque versions where the narrator thought it a good idea to realize this possibility inherent in the constellation.[203] It is also no great jump when someone who is to fetch a beautiful bride from afar for someone else ends up with her himself, whether because the young woman knows how to eliminate the king who originally gave the commission, because the intermediary himself assumes an active role (as with Tristan in the romance), or because the magnanimous prince offers his bride to the loyal helper, as in some versions of *Faithful John* (where, of course, the helper, just as magnanimous, refuses the woman). That the intended husband should hit on the idea of turning the successfully won beauty over to the helper because the latter really deserves her, is as much a possible development which individual narrators will pursue as the other, where the bride falls in love with the helper. Developing given narrative kernels is probably the most significant freedom which is open to the narrator. The natural development of the narrative in its passage from one renderer to another, whether it involves popular tellers, collectors, or writers like Andersen, is an inherent dynamic feature, something counter to its likewise characteristic stability.

Stasis and dynamism are also characteristic of the individual fairytale. Both factors are present in the consequent plot development, which never gets bogged down in description, and in the easily moving figures, who display no psychological complexity. The persons are caught up neither in their social and physical environment nor in their past; the props play their role only at some particular point—that the hero in many fairytales forgets the gift received until an emergency, when it pops back into his mind, is representative of the pure separation, of the tendency to isolation, which contributes so greatly to the sharpness of the narration and thus to the compactness, to the stability, of the phenotype. Working to the same end is the tendency to factor complexes into juxtapositions (instead of one complex character, two contrastive figures) or sequences (varying repetition instead of concentrated intensity) and the use of step-by-step progression from station to station instead of gradual development, of the sudden transformation instead of slow change. (In the sequence and in the transformation, there is still the complementary element of dynamism.) The stability of the figures and objects, however, is expressed not only in their straightforwardness but also in the fact that they are not influenced by the passage of time. Sleeping Beauty and her fellow castle dwellers are still just as young or old after a hundred years as they were before; and the girl who is hung up in the chimney in a barred crate as a result of the machinations of her hostile mother-in-law, after three years has neither died nor gotten older, but has instead "become, as a result of the smoke, much more beautiful than she was before."[204] Gouged-out eyes do not decompose, even though the wicked witch has stashed them "behind the stove"; when they are put back in, they do not see worse than before but, on the contrary, better, the left seven times better and the right yet seven times better than the left.[205]* Copper, silver, and gold forests are also obviously incorruptible and unfading. The special preference in general in the fairytale for metallic and mineral transpositions contributes much to making the fairytale world firm and stable. The fairytale castle, in contrast to the ruin of the local legend, is ageless and perfect. People who have been turned to stone show no signs after their disenchantment of the terrible experience lying behind them; like Sleeping Beauty, they are as young and full of life as before. That the fairytale says so much more about clothing, armor, and shoes than about bodies and builds reinforces the total impression of stability and inflexibility—the "gallery of bare human arms" that in Jean Cocteau's film *La Belle et la bête* (1945) "reach out of the wall" produces very little in the way of a fairytale effect.[206]

The inflexibility of materials finds its counterpart in the inflexibility of the formula: conventional openings and closings; the stereotyped reappearance of the same or similar happenings (similar to those in the same narrative, as well as to what is narrated in other fairytales); repetitions and variations structured through the conventional as well as symbolic use of patterns of threes and twos; and the high degree of formal completion in general, the striving for perfection, and the respect for measure (for the notion of measure as the polar opposite of intensification, see p. 110). The dominance of the visual in the European fairytale also fosters the impression of stability. Music and sounds, scents and odors are fleeting, prototypically transitory; the visual, however, remains.

Some of the things which we have mentioned as indicators of the stability, compactness, or even inflexibility of the fairytale have another side, however. The isolation of figures and objects leads, on the one hand, to the graphic sharpness of the conceptual representation, but it is, on the other hand, the basis for the separability, the mobility, especially of the figures. Mobility and movement are in the fairytale the polar opposite of the static. The leaving home of the hero or heroine, his or her wandering or being transported across wide stretches, not only to the end of the world but into otherworldly spheres, into the world above or the underworld, is the most noticeable and remarkable indicator of dynamism in the fairytale. The isolation of the figures and objects means at the same time that they are unburdened, ready and free to enter into any combination. The transformation, the enchantment and disenchantment, which also lends visual sharpness and thus compactness to the fairytale, is, as we have already noted, likewise a dynamic element. Stability is in the fairytale—and not just in the fairytale—a direct prerequisite for the dynamic.

The firmly outlined, stable figures and objects are, precisely because they are such, capable of being used to indicate likewise sharply visible changes—changes of place, form (transformation, whether voluntary or involuntary), rank, and condition. Regardless of how one interprets from the point of view of content the changes of social status—the elevation of the poor girl to prince's or king's consort, of the poor boy to prince consort and coregent or king, and the likewise not uncommon fall of a king, queen, or rich man—regardless of what sort of psychological and political meaning and effect they have, esthetically they are dynamic moments. In addition, the bits of fun, and humor in general, produce a dynamic effect within the cheerful but still serious fairytale of magic. (We offer no examples here, since they turn up of their own accord in the reading of even a few fairytales, and since examples appear on more than one page of this book.) The use of rapidly alternating dialog—of the sort popular in many fairytales and especially in those of Romance origin—also has a looseningup and dynamic effect. And when one considers the mimicry and gestures and acting of the narrators, which have been made familiar to us through the reports of many collectors and through photographs and films, one has the proper idea of the animation which can also be brought into the narrative from outside. "At times the narrator springs up from his chair and directly acts out—taking now one part, now another—individual bits of the story," writes the Austrian fairytale scholar Karl Haiding.[207] And Waltraut Werner in her "Portrait of a Hungarian-German Fairytale Narrator" says:

> Even when speaking purely expositorily, when he narrates sitting down, at no time does he speak without gesticulating. But when what he says is imperative, interrogative, or interjective, he intensifies his facial expressions and eye movement and his hand gestures to produce the appropriate impression of commanding, asking, or commenting. For this sort of emotional gesticulation, he has available in his repertory a large number of little formulaic gestures suitable to the formulaic expressions of his vocabulary.[208]

Thus also in gesture and movement, dynamism (physical liveliness) is brought together with stability (firmly established formulaic gestures). The twenty-one-year-old Sardinian/South Italian sailor Marco Sulis, whom Felix Karlinger heard narrating during a voyage ("the listeners were all men, largely sailors"), "had the habit of not sitting still for a single moment but rather moving around among the circle of listeners and emphasizing everything with lively gestures and mimicry."[209] Tools that just happen to be handy can become magical props. This sailor "used a wineglass first as a ship, then as an animal, while the table served as the stage over which he had his things run or travel." Thus "the surrounding space" about the narrator can be "transformed into the world of the adventure."[210] That the dialog should offer the opportunity to alter the voice for dramatic effect, that occasionally dialect and the standard, Sardinian and Italian, should be deliberately thrown off against one another, offers no further grounds for surprise.

More important, however, is the inner dynamism of the narratives. There are restrained narrators who nonetheless achieve a powerful effect. Even with broad farces, which indeed most readily encourage drastic gesturing and mimicry, "they do not go in much for animation." "While their listeners break out in peals of laughter, they display only a faint grin" (Haiding). "One finds men and women who bring their stories across stumblingly and apparently dryly but who still manage to generate tension through the organization of the content of their material" (Karlinger). The tension of fairytales, their inner dynamism, depends very little on the question "What's going to happen?"—for the outcome is more or less clear to the accustomed fairytale listener, especially because the happy ending for the hero or heroine, with whom the male and female listeners respectively can identify, is as good as certain. That the same listener wishes to hear the same fairytale several times—completely in contrast to the case, say, of the joke—shows that it sets in motion a pattern of internal experience, sets off a sequence of tension and relief of tension, of concentration and relaxation, similar in effect to that of a musical work, whose interest is also not exhausted by a single hearing and which one needs to hear time and again, since the effect is deepened through repeated listening.

Dynamism results further from the delight in anticipations, from the many forms of foreshadowing, of taking aim at what is to come (in this regard, see p. 91). The tiny loss, on the other hand, the tiny flaw—the wing instead of one arm—is a remnant of past dynamism: the making concrete, the making permanent, of a dramatic occurrence from the past. And in the framework of the act of telling (the "performance"), it is not only mimicry, gesturing, and the making use of one's own body, of the listeners, and of objects accidentally standing or lying about, that is dynamic and dynamicizing; on the verbal level, dynamism also results from improvisation, both voluntary and involuntary: sudden change of tense ("Now he lets himself down again; he'd become tired");[211] the alteration of intonation and the tempo of narration; or the sudden shift from third to first person, from "He" to "I,"[212]* so that the narrator has, unawares, himself become the hero, the internal identification being externalized (while at the same time the identification of the listener with the hero, precisely because of this, is possibly made more difficult). When a fairytale is printed, the nonlinguistic devices of the narrator, his facial expressions, gestures, comings and goings, and limping around (by which he imitates and represents some of his figures) are lost, and the more so are the reactions of his audience, which *also* belong to the narrative experience. Maja Bošković-Stulli reports:

> During a sad story about a dead child, a young woman with two small girls on her knees wept and said over and over again: "Alas, poor me. Alas, unlucky me." And these words wove themselves rhythmically into the narration like an integral part of the narrative. One felt that they had a personal meaning for the young woman. For the rest of us listeners, the story would have been some other, something more neutral, without her participation.[213]

Many of the linguistic devices of the narrators also fail to come through in the printed fairytale. The position of pauses can be suggested, but not changes of pitch or intensity, of voice coloration, or of variation in narrative tempo. Still, argues Bošković-Stulli, the faithful scribal transcription "with its colloquial authenticity" and its "departure from normative grammar" can have a powerful effect on the reader, "although it is orally structured, or perhaps precisely because it is."[214] There has been much talk of the "second life" of the fairytale in book form, and likewise much fun has been made of this conception, which corresponds to that of the "second life" of the folksong in the schools or in the youth movement of the first third of our century. But the fairytale as taken over into books is in fact one of the successor forms to the oral narrative, which in many places has died out and in other places is in the process of doing so. The success of the series of relatively literal fairytale renditions, which have been brought out by the most various publishing houses, speaks for the desire of adults to read fairytales, for the continuing vitality, the continuing influence, of the once orally transmitted stories which have now been carried over into book form.

There is *one* form of dynamism which the reader confronted with several variants of the same narrative type can experience even more clearly than the fairytale listener of earlier times: the striving of narrators to develop the narrative kernel contained in a motif or story, the striving for "end forms" *(Zielformen)*. I have attempted in various articles to show the dynamism of this process of development: The imagination of narrators does not expand something arbitrarily; it probes those places which directly cry out for elaboration.[215] Within the focus of this book, this seeking out of narrative possibilities turns up, among other places, where an exactly realistic imagination takes up a fantastic motif (see pp. 105–106) and in all those places where we have noted that something develops or might as well have developed in and of itself. Only a few additional examples will be mentioned here: Magical objects are happily stolen from the original owner and often used against him; a wishing table just waits to be stolen, a magical weapon to be turned against its owner (so that he has to give back the harmless magical object which he got in exchange for the weapon). The story of Aladdin goes one step further: The magic ring changes owners more than once. The possibility that the wife of the hero might be involved is obvious, and this possibility is realized in various ways in the various versions. Sometimes she gives away the magical object stupidly and without knowing, sometimes she does so out of faithlessness (AT 560, 561, 562; cf. 566, 567), both being possibilities which offer themselves voluntarily, partially because they follow from the constellation at the relevant point in the narrative, partially because the clichés both of the stupid wife and of the faithless wife are traditional and thus ready for use. The large number of narrators makes it probable that many relatively obvious possibilities will also actually be realized. Kurt Ranke has used the example of the farce fable about the bridge of lies to demonstrate that in this case the oral transmission has "made much greater use of the variation possibilities which the material and theme offer" than has the literary: because the *homo narrans* is really in many cases not only a *homo conservans,* but also a *homo ludens.*[216]* He can still allow himself to be animated by particular elements into giving short descriptions, although in the ideal type of the fairytale, description is out of place: In the *Cinderella* type, even just the word or the notion *beautiful* leads one narrator to talk of beautiful clothing, another to introduce a state-coach, which then leads to the idea of horses, coachman, lackeys, etc. The differing suggestive potential of words and of the ideas which they bring with them also comes out clearly in the two possibilities of either having Cinderella go to mass or to the ball: A dance in a lighted ballroom must be at least briefly described; the mass in the dark church makes no such demand.[217] The seeds of narrative dynamism are there ready in the narrative elements, but it requires talented narrators to hit upon and make use of them. If we can speak of frozen dynamism in particular forms of the tiny flaw (a wing instead of an arm: the remaining sign of a past occurrence, thus reference to the past—see p. 59), then here, on the other hand, it is a question of potential dynamism. The narrative possibilities inherent in motifs, features, and motif constellations wait to be discovered and realized; they refer not to the past but to the future.

# 3

## Technical Means
## and Artistic Effects

### REPETITION AND VARIATION

Whereas in the previous chapter the basic principles governing style and composition were outlined briefly, here some prominent special features will be examined. One of the most notable characteristics of style and composition in the fairytale is the principle of repetition. All oral narrative, whether strictly constrained or improvised, is dependent on repetition. It is one of the technical prerequisites of oral presentation, even with professional rhapsodists, and thus in works looked upon as higher literature—in Homer, for example, whose verbatim repetitions of and variations on individual verses and whole sequences are famous. One once said, "Homer nods" when such passages turned up and one seemed to be coming upon something which had been encountered before. The formula has its justification: Such repetitions allow the narrator to relax; they provide a pause in the process of creation. They relieve the listeners as well, allowing them a relaxation of alertness, and at the same time, since the listener, unlike the reader, cannot flip back a page or two, they constitute reminders or a renewal, an intensification, of the original experience. And to say "Homer nods" is to see only one side of the situation. The repeated verses and verse groups also provide pleasure; the narrator and listeners enjoy them, and not just as rest points. The return of the familiar provides a feeling of security, for the listeners as well as for the speaker, and has at the same time an organizing effect, providing form and shape and creating structure. The technical necessity leads to esthetic effects and psychological reactions, in simple folk narrative just as in orally presented verse epic, which one assigns to higher literature.

Repetition, both direct and with variation, is a universal principle. It is a fact of cosmic phenomena just as it is of human life, art, and culture: the alternation of day and night, of summer and winter, of sleeping and waking in plants, animals, and man; the regular (even if only apparent) returning of sun and moon; the regular appearance of hunger and thirst and the correspondingly recurring eating ceremonies which take place at set times; ceremonies and rites in general; festivals that recur each year; and the course of the day, which in its outer form repeats—one might even say imitates or copies—the course of preceding days. Further, when children imitate adults or members of their own age group, or even themselves to the degree that they have had success with a facial expression, a gesture, or any articulation, such imitation is a form of repetition. Every repetition imitates something previous. For the Middle Ages, the *Imitatio Christi* was a high ideal, so intensively pursued—and partially achieved—by St. Francis and other saints that the stigmata of Christ appeared on their hands and feet. In the framework of poetry, the repetition of sounds, syllables, words, and constructions can be a stylistic device; it can achieve specific effects, but it can also be a defect, a sign of lack of control or poverty of expression—when reading through one's own manuscripts, almost everyone stumbles on words which turn up only because they occurred one or two sentences before and now demand, as it were, to be reused. Everything that has once occurred seeks to recur. It is up to us to evaluate repetitions as positive or negative, to reject some as inappropriate, undesirable, or pointless, and to recognize others as life-giving, life-supporting, or structure-creating. One person imitates the other, partially with justification—all learning, all cultural transmission, is based on imitation and repetition—and partially illegitimately, for, within the limitations of established restrictions, man is called upon to exercise his freedom. Even in nature, where the range of freedom is more limited than it is with man, every leaf on the tree repeats the other and yet is not identical to it; each leaf is an imitation and variation of the other, just as every person is also like the other and still different from him, thus to a certain degree repeating and varying the other; just as, finally, in both man and animal, the one half of the body repeats and varies the other in mirror-image reversal and variation.

Art subscribes to laws similar to those of reality—similar, but not the same. For consciousness dwells within it. The artist imitates, varies, and transforms consciously, according to artistic feeling and artistic reflection. Symmetry is an especially well-known form of artistic repetition. Asymmetry, just like any small (often intentional) departure from strict symmetry, is effective only against the background of a conceptualized or represented symmetry, just as flaw and deficiency are recognizable and conceivable only in comparison to flawlessness and completeness, and just as anti-fairytale, anti-saint's legend, and anti-novel are viable only because of the existence of fairytale, saint's legend, and novel.

Other well-known forms of repetition in art are alliteration, assonance, rhyme, and meter in poetry, the repetition and variation of motifs in music, and rows of pillars and windows in architecture—for each of these examples there are also countless similar phenomena, not to mention the large-scale repetitions, the structural similarity of episodes, scenes, or musical movements, or even the similarity of houses, towers, churches, or five-act dramas based on repetition (and variation).

Thus it is not surprising that repetition and variation (which is nothing other than modified repetition) also play an important role in the fairytale. Moreover, by direct analogy to life, to reality in general, they play the governing role. It is only that they are more noticeable, more clearly recognizable in the fairytale than in an outer reality which is difficult to survey and which has become by and large something we are accustomed to, which we look upon largely without seeing, since we generally take it for granted. The fairytale makes the structural elements of existence visible; it shows itself to be an organ of knowledge, as indeed a knowledge function has been attributed to literature by some theoreticians. "The mission of art is . . . to make it easier for us to focus our attention," says Lessing in the seventieth piece in his *Hamburgische Dramaturgie*. In Novalis one finds a sort of anticipation of the Brechtian theory of alienation: "The art of alienating in an agreeable way, of making something strange and still familiar—that is romantic poetics."[218] Brecht himself says in his *Kleines Organon für das Theater:* "Art does not become unrealistic when it alters proportions" (par. 73). The theater should, "by making use of the technique of alienation of the familiar," develop in its portrayals of human society "that alien look with which . . . Galileo observed a chandelier which had been set swinging" (par. 44). Brecht is interested primarily in insights into social reality and in "impulses" leading to its modification; like Lessing, however, he sees art as a means to knowledge. The fairytale is, in a completely nontendentious sense, an organ of knowledge: It stylizes reality simply because of the demands of technique—to this degree it does so "unconsciously," and without purposely trying—making in this way part of the structure of reality visible, for example, just by allowing repetitions and variations, which as such represent a basic principle regulating reality, to become the conscious experience of the listener.

Repetitions and variations occur in many forms in the fairytale, and on several levels. Within the individual fairytale, words, word groups, formulas, and also patterns of behavior and plot sequences (episodes) are repeated, either exactly or with slight variation, and along with them, naturally, the same or similar figures also turn up: the same little old man three times, three dragons, three princesses, three brothers, etc. The same fairytale is also told again and again—at one time in traditional storytelling settings, today in the nursery—and there is the recurring wish to hear it again. And finally, in various stories of the same or some other type, well-known themes, motifs, and individual features familiar from other fairytales keep turning up. The fairytales of magic, moreover, are so similar in style and structure that here as well it is necessary to speak of repetition; the method of narration and the narrative structure repeat themselves in each individual fairytale. For this reason, Propp could state directly that instead of many types of the fairytale of magic, there is basically only a single type, which is realized in countless variations and transformations. All told, one is tempted to speak of a virtual orgy of (partially strict, partially varied) repetition in the world of the fairytale. The term *orgy* is deceptive only insofar as everything orgiastic is absent from the fairytale. It speaks with epic calm, self-confidence, and matter-of-factness; confusion is entirely foreign to its repetitions and variations.

Of a special sort, and especially obvious, is the delight in repetition found in the *farce fairytale*. Many farce fairytales occur in the form of chain fairytales *(Kettenmärchen)*; one prank follows the other in chainlike sequence, without limitation and structuring on the basis of tripling: for example, "Lucky Hans" (KHM 83, AT 1415), "The Death of the Little Hen" (KHM 80, AT 2022), and *The fleeing pancake* (AT 2025). Children, who already at the babbling stage produce endless variations on sounds and sound groups and who later, though on a different plane, practice something similar in their verse games and other little rhymes, take special pleasure in such stories. When the sound patterns in his counting and banter rhymes no longer just randomly multiply but become formed, organized, and filled with sense or nonsense, the playful child finds something comparable, but on still a higher level, in the chain fairytale. There one finds not only varied repetition on sound groups, words, and word groups, but on action sequences as well, and play on words, word constellations, and sentence structures can also be brought in. An example would be a Norwegian version of *The fleeing pancake*. As introduction to the word game, the baking mother is begged by the first child: "Give me a little bit of pancake, Mother; I'm so hungry." "Dear Mother," says the second. "Dear, lovely Mother," says the third. "Dear, lovely, good Mother," says the fourth. "Dear, best, lovely, good Mother," says the fifth. "Dear, best, lovely, good, dearest, sweet Mother," says the seventh. The substantive is thus repeated along with all of the adjectives already said, with a new one added each time. An accumulation is added to the repetition, also in the form of repetition to the degree that in the case of the new word, the same word category, the adjective, always reappears. Correspondingly, there is repetition in the further course of what happens, each time a new partner appears: The pancake which the children were supposed to get leaps out of the pan; he gets away from one pursuer after another, until he is finally eaten up, in Norway by a clever pig, elsewhere by a fox. At each station, the fleeing pancake triumphantly recites the list of all who have already sought in vain to catch him. Thus a word-for-word report of past events is given six times. At the end of each, the preceding episode is included—thus here as well an accumulation develops along with the repetition, one that is linear and not interlinked.

> "Dear, good Pancake, don't roll so fast. Wait up a little, I want to eat you," said the gander. "I have already left behind Lady Grady, Grandpa, too, and seven loudmouths, Master Raster, Henny Penny, Rooster Brewster, Duck Wuck, and Goose Bruce, so I can probably escape from you, too, Gander Leander," said Pancake, and began to roll as fast as he could.[219]

In Russian the boasting is rendered in verses to be sung; the first six verses are repeated at each station, and each time another is added to them:

> I am scraped together from the barrel,
> I am brushed together from the pantry,
> I am mixed with thick milk,
> And baked in rich oil,
> Then cooled on the windowsill;
> I got away from Daddy,
> I got away from Mommy,
> I got away from Rabbit,
> I got away from Gray Wolf,
> I even got away from Bear,
> And you, Fox, aren't about to get me.[220]

"Chain fairytales," says Archer Taylor in his excellent article "Formelmärchen" [Formula fairytales], "are told less as stories than as memory exercises. Often they have to be repeated without mistakes, or else the speaker has to pay a penalty."[221] In those of our pancake stories deriving from Scandinavia, Russia, Germany, and England, however, memory exercise and test of tongue agility are combined with an attractive plot; the result is enjoyed as a unity, that is, as a story—by adults as well as by children. The memory exercise is, as in many such cases, a memory game. The very ability to recall and the experience of being able to recognize repetition give the child a feeling of pleasure. Remembering is prerequisite to any repetition. And the ability to recognize repetition is a basic element of knowledge itself. The word compare (vergleichen) demonstrates that one seeks to find in the new something comparable, something like what is already familiar. The constant amid the changing, the known among the unknown, the invariable within the variable, and the seeking of such constants and the joy at their appearance and reappearance—these things are associated with the music of a Bach or a Mozart, with music in general, just as they are with the simple children's song or game and with the simple chain fairytale.

With stories like those of Lucky Hans or Jockel ("Joggeli"), who is supposed to shake the pears down from the tree ("Joggeli wott ga Birli schüttle," AT 2030, KHM [1812], nr. 72, taken down in Switzerland), the links in the chain are not simply hung onto one another, as in the story of the pancake, but actually interlinked; every element presupposes the previous one. It is only because Hans has a gold nugget that he can make a trade for a horse, and that is the prerequisite for the next trade. The fire sent out by Jockel's master is linked to the disobedient club sent out before, then the water to the disobedient fire, the little calf to the disobedient water, the butcher to the disobedient calf, etc. But even with such tightly linked chains, one feels and enjoys the easiness with which the story rolls on. That everything that comes should follow "logically" from what precedes, is in no way felt to be constraining; it seems much more to develop in and of itself. It is no accident that the chain, the stringing of things together, is popular in the farce; even from the point of view of content, it prefers to be concerned with things that, when the prerequisites are only present, require no effort and cause no problems: eating, drinking, sleeping, digesting, etc.[222] Fairytales of magic are more complex, more differentiated, and at the same time more moderately designed than chain farces. Roman Jakobson especially emphasizes that in the speech development of the child the phase of exuberant, undirected playing with sounds is succeeded by one of using sounds that are more carefully selected, limited, and structured;[223] and Goethe observes something comparable in the plant world. Correspondingly, a more highly developed state can be seen to be represented in the fairytale of magic than in the chain fairytale. This observation is not intended to argue that the chain fairytale in its present form represents historically an earlier stage, but only to call attention to the differences in structure and to the respective levels of artistry. Goethe sees in the development of the flower a metamorphosis of the exuberant sprouting of the leaves.

> . . . auf mastig strotzender Fläche
> Scheinet die Fülle des Triebs frei und unendlich zu sein.
> Doch hier hält die Natur, mit mächtigen Händen, die Bildung
> An und lenket sie sanft in das Vollkommnere hin.
> Mäßiger leitet sie nun den Saft, verengt die Gefäße,
> Und gleich zeigt die Gestalt zärtere Wirkungen an.

> . . . on the vastly exuberant surface
> the luxuriance of the sprouting appears to be free and unending.
> Yet here Nature, with powerful hands, halts the development
> And leads it softly on to something more perfect.
> More moderately she directs the sap, narrows the arteries,
> And immediately the form shows more delicate reactions.[224]*

*Fairytales of magic, novella fairytales,* and *religious fairytales* are not, however, a metamorphosis of the chain fairytale; they constitute genres in their own right. It is true that they may contain chains, but only as subordinate components, as is the case in the story of the magician and his pupil (AT 325, KHM 68). As Archer Taylor emphasizes, again there is the "characteristic interdependence of the links: The boy transforms himself into a bird, the sorcerer into a hawk; the bird into a fish, the hawk into a larger fish; the fish into a ring, the larger fish into a merchant; the ring into a pile of grain, the merchant into a rooster; and the grain into a hawk, which eats up the rooster."[225] In the *external soul* fairytale type (life outside the body, life in an egg, AT 302), the life or soul of a monster is hidden in an egg, which, however, can only be got at by way of detours. In a Russian version an oak must be uprooted; the box hidden in its roots must be raised; out of it springs a hare; a bitch must catch the hare; out of the slaughtered hare flies a duck; an eagle catches it; but the egg falls out of its ripped-open innards and into the sea; a pike—as the third in a series of "grateful animals"—brings it to the hero; and he can now at last cast the egg against the forehead of the monster and by so doing kill him.[226]

In the fairytale of magic, chains of this sort are built as motif complexes into a larger whole. To this degree one can speak of repetition with variation when what is really the same action is repeated again and again, always in a different but yet similar form. The fairytale of magic, however, is characterized by repetitions and variations of a stricter sort rather than by such chain episodes. These mainly follow the law of tripling. Tripling provides the narrator with technical help: He knows he has to narrate three episodes, no more, no less—and in case he might have forgotten one, an experienced and talented narrator can easily construct a substitute episode on the basis of motifs or individual features familiar to him. Tripling, however, also has esthetic value. It represents plurality in a clearly surveyable form, and, because it is a well-known fact of the fairytale (and not just of the fairytale), it is an element familiar to the listener, a constant which he expects and which he savors (see pp. 64–65, 69–70).

Within the fairytale of magic, the novella fairytale, the religious fairytale, and many a farce fairytale, the stringing together of two or three identical or similar episodes or episode groups is the most important form of repetition (taking repetition to include both direct repetition and repetition with variation). Three brothers leave home, one after the other, to undertake the same task (*three brothers* fairytale, e.g., AT 550, KHM 57, "The Golden Bird"), or three wandering companions are each confronted with the same difficulty (e.g., *The bear's son* fairytale, AT 301, KHM 91); two sisters have to undergo the same adventure (e.g., AT 480, KHM 24, "Frau Holle"), or two brothers have to cope with the arts of a witch (*two brothers* fairytale, AT 303, KHM 60). Or, one figure is confronted with a sequence of similar tasks. Thus under the fairytale type first mentioned, the hero of "The Golden Bird" must three times in sequence steal a living creature—the golden bird, the golden horse, and the beautiful maiden from the golden castle; and in the Frau Holle fairytale, both Goldmarie, the heroine, and then Pechmarie, the antiheroine (both names deriving from Bechstein), are supposed first to take bread out of the oven, then shake apples down from the tree, and finally serve Frau Holle. The degree to which the word sequence is also repeated in such analogous episodes, especially (though not exclusively) in direct discourse, can be shown in two stories from Schleswig-Holstein. In a fairytale of the *water of life* type (AT 551, KHM 97) the youngest prince comes

zu einem kleinen Hause, darin wohnte eine steinalte Frau. Er klopfte an, sie tat ihm auf, und als sie ihn sah, verwunderte sie sich und sprach: "Mein Sohn, wo kommst du her? Es ist hier in manch hundert Jahren kein Mensch zu mir gekommen." Er sprach: "Ich bin des Königs jüngster Sohn und bin ausgesandt, das Wasser des Lebens, das Wasser der Schönheit und das Buch der Jugend für meinen Vater zu holen." Ihm entgegnete die Alte: "Mein Sohn, ich kann dir nicht helfen. Aber ich habe eine Schwester, die wohnt 200 Meilen weiter von hier. Vielleicht weiß die Rat." Da erschrak der Prinz über den weiten Weg und sprach: "Wie kann ich schnell die 200 Meilen machen?" Die Alte aber sprach: "Ich habe ein Pferd im Stall, das kann die 200 Meilen in einem Tag machen, das will ich dir überlassen." Des war der Prinz zufrieden. Die alte Frau labte ihn mit Speise und Trank, und er übernachtete in ihrem Hause.

Am andern Morgen empfing er das Pferd der alten Frau und ritt so schnell, daß er noch am Abend bei ihrer Schwester eintraf. Er klopfte an, und da sie ihm öffnete, verwunderte sie sich und sprach: "Mein Sohn, wo kommst du her? Es ist in manch hundert Jahren kein Mensch in dies Haus gekommen." Der Prinz antwortete: "Ich bin des Königs jüngster Sohn und will für meinen Vater das Wasser des Lebens, das Wasser der Schönheit und das Buch der Jugend holen." Die Alte sprach: "Da kann ich dir nicht helfen. Aber ich habe eine Schwester, die wohnt dreihundert Meilen von hier. Vielleicht weiß die zu helfen." Da sagte der Prinz betrübt: "Wie soll ich diesen weiten Weg machen?" Sie aber sprach: "In meinem Stalle steht ein Pferd, das kann die dreihundert Meilen in einem Tage machen. Das will ich dir mitgeben." Des freute sich der Prinz. Die Alte setzte ihm Essen und Trinken vor und gab ihm Herberge in ihrem Hause.

Am andern Morgen bestieg er das Roß der alten Frau, und es lief so schnell, daß er noch am Abend bei der Schwester ankam. Er klopfte an, und als sie ihm auftat, verwunderte sie sich und sprach: "Mein Sohn, wo kommst du her? Es ist in manch hundert Jahren kein Mensch zu mir gekommen." Er antwortete: "Ich bin des Königs jüngster Sohn und suche das Wasser des Lebens, das Wasser der Schönheit und das Buch der Jugend für meinen Vater. . . ."

to a little house, where lived a woman old as the hills. He knocked, she opened the door, and when she saw him, she was astonished and said, "My son, where have you come from? In lo these many hundred years no one has come to me." He said, "I am the youngest son of the king and was sent out to fetch the water of life, the water of beauty, and the book of youth for my father." The old woman answered: "My son, I can't help you. But I have a sister who lives two hundred miles further on from here. Perhaps she has some advice." Then the prince was horrified at the great distance and said, "How can I cover the two hundred miles quickly?" And the old woman said: "I have a horse in the barn that can cover the two hundred miles in one day; I will give it to you." The prince was satisfied. The old woman refreshed him with food and drink, and he stayed overnight in her house.

The next morning he got the old woman's horse and rode so fast that he was already at her sister's by evening. He knocked, and when she opened up, she was astonished, and said: "My son, where have you come from? In lo these many hundred years no one has come into this house." The prince answered, "I am the youngest son of the king, and I wish to fetch for my father the water of life, the water of beauty, and the book of youth." The old woman said, "I can't help you there. But I have a sister who lives three hundred miles from here. Perhaps she knows how to help." Then the prince said sadly, "How am I supposed to cover this great distance?" And she said: "In my barn is a horse that can cover the three hundred miles in one day. I will give it to you." The prince was happy. The old woman laid out food and drink for him and gave him shelter in her house.

The next morning, he mounted the old woman's horse and rode so fast that he was already at her sister's by evening. He knocked, and when she opened the door, she was astonished, and said, "My son, where have you come from? In lo these many hundred years no one has come to me." He answered: "I am the youngest son of the king, and I seek the water of life, the water of beauty, and the book of youth for my father."

In one version of the fairytale about the search for the lost mate (*Amor and Psyche* type, AT 425; cf. KHM 88), the heroine comes

an ein kleines Haus. Darin wohnte eine alte Frau, zu der sprach sie: "Ach, liebe Frau, laßt mich zur Nacht ein wenig in eurem Hause ausruhen."— "Nein," sprach die Frau, "das geht nicht, denn mein Sohn, der Wind, wird bald nach Hause kommen. Der kann es gleich riechen, daß du hier bist, und dann wird es dir schlimm ergehen." Da erzählte die betrübte Frau ihr ganzes Unglück und weinte so sehr, daß es der Alten zu Herzen ging, und sie verbarg die Frau unter dem Bette.

Als nun der Wind nach Hause kam, rief er gleich: "Ich rieche! Ich rieche!" —"Was riechst du?" fragte die Alte. "Hier ist Menschenfleisch im Hause!" —"Nein, mein Sohn," sagte die Alte, "es ist wohl ein Rabe übers Haus geflogen, der einen Menschenknochen im Schnabel hatte."—"Das kann auch wohl sein," meinte der Wind, gab sich damit zufrieden und setzte sich zum Essen. Als er satt war, sprach die Alte zu ihm: "Mein Sohn! Ich habe dir etwas zu sagen. Du mußt nun nicht gar zu böse werden."—"Was gibt's denn?" —"Ich habe eine arme Frau im Hause versteckt, die ausgegangen ist, ihren Mann wieder zu suchen, den sie verloren hat." Der Wind verlangte sie zu sehen, und die Frau mußte hervorkommen. Sie erzählte alles, wie es sich zugetragen hatte. Der Wind tat ihr kein Leid, sondern versprach ihr seine Hilfe. Am andern Tag blies er mit solcher Kraft wie nie zuvor, aber auch er fand den verlorenen Mann nicht, und die betrübte Frau mußte weiter wandern. Als sie fortgehen wollte, sprach die Alte: "Ich will dir etwas schenken, das kann dir noch von großem Nutzen sein!" und gab ihr ein schönes Silberkleid.

Die Frau bedankte sich aufs beste und zog weiter, den verlorenen Mann zu suchen. Am Abend kam sie wieder an ein kleines Haus. Sie ging hinein und traf eine alte Frau, zu der sprach sie: "Ach liebe Frau, laßt mich doch diese Nacht in eurem Hause zubringen!" Die Alte erwiderte: "Nein, das geht nicht, denn bald kommt mein Sohn, der Mond, nach Hause. Der wird sogleich merken, daß du hier bist, und dann wird es dir übel ergehen." Aber die Frau erzählte ihr großes Unglück und weinte so heftig, daß es die Alte dauerte, und sie versteckte sie unter dem Bette. Bald kam der Mond nach Hause, und als er kaum eingetreten war, rief er: "Ich rieche, ich rieche!" und fing an zu suchen. "Was riechst du?" sprach die Alte. "Du hast Menschenfleisch im Hause!"—"Nein," sagte die Alte, "es wird wohl ein Rabe übers Haus geflogen sein, der einen Menschenknochen im Schnabel hatte." Der Sohn gab sich damit zufrieden und setzte sich zum Essen. Als er satt war, fing die Alte an: "Mein Sohn! Ich habe dir noch etwas zu sagen. Du mußt nur nicht gar zu böse werden."—"Was hast du denn?"—"Es ist eine arme Frau hier, die ist ausgegangen, ihren verlorenen Mann zu suchen."—"Wo hast du sie?" sprach der Mond. Und nun mußte die Frau hervorkommen und genau erzählen, wie es ihr ergangen war. Als der Mond alles vernommen hatte, versprach er ihr zu helfen, und in der Nacht schien er so prächtig, daß die Leute meinten, es sei heller Tag geworden. Doch den verlorenen Prinzen konnte er auch nicht finden. Da sank der armen Frau der Mut immer mehr, und am andern Morgen wollte sie sich in großer Betrübnis weiter auf den Weg machen. Da sprach die Alte zu ihr: "Ich will dir etwas schenken, das kann dir noch großen Nutzen bringen," und reichte ihr ein überaus prächtiges Goldkleid.

Die Frau bedankte sich vielmals und zog weiter. Am Abend kam sie nochmals zu einem kleinen Haus, und als sie eintrat, fand sie wieder eine alte Frau; zu der sprach sie: "Ach, gute Frau, laßt mich doch diese Nacht in eurem Hause ausruhn."—"Nein," sprach die, "das geht nicht an. Denn wenn mein Sohn, die Sonne, nach Hause kommt, wird er es gleich merken, daß du hier bist, und dann sieht es schlimm für dich aus." Da erzählte die arme Frau ihren Kummer und weinte so sehr, daß es die Alte dauerte, und sie verbarg sie unter dem Bette. Als nun bald darnach der Sohn nach Hause kam, rief er gleich: "Ich rieche, ich rieche!"—"Was ist?" fragte die Alte. "Es riecht hier nach Menschenfleisch."—"Mein Sohn, es wird gewiß ein Rabe übers Haus geflogen sein, der einen Menschenknochen im Schnabel hatte." —"Kann sein," sprach der Sohn, beruhigte sich dabei und setzte sich zum Essen. Als er satt war, sprach die Alte: "Ich habe dir noch etwas zu sagen; du mußt nur nicht gar zu böse werden."—"Laß Hören!" sprach die Sonne, und die Alte fing an: "Ich habe eine arme Frau im Hause versteckt, die ihren Mann verloren hat."

to a little house. An old woman lived there, to whom she said, "Ah, dear woman, let me rest a little tonight in your house." "No," said the woman, "that's impossible, for my son, the wind, will soon be coming home. He can smell it immediately if you are here, and then it will go badly for you." Then the sad woman told of her whole misfortune and cried so desperately that it touched the old woman, and she hid the woman under the bed.

When the wind came home, he immediately cried: "I smell something! I smell something!" "What do you smell?" asked the old woman. "There is human flesh in the house!" "No, my son," said the old woman, "it must be that a raven which had a human bone in its beak has flown over the house." "That may very well be," said the wind, satisfied, and sat down to eat. When he was full, the old woman said to him: "My son! I have something to say to you. Now, you must not get too angry." "What is it, then?" "I have hidden a poor woman in the house who has set out to find her husband, whom she has lost." The wind demanded to see her, and the woman had to come out. She told everything that had happened to her. The wind did not harm her, but promised her his help. The next day he blew with such power as he had never used before, but even he did not find the lost husband, and the sad woman had to wander on. When she was ready to go, the old woman said, "I want to give you something that can in future be of great value to you!" and gave her a beautiful dress of silver.

The woman thanked her kindly and went on to seek her lost husband. In the evening she again came to a little house. She went in and ran into an old woman, to whom she said: "Ah, dear woman, do let me spend the night in your house!" The old woman replied, "No, that is impossible, for my son, the moon, will soon come home. He will note immediately that you are here, and then it will go badly for you." But the woman told of her great misfortune and wept so hard that the old woman had pity, and she hid her under the bed. Soon the moon came home, and when he had scarcely come in the door, he cried, "I smell something, I smell something!" and started looking around. "What do you smell?" said the old woman. "You've got human flesh in the house!" "No," said the old woman, "it must be that a raven which had a human bone in its beak has flown over the house." The son, satisfied, sat down to eat. When he was full, the old woman began: "My son! I have something to say to you. Now, you must not get too angry." "What's up, then?" "There is a poor woman here who has set out to seek her lost husband." "Where do you have her?" said the moon. And then the woman had to come out and tell exactly what had happened to her. When the moon had listened to everything, he promised to help her, and during the night he shone so magnificently that people thought that it was broad daylight. Still, he also could not find the lost prince. Then the poor woman became even more dejected, and the next morning, in great sadness, she wished to continue on her way. Then the old woman said to her, "I want to give you something that can in future be of great value to you," and handed her an especially magnificent dress of gold.

The woman thanked her many times and continued on her way. In the evening she once again came to a little house, and when she entered, she again found an old woman, to whom she said: "Ah, good woman, do let me rest tonight in your house." "No," she said, "that is impossible. For when my son, the sun, comes home, he will immediately notice that you are here, and then it will look bad for you." Then the poor woman told of her sorrow and wept so desperately that the old woman had pity and hid her under the bed. Soon after, when the son came home, he immediately cried: "I smell something, I smell something!" "What is it?" asked the old woman. "It smells here of human flesh." "My son, it must be that a raven which had a human bone in its beak has flown over the house." "That may be," said the son, calming down, and sat down to eat. When he was full, the old woman said, "I have something to say to you now; but you must not get too angry." "Let's hear it!" said the sun, and the old woman began: "I have hidden a poor woman in the house who has lost her husband."[227]

With such a high degree of similarity in word sequence, one can again speak of a feat of memory (see pp. 79–80), and still the narrator acts as if he had not said everything once already but had to tell everything word for word anew. In the second text only two small connectives, *wieder* "again" and *nochmals* "once again," refer to what has gone before; otherwise each episode is independent. Each in its own right, so to speak, has a claim to being fully developed—examples of the stylistic principle of isolation, which pushes the independence of the parts to the extreme, and at the same time evidence of respect for the suitable word sequence, once it has been discovered. If they wished, even weaker narrators could easily use variations here and there, but their feeling for style apparently demands something else. With many narrators one can also find formulations like "Everything happened as it had the time before" (often prefaced by "In order to make a long story short"), but which sort of narration is the more impressive artistically can be judged not only by the listener with respect to an oral narrative but also by the reader of the printed fairytale. But with oral narration, the involved repetition has the additional advantage of extending the narrative, to make it, so to speak, evening-filling— here, as well, an external, one might say technical, requirement leads to an artistically effective result. It is the more effective insofar as the repetitions are generally not stretched out of proportion and, through tripling, not only limited, saved from endless multiplication, but also formed and structured. The pattern of threes, moreover, is in general internally differentiated: It is only the third helper that has advice; the first two brothers fail, the last proves successful; the hero himself fails twice, but is successful the third time. In this way a polarity is established within the pattern of threes, with the third segment standing over against the first two—polarity thus occurring not only in fairytales with two main figures (two brothers, two sisters), but often in those with three active figures. In other cases, intensification occurs instead of polarity: The tasks become increasingly more difficult, the adventures more dangerous, the princesses or metallic cities or bridges ever more beautiful, the advisors more knowledgeable, the dragons more ghastly—the first has three heads, the second six, the third nine. Scholars speak of the preference of the fairytale, and of many types of folk narrative in general, for emphasis on the final element.[228] That emphasis should fall on the last segment of a plot sequence is of course an obvious possibility, to a certain degree something developing in and of itself: The conclusion must be marked in some way, and it can be done most easily by using contrast, intensification, or diminution, as our examples of the chain fairytale have already demonstrated. After the final trade, Lucky Hans not only has less than before, as in every previous case, but nothing at all—the last step is not just an extreme, but indeed an absolute. It is exactly the same with the fleeing pancake (AT 2025), only here the last link does not bring an intensification of what has gone before, but rather a contrast, so that a polarity involving success and failure results; the concluding failure is decisive—the pancake is eaten up. In the type represented by "Joggeli wott ga Birli schüttle" (AT 2030 D, E), the final link is also the decisive one; it is not the end, of course, but the turning point: The whole chain is now run through in reverse. One can speak with justification of emphasis on the final element not only with intensifications but also, as has just been established, with groups that are in polar relationship to one another, already the case in chain fairytales but even more so in more richly structured fairytales. The first two episodes can be put on a par with one another; the second brother or comrade behaves just like the first and is just as unsuccessful. Here it is thus not possible to speak of intensification or other differentiation, but it is of emphasis on the final element. The last, the concluding, sequence (and along with it the last figure to appear) is different from both the others and thereby carries more weight. In this way the tripling pattern of the fairytale turns out to offer a concisely constructed design, even though it relies upon repetition; the tripling in and of itself already provides certain organizational resources, but they are further increased by differentiation, polarization, intensification or diminution, and by accentuation in the form of emphasis on the final element.

It goes without saying that there will be verbatim repetition in magical verse, for the magic is dependent on the form, and within a formula, repetition is something appropriate to the style of the fairytale for expressing the intensity of the magical proceedings: "Weh, weh, Windchen, nimm Kürdchen sein Hütchen. . . ." ("Blow, blow, little wind. Take Curt's little hat away. . . .") (KHM 89). The fact that verbatim repetition should appear in other sorts of direct speech is less obvious than it is with magical formulas, and it is still less obvious with sequences of pure reporting, but also in these instances many narrative segments are repeated verbatim, as the examples printed on pp. 83–87 show. The fairytale narrator leans toward quasi-ritualistic repetition. The word sequence, once it has been spoken, has the authority of authenticity. In direct speech, verbatim repetition may recommend itself for other reasons, as is the case in our model narrative (pp. 2–5), where it brings out the obstinacy of the denial: The beautiful girl must keep silent about the fact that she has observed the secret, compromising doings of the sorcerer (the flogging of fifty corpses). She thus dare not confess that she lost one of her golden shoes at that time. She maintains: "I lost it when I went to milk the cow." The sorcerer threatens her with death, but she answers: "I can tell you nothing other than what I have already told you. I lost it when I went to milk the cow." She gives the same answer after the second death threat. And after "several years," when her master, the sorcerer, repeats his question, her answer is: "I can tell you nothing other than what I have already told you. I lost it when I went to milk the cow." Some years later, when she is asked one last time, she answers again in the same words, only she replaces "already told" with "always told." Thus here the verbatim repetition not only has organizational and, one might say, ritualistic significance, it indicates at the same time the degree of resistance of the woman, who, despite the worst threats and actions of her tormentor (he takes away her children and makes her appear as their murderer), sticks by her story.

In a Rhaeto-romance version of the already often-mentioned *Faithful John* type (AT 516), master and servant, after winning the "most beautiful girl under the sun," stay overnight on the way home in the same magic castle of the three black maidens where they stayed on the way out.

> When they had gone to bed, the black maiden came back and said: "Prince Ludwig is sleeping, and the servant, John, as well. And the most beautiful girl under the sun is in another room."
> Meanwhile, the sister comes in: "Good evening, sister."
> "Good evening, sister."
> And she says: "Have they come with the most beautiful girl under the sun?"
> "Yes, they have brought the most beautiful girl under the sun with them."
> Later, the third also comes in: "Good evening, sisters."
> "Good evening, sister."
> And she says: "Have they brought her here, have they come with the most beautiful girl under the sun?"

Second night:

> And in the evening, after supper, when they had gone to bed, the black maidens came again.
> And the first one came in and said: "Prince Ludwig is sleeping, and the servant, John, is sleeping as well, and the most beautiful girl under the sun is in another room."
> Meanwhile, the sister comes in: "Good evening, sister."
> "Good evening, sister."
> . . . and says: "Are they still here with the most beautiful girl under the sun?"
> Then the third comes, as well: "Good evening, sisters."
> "Good evening, sister."

. . . and says: "Are they still here, Prince Ludwig and the servant, John, with the most beautiful girl under the sun?"

"Yes, indeed," said the eldest, "the servant, John, is not feeling very well, and thus they have had to stay here."

Third night:

After supper they again went to bed, and shortly thereafter the black maiden came in: "Prince Ludwig is sleeping, and the servant, John, as well, and the most beautiful girl under the sun is in another room."

Meanwhile, the sister comes: "Good evening, sister."

"Good evening, sister."

. . . and says: "Are they still here with the most beautiful girl under the sun?"

Later, the third also comes: "Good evening, sisters."

"Good evening, sister."

. . . and says: "Are they still here, Prince Ludwig and the servant, John, with the most beautiful girl under the sun?"

"Yes, indeed," said the eldest, "the servant, John, is not feeling very well, and thus they have had to stay here."[229]

Here the verbatim repetition is not demanded by magical activity, by anything in the content, or for any other reason; but it is still brought in despite the trouble it takes. Direct speech, extensive use of dialog instead of simple report, lengthens the story, and that was an important consideration for the narrator in the story-telling context. But the almost ritualistic inflexibility of the repetition also has its own special esthetic effect. It is possible that the content here is somehow a factor: The compulsive repetition in the three-way conversations may indicate that the three black sisters are otherworldly beings, may reflect the spell which they are under. But the inflexibility in the presentation of the dialog in all of its reprises fits in well with the metallic-crystalline overall style of the fairytale.

Another variety of repetition, the imitation of the spoken word through action, can be illustrated with the Grimms' version of *Faithful John* (KHM 6). At the beginning of the story, the old king commends his son to the faithful servant:

"After my death, you are to show him the entire castle, all the rooms, halls, and cellars, and all the treasures that lie therein; but the last room at the end of the long hall you are not to show him, the room where the picture of the princess of the golden roof is hidden. If he sees the picture, he will fall hopelessly in love with her and swoon dead away and face great dangers because of her. You have to protect him from this."

That is exactly what will happen; the plot brings the realization of what has been prefigured in words. Later, Faithful John hears the raven foretell what is to come, and in the Rhaeto-romance version, as well, Giovan overhears what is to happen and what is to be done. In the formulation of Bennison Gray: *Incident repeats narration.*[230] This phenomenon, in either rudimentary or fuller form, can be observed in almost any fairytale. Just as prophecies and dreams play a large role in the classical tragedy (and in the renaissance and baroque tragedies which were influenced by it), anticipation of what is to come is also characteristic of the fairytale, be it through the spoken word or the fact that the figure of the princess is anticipated in a painted picture, as happens in *Faithful John* and other tales. Prohibitions are also anticipations. They state negatively what will with certainty happen later on; to this degree the later event is a repetition of what was announced in the prohibition. Every foreshadowing, whether it is an announcement, a directive to act, or a prohibition, creates expectation; tension results. Every anticipation, even one with minus sign—indeed, especially this sort—cries out for realization. Even when one knows in advance that something will come to pass—as can be assumed to be the case with the accustomed fairytale listener or reader— one remains, so long as the realization has not occurred, in a state of suspense, which is relieved only when what has been anticipated actually occurs, when the expected chord sounds. The important role which various kinds of anticipation play in the fairytale is also of anthropological significance—they reflect man's way of thinking. That man is quite specifically characterized by the ability to previsage, to anticipate, to project, is something that not only Ernst Bloch has tirelessly pointed out; the much-neglected Swiss philosopher Carlo Sganzini has just as impressively and persistently illustrated it in another way, with other emphasis, and completely independently of Bloch.[231]

*Narration repeats incident,* where what has happened is recapitulated, is the complementary converse of *Incident repeats Narration. Faithful John* again offers an example: After the faithful servant has three times managed to avert disaster, he tells about doing so and why. We thus have in the same fairytale—and not only in the Grimms' version—the three corresponding elements: First the events are prophesied, i.e, the dangers threatening the homeward-bound pair; then they occur; and finally, in a sort of finale, they are recapitulated. This tripartite scheme is present in many fairytales, in either embryo or developed form. One of the most pointed and well-known forms of recapitulation is the question about what somebody deserves who has done a particular deed. Villains or evil queens are presented with a precise formulation of their villainy, and they must render their own verdict in the matter. Occasionally one runs into a more long-winded variety of recapitulation in the fairytale, the repetition of events in so many words: In the locked hall, either the hero or the king at the hero's request announces, "Now everybody has to tell a story." When the hero's turn comes round, he begins, "Now I will tell you my

story, and no one is to . . . get up . . . from the table before I am finished!"
He relates what has happened to him, and the male or female villain,
whose evil deeds are being revealed to the assembled court, sits there on
pins and needles and asks to no avail to be allowed to leave the hall
because of a headache or some other (often graphically portrayed) press-
ing call.[232] There are many ways to bring such recapitulations into the
story. In the Grimms' fairytale, the goose-girl first complains to the iron
stove about what she has had to endure (KHM 89, AT 533),[233]* then the
old king, who has overheard, relates it to his son, and finally he repeats it
before the whole court and the invited guests, addressing himself to the
"false bride." And even if here, as in many other instances, the whole
thing is not repeated in so many words, what happened is still reported
three times, so that the telling, the narrating within the narrative, the
verbal recapitulation of what has happened, is set in motion and fully
carried through. Instead of words, a paintbrush can also be used to convey what has happened: "The king . . . gave him the task of decorating two
rooms and a hall," and he depicted the "story of his life." "He painted
himself as tailor's apprentice, how they had pulled his ears, what he had
gone through, how he . . . overcame the lion . . . and how the minister
had cast him in the sea." And then it goes on: He opened up "the rooms
and the hall and explained everything. And the minister was standing
there. Voices were immediately raised, asking, 'What does such a person
deserve as reward?' 'Nothing short of being torn to pieces by four
oxen.'"[234]* Another form of recapitulation of a preceding sequence of
events is familiar from the riddle fairytale (Rätselmärchen), where the
experiences of the hero and his companion are presented as such a complex riddle that the princess is unable to solve it, as in this example from a
fairytale from Brittany: "When we left home, there were four of us. Of the
four, two died. Of the two, four died. Out of the four, we made eight. Of
the eight, sixteen died. And now we four have come to you."[235] The riddle,
which the clever servant has invented and with difficulty drummed into
the head of the stupid nobleman, reports in coded form the things that
have happened to master and servant on the journey to the royal city,
things which are known to the listener but not to the princess, who is
supposed to solve the riddle. As in various other farce fairytales, the hero
is finally supposed to fill up a sack with bits of truth. Here he does so with
telltale bits of clothing; in other fairytales, he begins to tick off the embar-
assing things that have happened to the king and his daughter. The king
orders him to stop, explaining that the sack is full. Stories of this sort have
led Marie-Louise Ténèze to characterize the fairytale, in which the gift so
often precedes the task, as follows: "The fairytale of magic . . . has the
answer precede the question."[236] The recapitulation of prior events is
anthropologically as important as the anticipation of coming events. Man

is called upon not only to plan the future, but, as a basis for doing so, to have access to the past.

One can call the narrative within the narrative the narcissism of the narrative, just as Ernest Dutoit has called the tendency toward the play within the play, theater within the theater, "le narcissisme du théâtre."[237] It is not surprising that the narrator repeats not only already-pronounced sounds, sound groups, and words a second and a third time, but whole parts of his narrative, as well. When he does not wish to repeat them himself, he at least reports that they have been repeated, in whatever form may be appropriate in the framework of the narrative sequence. The internal narration is especially lavish where an inn, a public baths, or a hospital has been built or opened, and the guests (passing wanderers) or patients are not asked to pay anything, but instead to relate something from their life story. By this means, the woman proprietor of the hotel or baths hopes to find her lost husband or lover (Motif H. 11.1.1, AT 304, KHM 111). One runs into this motif in the Arabian Nights, in the folk book about the beautiful Magelone, in Basile, and in many fairytales: Turkish, Greek, Italian, Rhaeto-romance, etc. Finally, someone always comes along whose story proves him to be the one sought, or who at least brings news of the one sought. This model is especially nicely developed in a Chilean story about the missed rendezvous (AT 861). At the free hostel with the sign "Hostel for Poor and Rich—Stable and Everything Available," the robbers narrate first, then the princess, who runs the hostel, gradually coaxes out of the poor prince, who has to serve the robbers and gets his share of beatings in the process, the complete story of his misfortune. The princess is able to say: "How beautiful this story is! Please go on," for, without recognizing her, he tells her of everything that they had once experienced together, something that the fairytale listeners or readers have already heard or read.[238] She listens to it happily, and we do, too—she, because for her the past again becomes the present; we, because we enjoy esthetically the pleasure of the narrative within the narrative, the narration to the second power, the metamorphosis of the real into the narrated, and the corresponding effect of this reality cum narrative on the present. "Ernst ist das Leben, heiter ist die Kunst" ("Life is earnest, art is cheerful"). It is not just that the fairytale itself is art. As part of its art, the fairytale happenings, the fairytale reality, are again filtered, and because of the altered context, the difficulty experienced is transformed, also from the point of view of content, into its opposite. It is as if this South American fairytale wished, in its own way, to exemplify and interpret the statement of Schiller quoted above.

We have repetition as narcissism, imitation, renewal, and variation and transformation. Completely rigid, verbatim repetitions of long passages scarcely ever occur, but slightly varied and even greatly altered ones often do. Thus almost every repetition is at the same time a variation; constants are bound to variables, the old to the new. And what is true of the individual fairytale is also true of the totality of fairytales at the disposal of a single teller and, in another way, of the listener, of one who knows his fairytales. It is not only that he gladly tells or hears one story again and again; the other fairytales are also variations on the same structure, course of events, individual motifs and features, and mode of representation. Whether repetition and variation should be called a structural principle is a subject of controversy, but it is a controversy over words. When Propp states that they are not relevant to structure, that is certainly true as far as it goes, since the repetition or variation does not really advance the plot— it constitutes no *new* structural element. In the farce fairytale about the rabbit-herd (AT 570), it changes absolutely nothing with respect to the basic pattern *(Ablauf)* of the plot whether a hare is bought from the hero three times in sequence, as is usually the case, or whether it is shown just once how the keeper of the one hundred hares can call back the one he is missing by using his magic whistle[239]—but it does affect its realization *(Verlauf)*. The retardation effect which is engendered by the variations gives the story a different character. Thus one may join Lutz Mackensen in calling tripling a "structural formula," a construction feature.[240] A fairytale is differently constructed when it is told as a single sequence than when we are allowed to experience that particular sequence within the framework of trebled variation—however primitive it may be: The first hare is called back when the buyer is still close by, the second only later, and the third when he has almost—or even actually—reached the castle.[241] The repetition of sounds, words, and word groups (formulas), both within the individual fairytale and beyond the boundaries of the individual story, is a fundamental stylistic principle of the fairytale; the repetition of whole episodes, mostly in slightly varied form, is one of its most important construction principles. Both types of repetition and variation answer technical and esthetic demands. What is demanded by narrative technique can as such have an esthetic dimension, just as a demonstration model or any other functional structure can have beauty. The teller is encouraged to go a step farther, i.e., to bring in repetition and variation of a more refined sort, as art for the sake of art, even where it would no longer be necessary purely from the point of view of narrative technique.

## CONTRASTS, POLARITIES, AND EXTREMES

Since contrasts provide the counternote to repetition even within repetition patterns built up on the basis of groups of twos and threes, it is scarcely conceivable that they should be absent within a whole fairytale narrative and, yet wider, in the total corpus of fairytales known to narrator or listener. Without contrasts, the fairytale would lose its distinctive character. They are something which derive from its tendency toward extreme completeness of form, and they come into being, like so many other things in the fairytale, to a certain degree in and of themselves, as a consequence of this tendency to the extreme, to vigorous stylization. Beautiful and ugly, good and bad, success and failure, helplessness/perplexity and successful outcome, emergency and rescue, enchantment and disenchantment, reward and punishment, gold and pitch, death and resuscitation, appearance and reality, high and low, magnificent and dirty, small and large, real and unreal—these and other polarities run through the world of the fairytale in manifold variations, and they frequently occur with respect to the same figure: The goose-girl is secretly a princess; the scald-headed boy secretly has golden hair; Cinderella has magnificent clothing at her disposal. It is unnecessary to provide examples for all these contrast polarities; they lie about on the street, on the fairytale street. The fairytale narrator or fairytale inventor need only pick them up. But a talented narrator does not pick them up at random; he does not stuff his narrative full of them. Here, as well, measure is the rule. By no means do all the polarities mentioned—and those not mentioned but still possible—appear in a single concrete fairytale.

The polarities come into being in and of themselves, according to the law of opposite word meanings.[242] Whoever says *beautiful* says or thinks *ugly* as well; *reward* calls forth its opposite, *punishment*. It also follows in and of itself that the narrator, in accord with the overall style of the fairytale, something with which he is familiar, should push the poles far apart: not simply reward and punishment, but the highest reward and terrible punishment; not just high and low, but princess and poor boy, king's daughter and animal child. Sharpening in this case also means making concrete—concrete not in the sense of the opposite to abstract, but as the opposite to general. *High-ranking* would be general, while *king's daughter* by comparison is concrete; *isolated* or *strange* would be general, while *animal child* is one of the possible concrete realizations of the notion. In another sense, *animal child* and *king's daughter* are, however, still in accord with the specifically abstract fairytale style: Sharpening, the driving of things up to the highest degree possible, to the utmost in perfection, is, at the same time, abstraction—neglect of nuance, individualization, and perspective depth.

Contrasts are the counterbalance to repetition. The two principles of contrast and repetition stand at opposite poles and are thus complementary. Not only does a contrast appear each time in the pattern of threes with the final repetition, which, because of its different character, balances out the two previous instances, but the fairytale, looked at from the point of view of esthetics, always strives for balance; the fact that repetition and contrast appear together is only one especially striking, generally observable form of such equilibrium. Contrast is not just some random counterbalance to repetition; it is rather that counterbalance specifically appropriate to it, for contrast is itself a sort of repetition with variation. Whenever one speaks of the variation of a theme in a fugue, its inversion is implied: Variations on the same note pattern result not only from increasing the intervals between notes—vertically, through proportional raising of the notes, or horizontally, through retardation, through lengthening the notes—but also from inversion—horizontal, so that the last note appears first (retrogression), or vertical, through the transformation of a note sequence rising from the first note (and then perhaps falling again) into one where, instead of rising to a peak, there is a progressive fall (and then perhaps a rise again). Fairytale narrators, who, unlike rhapsodists, are of course not limited to a verse pattern, make relatively infrequent use of strictly verbatim repetitions; mostly they vary the repetition a little, not only in terms of word sequence but in the action sequences as well (the hero must fulfill three different tasks or three tasks of different difficulty). Repetition, variation, and contrast constitute a sequence of steps; contrast is nothing other than an extreme variation. The hero fails twice in the face of similar tasks because he twice ignores the advice of an otherworldly helper; the third time he succeeds. Or the older brothers run afoul of the same difficulty; the hero overcomes it. In the Grimms' fairytale "The Golden Bird" (KHM 57), which can serve as an example for a whole type (AT 550), first the eldest, then the king's second son is supposed to guard the tree with the golden apples, but both fall asleep at midnight; the youngest, on the other hand, stays awake, and, shooting at the thieving bird, causes it to lose one of its golden feathers. When, with the help of a talking fox, he finds the golden bird, he takes it out of the wooden cage against the advice of the fox and puts it into a golden one—and thus gets caught. The same thing happens with the golden horse, upon which the hero, once more against the advice of the fox, decides to place a golden saddle. And it is the same again with the beautiful princess, whom he, once more against the advice of the fox, allows to say goodbye to her parents. As a result of the three failures, the hero is presented with another task, this time of a different sort: Within eight days he has to move a mountain away. Now it is the magical fox instead of the hero that solves the problem; instead of the pattern difficulty/failure, finally the contrastive pattern difficulty/success comes in, though not immediately: During the first seven days the hero accomplishes nothing; thus he appears again to be on the verge of failing at the task. Only on the last night, in keeping with the principle of "just barely," is the mountain successfully removed by the magical fox while the hero is sleeping—a further contrast, which can also be observed in other fairytale types, one which has surely not come into being as a result of artistic intent but which, in interaction with all the other contrasts, is artistically effective and for just this reason has been gladly maintained in numerous stories: The helper is active at full speed while the hero is fully passive (sleeping). Things are then—for just a while, of course—in order; on the way back home, they become confused again, providing "the moment of final tension" before the ultimate resolution,[243] before what is for the hero and the other positively represented figures the happy ending (while, on the contrary, the "godless brothers" are executed).

A favorite form of contrast used in the fairytale is the pattern of *unsuccessful imitation (mißglückte Nachahmung)*. Well known is the already-mentioned sequence in the Frau Holle story: The "bad girl" tries to no avail to do what the better sister has done (AT 480, *The tale of the kind and unkind girls*), and the "imitation" misfires (see pp. 82–83). The first part of the fairytale could also stand on its own; it would then be necessary only to muster up a prince who takes the "golden maiden" home with him, something like the way Two-eyes is chosen by a "handsome knight" to be his wife (KHM 130, AT 511). But everyone notices that the narrative is improved when the "story with a happy ending" *(Glücksmärchen)* or success fairytale is supplemented by a complementary anti-fairytale, i.e., by the unsuccessful imitation which is tacked onto the first part. This second part is not just the foil to the preceding success fairytale; it has a significance of its own, which is evident from the fact that it concludes the narrative. It is not the image of the golden maiden which stands at the end, but that of the pitch black one. This ending is so meaningful that one can do without all the princes and weddings: The two sequences balance one another, building together an esthetically effective contrastive whole.

But in the Greek narrative about the sweet husband whom the princess fashions out of almonds, sugar, and semolina, who is then stolen from her and recovered only after a long and strenuous search (*Amor and Psyche* type, AT 425 B; see pp. 12–13), the unsuccessful imitation is just a bit of closing decoration. Her rival, who steals "Mr. Marzipan" and then loses him, also fashions a man for herself. But while the first woman stood the marzipan or sugar man in front of the wall of icons and prayed on her knees to God for forty days and forty nights in order to bring the semolina doll to life, her imitator begins "with kneeling, but instead of prayers she uttered curses, and after forty days the man had become moldy, and they threw him away."[244] The anti-fairytale, the unsuccessful imitation, seems here to be almost a repudiation of the beginning: If we take the two dough kneaders (the imitator does not do the kneading herself, but characteristically turns the work over to her maids to do) as two sides of the same person, in the sense of Jungian psychology, then the ending would show that one should not just create a mate according to one's own heart's desires—and that one cannot: The original creator also loses the husband. Only after she has selflessly worn through three pairs of iron shoes in order to find and win back her mate does he really become hers.

The dirty maiden—Pechmarie, Harzebabi, or whatever the contrastive figure is called in the individual versions—also imitates her sister only imperfectly. She intends to reach the same goal as her sister, but because she is lazy and impudent, she neither can nor will put herself to the same trouble. There are much closer imitations, as in the case of real (magical) or apparent rejuvenation or beautification. The bride who has been brought from afar (thus apparently from some otherworldly place) does not wish to marry the king until he has taken a bath in boiling mare's milk. The king first has the hero of the fairytale climb into the bath. The hero comes out of the bath not only unharmed—because his magical horse blows on the boiling milk and cools it off—but also made more handsome; but the king, whose own horse is unable to help him, completely dissolves in the boiling milk—and then the beautiful girl can marry the young fellow that, on the orders of the ruler, had fetched her home.[245] In place of the nice mare's milk motif, which is common mainly in the Balkans, other, simpler methods can also turn up, as, for example, in the Grimms' fairytale about Ferdinand the Faithful (KHM 126), where the beautiful girl, who is skilled at magic, offers to chop off heads and put them back on again in order to be rid of the king, whom she cannot bear. She properly puts back on the head of Ferdinand the Faithful, who as guinea pig has to allow himself to go through the procedure first, but when the king then offers his, she does indeed chop it off—but: "Se doet, as ob se'n nig darup kriegen künne, und as ob he nig fest sitten wulle. Da ward de König begrawen, se awerst frigget den Ferenand getrü" ("She pretends she can't get it on and that it won't sit properly. Then the king was buried; she, however, married Ferdinand the Faithful"). Whereas the milk bath is well integrated into the course of the plot—it is allegedly intended to rejuvenate or beautify an old or ugly king—the decapitation here is offered and carried out as entertainment, simply as a "clever trick." Other versions are less farcical; instead of a simple magic trick, the water of life comes into play, or, as in the case of the imitator, does not come into play. The water of life, however, is a conventional fairytale element; bathing in mare's milk is more original, more strongly expressive, more graphic, and is often linked in several ways to the other events which occur. It was, in addition, a bit of their actual world in fantastic transformation for the original listeners, who were presumably nomadic horse breeders for whom mare's milk was not for bathing, but was instead a staple in their diet.[246]*

The actions of the Sicilian "Daughter of the Sun" have a similarly close association with the actual milieu of the teller, and are of similar vividness and original/moderated fantasy: She laid "her beautiful white hands in the pan and kept them there for a while, and when she took them out again, two beautiful golden fish were lying there, but her hands were completely uninjured." The wife of the prince wishes to imitate her, but she burns herself so badly in the process that she dies as a result. The same thing is repeated three times, in three variations. When the daughter of the sun creeps into the oven in which a bright fire is burning, she comes out again after a while "having become still more beautiful," but the second wife of the prince dies in her oven. "Lattughina, why do you kill my wives?" "It's their own fault if they want to imitate something that they are unable to."[247] In Turkish and Bulgarian variants, a doll that has been brought to life or a "girl of chalk" issues orders to things: "Fire, light yourself!" "Pan, come here!" "Bread, knead yourself!" "Needle, thread yourself!" The things obey the girl of chalk, but not her mortal imitator. The chalk girl or the brought-to-life doll cuts off her own nose with scissors and sends it to fetch something for her; then she puts it back in place. The other intends to imitate her, but her severed nose does not obey her and does not allow itself to be put back on again.[248] This variant sounds like a farcical modification of the Medea story. According to the classical saga, Medea calls Aeson, whom Pelias has killed (or driven to commit suicide), back to life, and thereby induces Pelias to allow himself to be cut into small pieces—but the daughters of Pelias fail with the planned resuscitation and rejuvenation after Medea (the daughter of Aeëtes, thus granddaughter of Helios, the sun) refuses to provide them with her magical aid.[249] Sicily experienced Greek cultural influence, and a connection is well possible. But independent of the question of the source of the fairytale motif is the fact that the unsuccessful imitation which appears in the two stories is both esthetically and anthropologically mean-ingful—esthetically as a qualified variation and contrast, anthropologically as a reflection of the linked possibilities success/lack of success, the two possibilities associated with anything attempted, of winning and losing, of standing the test, of realization, and of failure: a potential source of ten-sion which belongs specifically to the existence of man.

The model of unsuccessful imitation also appears in other folk literature genres, e.g., in religious tales, myths, and farces concerned with a dual-istic Creation: God creates man; the devil, who then also molds a form out of a chunk of earth and blows his breath into it, succeeds only in bringing forth the monkey, and instead of the bee, only the wasp; or he is able to form the creatures but unable to bring them to life. The example bee/wasp shows, however, that the imitation can also be differently inter-preted, not as unsuccessful but as evil imitation: God creates the dog, the devil the wolf; God the moorhens and hazelhens, the devil hawks, owls, and crows; and God's creatures are devoured by those of the devil.[250] The meaning can thus so easily change within the same pattern.

Unsuccessful imitation also occurs in the local legend: The boy cowherd who has to fetch the milkstool forgotten in the alpine hut, and thus has to climb up alone in the solitude, falls into the clutches of alpine spirits and is given the gift of yodeling. His master, who later also climbs up, not because he has to, but intentionally, in order to obtain a similar gift, is

torn to pieces by the spirits. One is reminded of the Frau Holle story—
the same conviction or hope or illusion, not limited by genre boundaries,
finds expression in the most diverse narratives: Anyone innocent who is
forced to place himself in danger does not come to harm but even benefits
from it, insofar as he behaves properly; but anyone who does so simply for
his own benefit comes to a bad end.[251] In the fairytale, this theme is
especially familiar to us from the story of the child of fortune: The boy
sent forth, supposedly to his death, by someone with evil intentions
survives all dangers and is even richly rewarded; but his master, who
wished to do him in and who now wishes to grab similar riches for himself, does himself in in the process or is forced into eternal slavery as a
ferryman (AT 461, KHM 29, "The Devil with the Three Golden Hairs").

Farces and farce fairytales are less concerned with such just deserts.
Along with greed, stupidity is the main force at work in them, and the
imitation is happily provoked by a clever instigator. In the farce about the
peasant Einochs (Unibos), which is known from the medieval period and
which is attested in countless variations (Andersen's farce fairytale about
Little Claus and Big Claus goes back to a Scandinavian version), the crafty
hero brings his partners to the point where they, supposedly in imitation
of him, kill their oxen or cows and calves (in order to obtain lots of money
from the hides); then they even kill their mothers, mothers-in-law, or
wives, and finally throw themselves voluntarily into the sea or river to
fetch themselves a herd of lambs, just as the hero has supposedly done—
but they find nothing other than their deaths. They have been
manipulated; they imitate not a real action but an imaginary one (AT 1535,
KHM 61). The situation is similar with the three stupid giants who give
the little tailor a headstart in the race: He cuts open his shirt, into which
he had earlier stuffed noodles during an eating contest. The giants see the
noodles lying alongside the road and the knife beside them, and a woman
wood-gatherer, before whose eyes the tailor had done everything, tells
them: "Because the noodles weighed him down and interfered with his
running, he slit open his belly. And as he ran on, he shouted: 'Ah, that feels
good!'" It continues as one would expect: "The giants' full bellies were
very much in their way as they ran. Just as they had heard in the old
woman's description, they took the knife and slit open their bellies so that
their innards fell out. 'Just keep cutting,' the one encouraged the other,
'the noodles are about to come'"[252] (AT 1088, *eating contest;* cf. K 81.1 and
J 2400–2499, *foolish imitation* and J 2401 and 2413.4, *fatal imitation*). In
the Grimms' version of the *Unibos* story ("The Little Peasant") we have,
strangely enough, an exact parallel to the last-cited sentence from the
Austrian giant-killer story. When the peasants come to the water out of
which they intend to bring up the sheep, "just then in the blue sky were
some of those little fluffy clouds that are called little lambs, which were
reflected in the water; then the peasants shouted: 'We already see the

sheep below on the bottom.'" In the Austrian farce, the supposed imitation is provoked through clever long-distance manipulation *(Fernregie)*: The cunning tailor reckons first on the reaction of the woman wood-gatherer who has observed his actions and then on the reaction of the stupid giants to her story. In this way he can fool and manipulate them without directly lying to them; he proves himself to be a subtle virtuoso, subtler than Little Claus or Little Peter. In the Grimms' story about the little peasant, which also tells of a purely imaginary imitation, the sky even plays along; it supports the manipulation of the clever little peasant, and this farce fairytale concludes with the words: "Then the entire village had died off, and the little peasant, as the only heir, became a rich man." The Latin Unibos farce in rhyming verse (an eleventh-century manuscript) already shows, if not the sky, at least the sea as accomplice.

> Motus marini personant
> grunnire porcos estimant.
>
> They took it to be the grunting of swine
> When the sea let itself be heard.[253]*

Whether such a single feature has been preserved, even if transformed, into the twentieth century through literary influence and oral transmission is an open question. There is also the possibility of polygenesis, for the imitation of an untrue, imaginary, or simply trumped-up happening is more likely when an actual or apparently actual bit of circumstantial evidence supports the manipulator's assertion. Whatever the case, whether the feature, even if in an altered form, has been preserved as a result of wandering and transmission or whether it has developed over and over again out of similar constellations, it has, in any event, been either preserved or developed only because it is impressive, because it is artistically efficacious.

The motif index of Stith Thompson brings together a number of the absurd attempts at imitation which can be found in farces (J 2400–2499). The unsuccessful imitation of a magical or faked rejuvenation, something which also occurs in the fairytale, figures among them. Of the others, only two will be mentioned here. In the first, a fool tears out his aching eye because he had earlier had an aching tooth extracted, and this had caused the toothache to cease (J 2412; *Hodscha Nasreddin*, I, p. 244, no. 136). The second involves an inadequate but surprisingly successful imitation: When his angry wife remains spitefully silent, the worthy husband, a sexton in the area around Lucern, remembers that the pastor, when his sermon began to flag, remedied the affliction each time with cherry spirits (brandy). The sexton intends to imitate this procedure, but since he has neither cherry spirits nor money to buy them, he cuts a thick branch from a cherry tree and uses it on his wife, which produces precisely the same effect as the cherry spirits with the pastor (J 2412.5; Pauli, no. 715). The imagination, disposed to dirty tricks, thus plays with the motif: The imitation is a failure from the point of view of form, but a success from the point of view of effect. In an example of unsuccessful imitation from the fable, an ass observes how the dog fawns on its master, jumping on him and being petted and rewarded as a result; but when the ass then jumps up on his master and lays his hooves on his shoulders, he is beaten (J 2413.1; Aesop/Halm, 331; *Gesta Romanorum*, no. 78).[254]

Even though the pattern of unsuccessful imitation also appears in other genres, in the fairytale it is particularly many-faceted, occurring in especially many variations and metamorphoses. It is the special peculiarity of the fairytale that it can pick up elements which occur in the real world or have actually been developed in other narrative genres and fit them in and adapt them to its overall structure. Moreover, unsuccessful imitation is brought in prominently in several well-known fairytales, as, for example, in the story about the two wanderers and related narrative types, where the hero or heroine overhears secrets told by witches, speaking birds, or similar otherworldly beings and makes effective use of them. The antihero betakes himself to the same place, and also eavesdrops—but the enraged secret tellers have now realized that their earlier conversation was overheard. They search around, find the unlucky second eavesdropper, and tear him to pieces. This pattern is in accord with both the Frau Holle pattern and the local legend about the origin of yodeling or cow-calling (see p. 99). Anyone who accidentally becomes an eavesdropper is reprieved. One who has been blinded by his evil wandering companions hears that he can use the freshly fallen dew to make his eyes see again, and he learns in addition how the ailing princess is to be cured and how the royal city can be supplied with water. "The grace of God luckily made it happen to me," says the "soldier who does what is right" in the Grimms' story "The Crows" (1815, no. 21, later replaced by "The Two Wanderers," KHM 107, AT 613). His two knavish companions then likewise set themselves under the gallows, but the crows peck out their eyes "and continued then to peck until they were dead." Here one has imitation in two senses: The crows, though unknowingly, imitate the actions of the two cruel soldiers, who (out of greed) had poked out the eyes of their comrade, and the two villains attempt to imitate their successful comrade and are done in in the process. Simple, if also unintentional, imitation (the crows) and intentional, though unsuccessful, imitation (the soldiers) are played off against each other—the motif is cleverly woven into the context of this story told by an unknown hussar, who was killed on the following day.[255]

Just as important and still better known is the story of Ali Baba and the forty thieves from the Arabian Nights, which is reflected in the Simeli

Mountain story (KHM 142, AT 676).[256]* The poor grain merchant of the Grimms' fairytale imitates the twelve robbers correctly and successfully; he fetches gold for himself out of the magic mountain. His hardhearted and greedy rich brother, however, who wishes to do what his brother did and more, remains trapped in the mountain, for he has forgotten the magic formula "Semsi Mountain, Semsi Mountain, open up!" He is caught and beheaded by the robbers, who take him to be the one who has several times plundered the treasure (the Arabian Nights version is similar, though further embellished). Here again we see the pattern showing through, which takes on ever varying forms: The poor man who accidentally comes into contact with another dimension profits from it; the greedy man, rich in worldly goods, who forces the encounter is punished. And here, just as in the Frau Holle story, stories of the *two wanderers (three crows)* type, and many other narratives going as far as farce fairytales of the *Unibos* sort (pp. 100–101), the motif "unsuccessful imitation" appears as the vehicle for the theme "Man lays out his own destiny"—his own actions lead him onto disaster. The same is found, though in harmless form, in the religious farces about the three wishes which bring good fortune to the good and the simple, but only trouble to the bad and calculating (AT 750 A), and about the earthly wanderings of Jesus and Peter, where Peter, who intends to imitate the Lord (or also some mortal who imitates Jesus or Peter), sits down in the nettles (AT 791, 785).

Taking into consideration the full spectrum of fairytales (fairytales of magic, novella fairytales, religious fairytales, farce fairytales, and animal fairytales), one finds, in addition to the many forms of unsuccessful imitation, something like *mißlingende Vorahmung* "unsuccessful premitation," if one wishes to use this unusual but appropriately descriptive neologism of Martin Luserke's to designate the phenomenon. In Shakespeare's plays, for which Luserke coined the term,[257] just as in musical works, there are any number of fore-echoes, prefigurations, suggestions, and premitations of a main theme or course of action, but in the fairytale one finds mainly the contrastive sequence which precedes the successful actions of the hero: The stepsister's imitation is inadequate, e.g., in the Frau Holle type; the two elder brothers rehearse the actions of the youngest in a likewise inadequate way. Similarly, the first part of the *two brothers* fairytale, depicting the progress of the first brother to leave home, presents a finally unsuccessful anticipation of the progress of the second brother, who later leaves home. (Looked at the other way round, the actions of the second brother can also be designated a correcting imitation of those of the first.) The attempt of the witch or ogre to demonstrate to the captive children how to creep into the oven or lay one's head on the block also appears to be a variety of unsuccessful anticipation—unsuccessful to the degree that not only do the evil beings fail to achieve their goal of instructing their victims and making them ready for the slaughter, but, quite the opposite, they die by falling into their own trap. Contrary to their expectations, the model sequence intended to be preliminary to the main plot becomes the actual main plot.

If repetition, variation, and contrast are the ever-present basic elements of the fairytale, then imitation and anticipation, as special forms of repetition and variation, are likewise of significance and importance, just as is the case with their still more special forms, unsuccessful imitation and premitation, representing as they do particularly impressive combinations of repetition/variation and contrast. The latter are a sort of miniature anti-fairytale within the framework of a fairytale narrative; they can, however, as is shown in the Frau Holle type *(kind and unkind girls)*, be established as an equally extensive and almost equally weighted countersequence, which is moreover placed in final position—almost equally weighted, for it is overshadowed both by the degree of elaboration and by the remaining effect of the recollection of the preceding positive sequence: It is not Pechmarie but Goldmarie who is the central figure; for once it is not emphasis on the last element that is paramount but emphasis on the first *(Toppgewicht)*. When Alan Dundes cautiously connects the noticeable frequency of unsuccessful imitation (sequence *success-failure*) in the published Lithuanian folk narratives with the political fate and the wishful thinking of the Lithuanians, thus seeking to explain the phenomenon psychologically and historically,[258] it remains a hypothesis. But since unsuccessful imitation is found over the full range of folk literature and in the fairytale, along with unsuccessful premitation, attracts particular attention, there is no question that it has esthetic significance—as a contrastive plot and a synthesis of the basic principles of repetition and contrast, which shape the overall character of the fairytale. Both repetition and contrast are elementary technical devices; both arise largely in and of themselves, and both can have an esthetic effect, as is true to an even greater degree of the combination forms unsuccessful imitation and premitation. Within the repertory of the narrator and listener, which varies with the individual, the negative character of the latter constitutes a sort of quantity contrast to the main plots, which generally develop positively. Within the individual story, the anti-fairytale segment, the unsuccessful premitation or imitation, usually takes up only a fraction of the narrative time. Premitation and imitation are foils of the main plot, but at the same time they call to mind or offer as experience the ever-present possibility of failure. Nonetheless, in the case of premitation one must not speak of an ascending plot, nor in the case of a concluding imitation of a descending plot (in the first case of optimism, in the second of pessimism): In both cases the main plot, which is carried by the hero, is ascending; the unsuccessful premitation or imitation is carried by the antihero, or by a hero whose failing is only temporary.

The art historian speaks of *quantity contrast* when a dash of color in a painting is especially prominent precisely because, in the midst of a large surface, it appears only in small quantity, for example as a small red triangle.[259]* Something similar, if not exactly the same, can be observed in the fairytale. Of twelve rooms, only one, the last, is important, and frequently only one particular place inside it, a feature, perhaps a picture (see p. 90). The other eleven rooms are of little interest. The three golden hairs of the devil offer an intensive small touch of contrast in this otherwise dark figure, as do the grandmother of the devil, the well-wishing housekeeper in the robbers' house, the helpful daughter of the demonic task giver in the other world, and Snow White among the dwarfs, who, in many variants, are man-eaters, or in whose place appear robbers and murderers. The tiny loss, the tiny flaw, is also a quantity contrast: The sister of the seven ravens or twelve swans (she is already a quantity contrast) must cut off a finger in order to open the glass mountain, or she is unable to quite finish knitting the shirts necessary for breaking the spell. Snow White has a tiny moral flaw: curiosity and disobedience, and the same flaw inheres in many a fairytale hero. Of the thirteen fairies, twelve bring blessings; the thirteenth brings the curse, and that is precisely what is decisive—just like the fateful twelfth room or the slipper which Cinderella loses. When one looks at the fairytale world as a whole, it is the negative amid the positive that stands out, the dark color amid all the magnificence and sparkle: witches, dragons, and plotters; the presence of evil, of failure, of the unsuccessful imitation, for example, which is really not *just* a foil, but, as the instantiation of a contrastive possibility, something in its own right. Failure, destruction (and other things that follow upon failure), the evil, the ugly and also the unpromising, and even blunted motifs are inseparable from the fairytale. The fact that these elements appear in lesser quantity than their contrasts does not raise them above the contrasts, but, since they persistently reappear, it does give them a peculiarly effective consistency.

The magical, wondrous phenomena which have given the fairytale of magic its name are also potent spots of color in the midst of a plot containing many realistic elements.[260] The fairytale of magic and wonders, as has often been established, is in no way a wild story of wonder stuffed full of supernatural happenings. Most of its props are of the worldly sort, most of its happenings possible in reality. Thus the individual places in the narrative where things occur that are foreign to reality stand out more prominently precisely because of the power of quantity contrast. The mixture of *much reality and starkly nonreal accents* is a mark of the fairytale as a genre and also as a work of art. Just as the magical elements generally stand out as a powerful quantity contrast within the parts of the narrative which conform to reality, the same can be observed with small scale contrasts of the reverse sort: During the search for his sister, who has been carried off, a boy must go over a "glass bridge . . . which ascends so steeply to the castle and is so slippery that no one can mount it." But the sun, offering advice, tells him to buy a black hen ("Do you have any money on you?") and to cook and eat it, but to save its bones and lay them piece by piece on the bridge. While in analogous cases, for example in variants of the *seven ravens* (KHM 25), it is accepted without question that one can simply lay the little chicken bones on the glass mountain or stick them into it, here, with exact, realistic imagination, it is remembered that some sort of glue is necessary: "Take . . . each time a little bone from the hen and dip it in syrup and lay it on the bridge; in this way you'll be able to step on it and thus go up." That syrup is not exactly an ideal sort of glue need not have been a secret to the narrator; perhaps like us he really had a sense of humor—but perhaps he meant it completely seriously: Within the magical world of the fairytale, syrup can be that magical means by which one can make something stick to glass bridges or mountains. In such a case, then, within the framework of this small bit of realism, a still smaller bit of magic would finally come into play. Moreover, syrup fits better than some sort of craftsman's glue into the fairytale, which concerns itself quite happily with things to eat, but shows little interest in the techniques of the craftsman. In the same story from which our syrup example is taken,[261] the wild and cruel wind, from whom his elderly mother initially hides the boy seeking his sister so that her son does not "tear him to pieces like a head of cabbage," first of all invites the boy to sit down and eat: "You must be hungry; sit down here and eat." Then, in the magic castle, the hero does not immediately locate his sister, but enters a room in which "a meal has been laid out" (a table laid in an empty or apparently empty castle or some other sort of dwelling is a motif that occurs in countless fairytale types—see pp. 119ff.); "he immediately sat down and ate." Another small touch of realism, a quantity contrast in the context of the magical otherworld, is the question asked by the beautiful and friendly Mrs. Sun (she "gave him something to eat"): "Do you have any money on you?" The boy has to "buy" the magical black hen in a completely realistic way, and to "cook and eat" it in just as realistic a way—that a magical element also originally stood behind this ingesting of the magical bird does not really come out in the fairytale.

An additional realistic touch that springs up in the middle of a marvelous happening occurs in the story of the three brothers who take turns watching the tree with the golden apples (or a grainfield): Each of the two older brothers falls asleep at the crucial moment, at midnight, for example; with the third brother, one is often told only that he did not let sleep "get the better of him" (see KHM 57).[262] Other narrators, however, ponder how he manages to stay awake, and in tune with the basic tendency of the fairytale style, with which we are already familiar, they bring in visible, external means instead of the (internal) force of will: The third son sets himself amid the thorns so that he does not fall asleep, or he places a hedgehog pelt under his chin so that when he begins to nod the quills wake him up,[263] or he slashes his little finger and binds it up with a bandage soaked in salt, which does not allow him even to reach the point of falling asleep.[264] The same result can be achieved by reading a book, etc.[265] Another third brother climbs the apple tree, wraps his hand around the one remaining golden apple, and is then awakened when the wondrous bird, intending to steal the apple, pecks him on the hand.[266] Still another takes a scythe with him and works with it in the garden[267] instead of lying down under the apple tree, while a very sly one does the opposite, lying down and immediately going to sleep so that later, in the second half of the night, he is wide awake.[268] Thus there is a wide range of possibilities for the imagination of the talented narrator. The sort of imagination at work here is not wild and uncontrolled but realistically exact. We might offer two additional examples: It often happens that a fugitive girl leaves behind in the dwelling of the witch a doll, some other object, or even her spittle to answer for her, and in this way the witch is fooled. In a fairytale from Sardinia, the heroine spits on the threshold of the stable, and when the witch then asks, "Dolores, what are you doing?" the spittle answers repeatedly and faithfully, "I am watering the horses." But the morning sun finally dries up the spittle, and no one answers the witch anymore.[269] In a Sardinian *Blue Beard* fairytale, the ears of the monster are stopped up with magical tree bark, so that he lies there as if dead and thus harmless—"but as luck would have it, there was a woodworm in the bark with which one of the ears was plugged, and it slowly ate at the wood of the bark until it finally fell in bits out of the ear." The demon wakes up and hurries after the fugitive girl.[270]

Such magical and otherworldly motifs within the framework of a fairytale world ranging broadly in conformity with everyday reality, and small bits of realism within otherworldly and magical motifs, have an esthetic effect above and beyond the meaning of the plot; they exemplify the many quantity contrasts which permeate the fairytale.

## ARTISTIC ECONOMY AND ARTISTIC PRODIGALITY

Artistic or literary economy is normally seen as the purposeful use of elements once they have been introduced. In the stricter sense, artistic economy is the use of the same motif, the same feature, for more than one purpose in the context of a narration or of an artistic work in general.

In a broader sense, and contrary to the usual assumption, even the use of repetition can be called artistic economy. It makes use several times of what has already been introduced, and just as is appropriate to the nature of the fairytale, in a sequence, which is a juxtaposition transposed onto the dimension of time. Repetition is prodigality and economy at the same time. It is prodigality because, when seen completely rationally, it is superfluous to show two or three times what is already clear the first time. But the fairytale—or, more precisely, the narrator, listener, or reader— enjoys playing with the superfluous, being no different from composers and music lovers. It is predictable that the young hero who manages to cope with the three-headed dragon will also get the better of the six- and the twelve-headed ones, especially for someone accustomed to listening to fairytales, who has often heard things similar and is acquainted with the ground rules of the art. It is not just the intensification that makes such a sequence interesting; the pure pleasure offered by the play of repetition and variation is also at work. The anthropological significance of intensification is obvious—it can be read directly and easily from such simple examples, from such a primitive technique: The listener recognizes in the progress from the victory over the first dragon to the conquering of the more dangerous second one and the most dangerous third one his own possibility of rising to progressively more difficult tasks, of gradually reaching ever-higher spheres (in the fairytale: ever more beautiful princesses). And the anthropological significance of repetition, of playfully varied repetition, is as little hidden as that of intensification. It reflects daily experience, the continual renewing return of a similar daily run of events (which is normally not found to be bothersome). But like intensification, only in a different way, it is much more a mirror of and— given the achievements of both narrator and listener—also an exercise of the human ability to master or create similar yet different situations. Perseverance and stamina are at work in repetition; and variation, which almost always goes along with repetition in one form or another, illustrates flexibility, the ability to come to grips with changing situations and tasks. Behind both is also the delight in the superfluous, which is fostered by the certain knowledge that man need not limit himself to what is absolutely necessary for life, but that he dares, and apparently ought, to go much farther in the experimental quest for what is important.

It is not only prodigality which is of existential significance, varied repetition in all its forms (including intensification and contrast), but also the ability to apply limitations, to economize. Like nature, the fairytale displays both excess and parsimony. We have already demonstrated that repetition is, in the broader sense, economical. But we also encounter artistic economy in the narrower sense in the fairytale. One constantly observes the use of a motif or feature on various levels. In the *dragon-slayer* fairytale (AT 300), the helpful beasts go into action during the battle, and later they also bring about the reunion of the hero with the bride by fetching their master food from the bridal table. In the related *two brothers* fairytale (AT 303), they bring about the resuscitation of the brother of the dragon-slayer, whom the latter has too hastily slain. In the same fairytale type, the sword not only sees action in the battle but later serves as a *signum castitatis*. A Greek dragon-slayer uses his knife to cut the tongues out of the seven heads of the dragon, and the same knife, instead of the sword, is then used again as a chastity symbol, in that even the first fisherman's son lays "his knife between himself and the bride" and turns his back to her, a contamination that occurs in other places as well.[271]* A Norwegian version has the usurper, who, as in many other instances, is a charcoal burner, thrust into the last charcoal kiln, where the bright flames close over him.[272] Thus the narrator does not make use of one of the well-known fairytale punishments; rather, the charcoal burner, who has maintained that he killed the troll and thus has the right to the hand of the princess, is drastically enough pushed back into his own environment. In the same Norwegian *two brothers* fairytale, the enchantress who turns the dragon-slayer and his animals to stone immediately after the wedding is not just some witch who has nothing to do with the dead dragon, as is the case in most of the other variants, but the mother of the slain giant troll. The charcoal burner's dying in a charcoal kiln has a still more striking parallel in the *Hansel and Gretel* type, where the witch is burned up in her own oven—more striking because she is hoist with her own petard, preparing through her stupidity her own demise—a narrative topos which is artistically impressive and anthropologically significant and which thus turns up in various forms in the most various places. We could cite numerous examples,[273] but we will confine ourselves to mentioning just two farce fairytales. In the Grimms' fairytale "The Peasant's Wise Daughter" (KHM 94, AT 875), a fishnet allows the heroine to fulfill simultaneously two of the absurd conditions she has been set, namely, to come to the king neither dressed nor naked and neither mounted nor in a vehicle: "Then she went forth and stripped herself naked—then she was undressed—and took a large fishnet, placed herself inside it, and wrapped it completely around her—then she was not naked." "And she hired herself a donkey for the money and tied the fishnet onto the tail of the donkey so that it had to drag her, and that was neither mounted nor in a vehicle." Later a fishnet is again utilized: When the king, in an absurd judgment, awards a foal to the peasant in front of whose oxcart it had lain down as if one of his oxen had given birth to it, the wise daughter, who in the meantime has become queen, then helps the rightful owner by advising him to cast a "large fishnet" in the middle of the street, and before the king's eyes, and act as if he were fishing: "It is about as likely that two oxen can beget a foal as it is that I can go fishing in the middle of this dry square." It is not the same fishnet as before, it is not a matter of the practical economy of the peasant's wise daughter, and perhaps it is not even the economy of the narrator, only coincidence, that here a problem can again be solved by using a fishnet—nevertheless, coincidental compression or even that resulting from lack of imagination also has (in effect, at least) the appearance of economy of technique; it

belongs to the attractiveness of the Grimms' story, not, of course, that a
particular fishnet should turn up again in the second part of the fairytale
but rather that the notion "fishnet" should, that use is made once more of
this already familiar feature. And what is attractive will also be happily
retold. In this way such real or apparent narrative economy can lead to
the perpetuation of a particular version. In a farce fairytale of the *golden
goose* type (KHM 64, AT 571) taken down in 1961, the golden duck not
only enables Dumb Hans to make the princess laugh, it also solves an
additional problem for him: He only has to put it in the water, and it
brings up the ring that had been cast into the deep lake.[274] In the same
fairytale, a chimney sweep is among those who find it reprehensible that a
naked girl is running after the hero. "Der mecht i den Hintern schworz-
mochen, wenn die sich niet schamt und laft nackert hinter dem Burschen
mit der Anten noch" ("I would like to make her behind black, because she
is not ashamed and runs naked after the boy with the duck"). Thus here,
just as in the case of the Norwegian charcoal burner, use is made of the
possibilities suggested by the occupation of a plot figure.

The inclination to prodigality makes its appearance in the fairytale
particularly in the use of the series, which, however, expands to comical
excess only in the farce fairytale (see pp. 79–81, "Lucky Hans," among
others); in the sterner fairytale of magic, and also in novella and religious
fairytales, it is held in check by the domination of patterns of twos and
especially of patterns of threes, at least in the western world. Measure
and moderation determine the construction of the European fairytale;
they also are a sort of economy, an economical use of the powers of
narrator and listener. There is economy in the vigorous, goal-oriented
formal structuring. The strong tendency of the fairytale to extremes, toward
pushing everything to the highest degree (of beauty, ugliness, evil,
strength, power, riches, etc.), can be viewed as a special sort of prodigality. But in contrast there is the clear, surveyable construction of the story,
which is cut to human proportions. Within the context of the narrative
*style*, the prodigal use of superlatives is in contrast to the consistent
avoidance of any sort of *stilus ornatus*—few decorative adjectives; parsimony, even abstemiousness, in the description of things, figures, and
settings; and the infrequent use of metaphor. Comparison, on the other
hand, is relatively frequent. We have already run into it as a means of
characterizing beauty (pp. 21–22), but it is also happily made use of in
other contexts, at times artlessly conventional: "old as the hills,"[275] "happy
as a fish in water,"[276] "He sleeps like the dead,"[277] "She took off like the
wind";[278] at times humorous or in some other way original: "a man as old as
bread and mush,"[279] "The little goat was as quiet as a fish in a boiling soup
kettle,"[280] "as quick as one thinks and doesn't think,"[281] "happy as the
pope,"[282] "He waited for the day like a dead man for the funeral meats,"[283]

"so poor that not even the flies stayed in the house,"[284] "as many kids as there are holes in a sieve,"[285] "What he said he only shook out as if it were bits of grain from a sack,"[286] "The emperor lives here like a post in a fence, coming into contact with no one,"[287] "I went by stiffly as if on a wire,"[288] "He watched him like the guards watched me when I was a robber, and I was allowed to turn neither to the left nor to the right, for otherwise I would have been shot," "At twelve o'clock the bells toll, as they also tolled at our place when the Americans came with the planes."[289] There is a counterpart from West Prussia (around 1940): "So they lived the way Switzerland lives, very quiet and without fear."[290] Not only politics but also modern technology forces its way into the comparison: "It was always bright like electric light."[291] Close by, however, is again something native: "He said nothing and gave no answer, either. It was as if one were speaking to the ground."[292] The immediately surrounding public can also be brought in: "He pretends that he is sleeping, and snores a little—like this old woman here."[293] But while one continually runs into comparisons, one has to look for metaphors—at least living, striking ones—with a magnifying glass. The shoemaker "would have liked to have grabbed his work by the throat and strangled it, if it had been possible to grab it."[294] Metaphors condense, create a complex whole; the comparison separates, sets up two poles. It is simpler than the metaphor, more artless; it corresponds to the tendency in the fairytale toward juxtaposition (parataxis, sequencing of episodes, good beside bad, beautiful beside ugly, etc.), while the metaphor creates a merger. In Basile one finds numerous instances of the piling up of comparisons; the fairytale narrator almost always contents himself with single comparisons. The comparison, like so much in the fairytale, serves the purposes of vividness and clarity, and its relatively artless character fits in with the overall style. Here as well the simplicity of technique leads to an artistic effect. Excessive delight in comparison, poetical metaphors, so-called poetic decoration in general, is alien to the fairytale narrator. Partially a result of lack of aptitude, it is still beneficial for the narrative. It is in this framework stylistically appropriate. Verbal exuberance, excess verbal power, and delight in prodigality are found primarily in particular introductory formulas—a sign that a different style is also possible for the folk narrator and also gives him pleasure (see in this regard pp. 24–25, 52–53 and note 112). Within the actual fairytale of magic, however, measure is maintained.

The maintenance or even insertion of blind or blunted (i.e., nonfunctional or incompletely utilized) motifs and features (see pp. 64–67) is another kind of prodigality; it conflicts with artistic economy. These blunted elements are often, though not always, a result of failure—they are maintained, however, for deeper reasons. A superfluous gift also serves to show the (male or female) hero specifically as one to whom gifts

are given; a figure having no function in the plot, if he or she is built into a
pattern of threes, also serves the purpose of giving the fairytale its appropriate contours.

Finally, *contamination* is also to be associated with the pole of prodigality. "Contamination is the essence of all folk literature," says Lutz
Röhrich,[295] and he refers here to the mixing of genre types, of local legend
and fairytale, for example. Within the fairytale genre, which, along with
the local legend genre, has been able to maintain itself in a relatively pure
form for centuries despite all the mixed forms, the contamination of two
or more different fairytale types is a favorite way of extending a narrative.
Many a commentator has observed that poorly structured conglomerate
fairytales can develop as a result, that the clear construction and style of
the fairytale can be interfered with and destroyed through the jamming in
of some motif familiar to the narrator. But there are also contaminations
that are successful; there is an art to contamination. Contamination, combination, is one of the possibilities at the disposal of a narrator who is
familiar with many fairytales and many motifs; he can use it or misuse it.
Successful contamination may be illustrated in detail by means of a single
example.

A short segment from the "Erzählstückl vom Grünhösler" [Little story
of Greenpants], which was taken down verbatim and so published by
Waltraud Werner,[296] shows immediately that three narrative types have
been combined in the story: *The dragon-slayer* (AT 300), *Strong John* (AT
650 A, *Jean le Fort, Jean de l'Ours, Bärensohn*), and *The youth who
wanted to learn what fear is* (AT 326, *Jeans-Sans-Peur*):

> No auf einmal kommt e Gebraus, hau, is der Drache komme. Der Drache
> hot si g'freit: "Ha, so krieg i glei zwei Speis auf einmal, nit nur die
> Königsdochder allein!" No hot der ober g'sproche: "Na wart!" Uffg'standn,
> die Eisenstange in die Hande genomme: "Dir wer' i den Appetit vertreibn!"
> Dann ham se ang'fange zum Kämpfe. Ja, aber der mit seiner Eisenstange der
> hot nur druffg'haut. Einmol is der Drache g'stürzt, a, kaputt! Na, jetzt hot
> die Königsdochder g'sogt ze ihm: "Jetzt woll mer heim un woll mer Hochzeit
> feiern!"—"Nein," hot er g'sogt, "un i heirat nicht, bis i mi net firchten dua!"

> Now suddenly there comes a great roar. The dragon came. The dragon was
> delighted: "Aha, now I'm going to get two meals at one stroke, not just the
> king's daughter alone!" Now the other said: "Just wait a second!" Stood up,
> and took the iron bar in his hand: "I'm going to spoil your appetite!" Then
> they began to do battle. Yeh, and the guy with the iron bar just swung away.
> Suddenly the dragon collapsed, done for, finished! And the king's daughter
> said to him: "Now, let's go home and get married!" "No," said he, "and I'm
> not going to get married until I know what fear means!"

The super-strong iron bar derives from the motif arsenal of *Strong
John;* the hero of our story, as is appropriate for this narrative type, has it

made especially for himself—he had found the first one to be too weak: "Wumm, wor sie ganz bogen" ("Wham, and it was all bent!"). Now he is properly armed. In the style of one who sets out to learn what fear means, once in the haunted castle he uses the bar to render harmless the unearthly man who comes piece by piece down the chimney and who intends to do him in; and finally it also comes in handy for him in the fight with the dragon. He needs no helpful animals; thanks to his iron bar, he is able to finish off the dragon by himself. Such self-confident independence is in accordance with the fairytale, especially the farce fairytale, just as is the dependence on a helper, which is especially conspicuous in the pure fairytale of magic.

The mixture with the farce fairytale about learning what fear means makes possible the humorous tone of the dragon-slayer: "I'll spoil your appetite!" And, more importantly, the refusal to get married immediately is now properly motivated; namely, the hero has sworn not to marry until he learns what fear means. In many other versions of the dragon-slayer story, the motivation is markedly weaker: "Ik will örs de Welt 'n beten besehn" ("I just want to see the world a little"). Or: "'Ne,' seggt he, 'eers will ik noch twee Jahr wandern'" ("'No', says he, 'first I still want to wander for two years'").[297] Or: "Es paßt mir besser, noch ein Jahr mit meinen Hunden herumzuziehen" ("I prefer to wander around for a year with my dogs").[298] Or simply: "Denn reist he wieder, un de Königsdochder kann ja weller to Hus föhrn" ("Then he travels on, and the king's daughter can just go back home").[299] These sorts of weak motivation are not in themselves less appropriate to the fairytale—*nonmotivations* help to create the isolating style. But the general human demand for motivation always competes with the style of the genre, and it is the battle between the two that gives life to the fairytale. Just as in the case of real versus nonreal, the fairytale has motivated and unmotivated side by side. Such is the situation in the "Little Story of Greenpants": We find out neither why the "man from heaven" haunts the castle and has to murder the visitors there nor why the "dragon . . . has to have a maiden to eat every day." Thanks to their knowledge of motifs, our narrator and his line of predecessors have been able to insert justifications wherever it seemed appropriate to them, justifications which are in accord with the fairytale specifically because they call to mind other fairytales, because they are the products of contamination. Thus in our story, which is a contamination of three fairytales, the mother sends her son, who intends to marry only after he has learned what fear means, into the churchyard—but not just like that; instead, she pretends to be ill (a feature which is familiar from the stories about the treacherous mother or sister, AT 590, 315) and insists that only water drawn at night from the spring in the graveyard can cure her. And the narrator—or one of his predecessors—is successful with still other logical connections because of his gift for combination: The future dragon-slayer has a reason not to return home but instead to wander out into the world, because, as a result of his churchyard adventure, he considers himself to be his brother's murderer. And that, in fact, also motivates him to save the maiden who is to be the prey of the dragon: The man in the haunted castle has instructed him that a murderer can find forgiveness in heaven if he saves someone from death. When our hero at last finds out that his brother is alive, he even regrets that he went to so much trouble to save the king's daughter. Thus this playing with contamination, which was born of superfluity, leads to a whole series of effects; the elements gained are used economically. It need not be just a single narrator who brings all of this about; he can take over a great deal from his predecessors. The contamination of the dragon-slayer with the boy who sets out to learn what fear means occurs frequently, and the affirmation of not wanting to marry is also traditional. But each new narrator can, on the basis of his stock of materials, come up with a new feature, a new motif which allows itself to be inserted with a happy result. The Hungarian-German Markus Schäffer, who subsequently moved to West Germany, took over the "Fürchtenix Grinhösler" [Fearless Greenpants] story from his father, a small farmer and minstrel from the Vértes Mountains. His fairytale has weaknesses in addition to its strengths. The masterfully applied art of contamination, however, is clearly one of its positive features. The story also demonstrates the possibility of the successful contamination of fairytale, local legend, and farce: The most impressive episodes of the fairytale about learning the meaning of fear, which forms the basis of the story's general structure, derive from the sphere of the ghost story, and they are handled in the manner of the farce, influencing the tone of the entire narrative.

# 4

## Interaction of Motifs and Themes

### MOTIFS AND FEATURES

Motifs and their individual features *(Züge)* lend life, vigor, and color to the fairytale; the themes which they carry or which shine through them give it meaning and significance.

We have already encountered a sizable number of motifs and features, both those which are widely spread, for example, the beautiful maiden who finds refuge with dwarfs or robbers and keeps house for them, the tree with the golden apples that must be guarded because it is being plundered (by a magical bird), or the sister who disenchants the brothers that have been enchanted because of her, and those which are less well known: the talking spittle on the threshold of the stable door, which then, however, dries out and is silent; the "magician" who every day gives the corpses of fifty hanged men fifty lashes each and evidently must do so, who knows why; the fastening of tiny chicken bones to a steep bridge of glass with the aid of syrup; the gift of being able to comb flowers out of one's hair, to generate flowers "wherever one walks," to produce roses whenever one speaks, etc. These few arbitrarily selected examples are reminders of what we have already observed, but they also provoke new conclusions: One designates as "fairytale motifs" chiefly those plot kernels that carry some sign of the marvelous, of the nonreal, which are directly characteristic of the fairytale of magic, or those like Snow White's stay and activities among the dwarfs, which correspond to patterns which occur in many and diverse fairytales. Motifs of this sort possess a certain radiance and can be built into the most diverse narratives. They are capable of being transformed; they take on various shadings and shapes and offer points at which humor can be introduced. The boundaries between the notions "motif" and "feature" are flexible—the bone fixed to the glass bridge, with syrup of all things, certainly would not have the status of a motif, but only of a motif segment, just that of a feature.

Talking spittle and talking housewares reflect age-old notions and modes of experience. It may be that a part of the power of such motifs derives from their origins. One may suppose that for cultures at early stages of development talking animals and objects were just about as "natural" as they still are today for the child in a particular phase of development.[300] Special powers were attributed to spittle and other bodily fluids, especially the blood: As *pars pro toto* they can stand in place of the whole person, the part standing for the whole.[301] Archaic notions of this sort may live on in us subliminally and give significance to many fairytale motifs or features—but in the fairytale, which takes over these elements and plays with them, they do not begin to have the significance they do in popular superstition or the local legend. The connection to reality has largely evaporated; anyone not otherwise knowledgeable about such beliefs and modes of experience would scarcely be able to infer them on the basis of the fairytale alone. Household goods that can talk are an amusing feature for the ingenuous listener or reader of fairytales today—it is no wonder that further comical ideas tend to turn up in such places, as in the *Rapunzel* story where the witch furiously throws to the floor the saucepan which has revealed the flight of the heroine, but only because it had not received any macaroni from her.[302] In the fairytale, villains especially are a favorite target for fun, just like the "stupid devil" in the local legend, who is duped time and again—like Ernst Bloch, one may see here a perhaps dangerous underestimation of the power of evil. The "magic flight" from the witch, which forms the second part of many versions of the *Rapunzel* type, often includes the favorite motif of the deaf person who misunderstands. The witch, in pursuit of the fleeing pair, asks a monk standing in front of the church if the fugitives have run past. "Mass begins in three minutes." A second attempt to obtain information about the fugitives evokes the response, "Mass will last about half an hour." The witch asks a third time "whether a lad and a maiden have passed by." "The lay brother stuck his finger through a hole in his habit and could thus truthfully say: 'No one has come through here.'"[303] The monk is thus not really hard of hearing, he is just pretending to be, and after the third question he allows himself a final joke of another sort, although in countless other instances the final answer also depends on actual or pretended deafness.[304] In French versions of the *Rapunzel* type, the witch keeps a parrot. On three separate days when she comes home, it tells her that the prince is in the tower. In order to determine whether it is telling the truth, she asks it about the weather that day, and each time it provides the wrong answer, as Persinette (the title figure) has seen to it that it should: One day she let water trickle down the window by the parrot, the next she sprinkled flour, and on the third, she sprinkled peas, so that the parrot was forced to believe that it had rained, snowed, and hailed respectively. The witch considers it to be a liar, and Persinette and her lover escape detection for the moment.[305] On the other hand, a Maltese version of *Rapunzel*, different from that cited above, has fun with Little Fennel, as the heroine is called, and her "handsome young man": Little Fennel, who has taken over something of the art of magic from the witch, quickly transforms her lover into a footstool when the old woman returns unexpectedly, whereupon the "Grandmother" decides to use specifically this footstool and no other. "The old woman put . . . her feet on the footstool and laughed, probably because she . . . knew who was hidden under the form of the footstool." Another time, Little Fennel turns the secret visitor into a needle, whereupon the old woman wishes to use specifically this needle as a toothpick instead of all the needles which Little Fennel offers her, for only this one "gets into all the crevices and best cleans my old teeth."[306]

Not only demoniacal beings but unwelcome suitors, as well, can be humorously resisted and gotten the better of. In various narrations about the forgotten or abandoned bride, the bride is courted by socially acceptable young men; she pretends to wish to accede to them, but before any one can lie down beside her, she asks him to close the shutters or the door, to put out a couple of lights, to wash his feet, etc. "Noble sir, the window is still open; wouldn't you like to close it before you come and lie down?" But whenever he closes one of the window casements, the other flies open and gives him a hefty blow on the chest; this cruel joke persists through the night, so that the poor man cannot get away from the window. This example is from a Sicilian version.[307] Basile (tale 9 of day 3) embellishes this theme: The gallant

> found her lying on a beautiful bed like a Venus upon a flowering meadow. In a gentle voice she asked him to please not lie down beside her until he had closed the door. That seemed to the cavalier to be a small thing to do for such a lovely jewel, and he went to close the door. But as often as he shut it, it flew open again. He pushed it closed, it opened again, . . . the whole night through.

The next morning he has to allow himself to be ridiculed by the beautiful maiden because he cannot even close a door, yet he intended to open up Love's shrine of joy. The Heinzian street sweeper, Tobias Kern from Ödenburg (Hungarian Sopron, in the neighborhood of Neusiedler Lake) is earthier than Basile. His Rosl makes a fool of the importunate Commis, asking him to take a (well-filled) chamber pot to the "privy"—where she "freezes him in place" so that he has to stand there all night with the chamber pot in his hand; only in the morning, when the master visits the privy, does she release him, and he lets the chamber pot fall.[308] The various tellers play with the motif with no less lack of invention than do the beautiful maidens with their suitors. The lovers are enchanted in two senses of the term, for the beautiful maiden is expert not only at love magic but also at completely different magical arts. The chore which she assigns seems easy, an ordinary, everyday task—but it proves to be undoable, a proper counterpart to the tasks which are only apparently undoable but which can then be done with the help of the task setter's daughter, who is skilled at magic: to cultivate a field with a glass hoe, to plant grapevines and the next morning deliver up ripe grapes and wine— tasks not only well known to everyone familiar with fairytales, but which often actually occur in the first part of the story about the duped suitor, as is the case in our Heinzian fairytale and in several Hungarian versions.[309] Thus, in the same fairytale the action of the first part, with its three undoable tasks which, however, turn out to be doable and which are not at all humorously narrated, is mirrored in the second part by apparently ordinary but actually undoable and undone tasks—an effective compositional ploy which is seldom directly aimed at and rather appears to be accidental: a sort of contrast *imitatio,* an unsuccessful imitation of what happens earlier.

In other cases, the humor is expressed not by means of an actual, fully developed motif but only in a small motif segment, in a simple narrative feature, or even in a remark of the narrator's standing outside the narrative. When the king of Greece wishes to hear yet a third time that there is no more beautiful maiden than his daughter, the hero, "the king's son from Ireland," loses patience. "Leave me alone; I saw a woman whose little toe was more beautiful than her face and brow."[310] When a dragonslayer cuts the tongues out of a twelve- or even a fifteen-headed dragon so that later he can prove that he was the true slayer, he must, of course, number both the heads and the tongues in order to put the latter back properly.[311] Here it is the exact and realistic sort of imagination which produces the comic effect—the small bit of realism within the context of a fantastic motif which we encountered earlier (pp. 105–107) and which can be encountered time and again. In one of the numskull fairytales told to the Brothers Grimm by the Hassenpflugs in Kassel, the small, crooked, hunchbacked hero conjures up a child for the princess (see p. 136). When the princess and the numskull are later set adrift at sea in a barrel, he reveals his magical gift to her. "'If that's true, conjure up something here for us to eat.' 'That I can also do,' said Dumb Hans, and he wished for a bowl full of potatoes. The princess would have liked something better, but since she was so hungry, she helped him eat the potatoes."[312] He thus uses dry humor to punish her for her haughtiness, and that satisfies him, whereas King Thrushbeard causes a great to-do. The affair with the chamber pot in the Heinzian version of the "duped suitors" motif can suffice as an example of earthy humor. Humor outside the actual narrative occurs not only in introductory and concluding formulas, but naturally also in inserted asides. In the Irish story about the daughter of the king of Greece, when the hero's magical female helper puts "healing balm on his wounds" after the battle, the narrator makes no aside. But a Rhaeto-romance narrator feels it necessary to comment on the sort of tin of salve one would have to get so that Faithful John, who has been turned into a pillar of salt, could be smeared *(strichar)* with salve between twelve and one every night for six nights: "It will have been a kilo tin" (*"Sara üna trocla d'ün kil"*).[313]

One may also mention just a few of the serious scenes which leave an indelible impression on the memory. There is the empty house or castle which the hero or heroine enters, having traveled from afar—not a sound is to be heard, not a living soul to be seen, yet there is a table set with food and drink. Volker Roloff speaks of an "esthetic of silence."[314] In the fairytale there are many examples of it. The silence of the figures of the *Our Lady's child* sort is presented with impressive intensity (as contrast: the blabbing of the little girl caught by the witch in the Grimms' narrative "Frau Trude," KHM 43), and this is true as well of the slandered sister of the six or the twelve swans, all the girls who suffer in silence, and the heroically faithful John, just as it is of many other forms of being silent or mute.[315] The silence in an apparently uninhabited house is a peculiarly forceful realization of the poetic of silence.

In a Rumanian fairytale of the *Faithful John* type (AT 516, 516 B),[316] the hero comes into a city.

> At the edge of the city, he entered the first house to ask for something to wear, so that the people wouldn't see him in his nakedness, bareheaded and with bare feet, wearing only a nightshirt. In this particular house, he calls out for somebody, but no one is there: no cat, no dog, no cow, no hen—nothing. He didn't dare take anything. He went into the second house, but there it's the same as in the first, and in the third, as well. "Well, but there must be someone there." Then he got up the courage to go into a house and put something on. . . .

Even here, where it is just a matter of completely ordinary houses, the emptiness and silence come across as eerie. The contrast between the fact that a house is meant to be lived in and the unexplained absence of anyone living there, of any house pet, constitutes an absurdity. Only later does the hero learn, and along with him the listener, as well, that the residents—no mention is made of the house pets (a blunted element)—have all converged on the market-place in the center of the city, and why they have done so ("There were as many people there as hairs on one's head": the complementary contrast to the empty houses at the edge of town). In the same story, however, the other form of this motif, which was sketched previously (pp. 105–106), has already appeared, as well.

> He travels through the wilderness over a long and difficult path. God knows how long he was underway. . . . Already on the verge of starvation, the poor

fellow spies a palace standing in a large field: "Oh God! What's going to be in this palace? . . . good people . . . or dragons? Whoever it may be, I'm going in in order to finally get my fill to eat, then I can die in peace!" When he goes inside, he finds all the gates, doors, and windows open, no dog, no cat, not a soul, no one is there. He calls out three, four times. Then he went in. When he is inside, he sees a table all set; the food has already been brought on, but not a soul, no cat, no dog, no one is there! He sat down and ate. "Hey, isn't anybody here? Either I'll work for my meal or I'll pay!?" No one. He continued to go forward and not back. . . .

Nothing has happened in the magical palace, although he was evidently expected there; the table appears to be set for him, and especially for him. The unexplainable emptiness and silence, yet a carefully prepared meal on the set table, apparently intended for the caller, is an absurdity which also has its own fascination, so that it is inserted by individual tellers at some appropriate place or simply left where it is, even when it has no function in the plot or when this function has been lost in the course of transmission. Usually, of course, after a time something comes to pass in the empty castle, as is the case in the Grimms' fairytales "The Gnome" and "The King of the Golden Mountain" (KHM 91, 92) or in the animal bridegroom and animal bride fairytale, from "La Chatte blanche" and "La Belle et la bête" (seventeenth/eighteenth century) right up to "The White Cat" (AT 402) told in Morissen in Rhaeto-romance in 1956 and taken down on tape by Leza Uffer. Here, just as in the two French stories mentioned, the person entering the castle is guided and waited upon by hands—by hands, not by bare arms as in the Cocteau film (see pp. 70–71); in Mme d'Aulnoy's "La Chatte blanche" there are twelve ("une douzaine de mains en l'air, qui tenaient chacune un flambeau"), in Duona Maria Luisa Caduff-Camenisch's "La gat'alva" only four (a reduction completely in tune with the folk narrative); the bodies they belong to are not visible.[317] In a Rhaeto-romance variant of *Faithful John*, there are "two black arms."[318] In the Heinzian fairytale about the twelve brothers, a stable ready for exactly twelve horses is found at the magic castle; at the table set up in the dining hall, however, there are twenty-four chairs; and at midnight twelve black ladies come to dine with the twelve hussar brothers.[319] Here and in a related Serbo-Croatian fairytale, a pledge of silence is laid upon the brothers, who are to disenchant the black ladies— in the Balkan story, one of seven years: Eleven of the brothers succeed in holding to it until fifteen minutes before the allotted time is to expire (the tiny flaw), then they begin to speak and are turned to stone; only the youngest holds out (the small exception within the group!) and then disenchants his brothers along with the black maidens.[320] The silence motif thus turns up in doubled form, first the silence in the empty castle, then the silence of those called upon to bring about the disenchantment; a presumably unintentional yet efficacious echo effect, which, like other mirroring phenomena in the fairytale, has a part in the esthetic realization of the story.

The empty castle may originally have belonged to the otherworld—the residents are frequently the dead who are in need of release; and St. Brandan and his companions encounter it on a journey to the otherworld as a residence of the devil.[321*] But in the fairytale it is just an enchanted castle; the black ladies are rarely explicitly identified as atoning dead. The motif is, in a way, sufficient in itself; only in stories leaning toward the local legend is its significance more or less made clear.[322] In the normal fairytale it remains entirely or practically unexplained, a blunted or partially blunted motif, as is appropriate for a genre which is precisely for this reason so mysterious. Within this context, the esthetic of silence speaks more directly to us than does the evocation of the otherworldly.

Impressive action pictures: The hero turns himself into an ant and creeps through the keyhole to get into the room of his sweetheart (West Prussia),[323] or through a small hole in the glass mountain, where there are twelve brothers who have been turned to stone and twelve enchanted maidens to be rescued, as in the Serbo-Croatian fairytale just mentioned. But where does he get the power to turn himself into a little ant? A lion, an eagle, and an ant, among which he had equitably divided up a dead horse, have in gratitude given him a hair, a feather, and an egg respectively, by means of which he can turn himself into the respective giver— this transformation into a tiny ant, by means of an ant egg in the Serbo-Croatian, with the help of the little back leg of an ant in the West Prussian, is especially amusing; it impresses with its fairytale-like extremism, underscored by emphasis on the final element. Motif or part of motif? One can call the transformation into the form of a thankful animal a motif, that into the form of a special animal, a specified or individualized motif; the tripling (Serbo-Croatian) or quadrupling (West Prussian), likewise traditional, can also be considered a *single* internally organized motif—to find and use a particular name for all special possibilities (perhaps larger motif or motif pattern, group motif, lesser motif, or special motif) would be sensible within a systematic categorization, but in our cursory presentation it would be only confusing; we will consider all of these categories and subcategories to be "motifs." But since the ant's gift sometimes consists of a little back leg, sometimes of an egg, both operating as *pars pro toto*, these constitute two different "features," neither independent nor even relatively independent motifs. The possibility of the hero's changing himself into the helpful animal shows the close relationship that he has to the animal—no fairytale heroine or hero changes into a helpful fairy or a helpful old woman or a helpful little gray man; the figures mentioned also do not constantly accompany the fairytale hero the way the animal helpers do the dragon-slayer. Helper figures are simply not arbitrarily substitutable for one another.

A forgotten or displaced bride can end up in the house of an old woman as a rose, a chestnut, or a twig from an apple tree and, in the old woman's absence, take care of the household:

> The old woman . . . laid the chestnut on the window sill and paid no more attention to it. But every morning, when the woman went to mass, a girl climbed out of the chestnut, built a fire on the hearth, cleaned the house, and prepared something to eat, so that when the woman came home, she found the table already set. The girl, however, always slipped back into the chestnut in time, and the woman was amazed . . . and did not understand what was actually going on.[324]

In the same fairytale from Abruzzi, a very well-known motif—the male or female evil-doer must pass judgment on himself or herself—takes on an unusual form, though one encountered here and there. The usurper, who had changed the real bride into a dove, pronounces her own punishment in the full realization that she is to undergo it: "The prince . . . said . . . to the ugly Moorish woman, 'I do not want to condemn you, . . . you are to pronounce the judgment yourself.' When the ugly Moorish woman saw that there was no way out, she said, 'Have a shift made for me out of pitch, and burn me in the middle of the square.'" It is again only a particular variation on a motif, only a feature, when here the punishment is not the same as occurs elsewhere, e.g., being pulled apart by four horses or being rolled in a barrel which has been studded with iron barbs, just as the conscious self-condemnation instead of the nonconscious is only a variation, a special feature, and not an independent motif.

That impressively formed motifs imprint themselves especially strongly on the memory and can lead a life of their own in one's recollection, largely independent of their function in the framework of a particular plot structure, is an indication of the intrinsic significance of the motif as such. In reaction to atomistic, decompositional methods of approach, particular emphasis has been placed in this century upon the interdependence of part and whole: "The whole takes precedence over the part," "The whole is more and something other than the sum of its parts," the function of the fairytale motifs is more important than the motifs themselves. It is the *revenge of the motifs* that they achieve independence in the memories of many fairytale listeners and readers, that they live on independent of the whole in which they were embedded. We play with the motifs, but they also play with us. Every artist is in a certain sense a perpetrator of violence. Adorno speaks of the "dying of the parts in the whole" ("Tod der Momente im Ganzen") in the integration of the individual element into the work of art. His "esthetic theory" does not include the key word *fairytale*. But there is scarcely any more convincing evidence than the life of the fairytale for the conflict he describes between the pressure in works of art to integrate every individual element, to "destroy everything within their reach" that has independent life, and the disintegrating pressure "of nature," which nonetheless exists covertly in the work of art, a centrifugal counterforce immanent in art.[325] The more significant narrators have selected from the large number of fairytale motifs and motif variants known to them those which seemed appropriate, and integrated them into their narratives. In other words, they liberated them from any firm context into which their predecessor had incorporated them, and they then reincorporated them. Fairytale motifs float—they are free to this degree and yet are still always ready to enter into a new synthesis, not unlike the fairytale hero, who within the narrative does not remain firmly fixed in stable situations or tied to stable settings, but, isolated yet capable of interaction, comes into contact with other figures and worlds. And if the whole tends to fade in the memory of the fairytale listener or, today, of the fairytale reader, while individual motifs are still fully remembered, this disintegration is not just a loss but a gain, as well. The motif is set free, but in the imagination or emotional life of the person who has taken it up, it is nevertheless ready and able to enter into new combinations. Whether the hero who changes himself into an ant is looking for a beautiful maiden or out to free his brothers from an enchantment is forgotten, a matter of indifference, but the image remains of one who is capable of turning himself into an ant or making himself tiny, who has the power to enter into the otherworld, despite the locked door or closing wall. For the clarification of such processes, a distant but rather illuminating analogy comes to mind: During the time of the popularity of *opera seria* and *opera buffa*, "preexistent musical numbers" were inserted into a new opera; they had then to be incorporated and motivated with new recitatives. Similarly, Johann Sebastian Bach turned the nonreligious shepherd's cantata which he had composed for a duke's birthday (27 February 1725) into an oratorio for Easter of the same year, a "little religious opera," "with a minimum of effort—the new recitatives are shorter than those replaced."[326] Significant motifs can be compared with arias and other "preexistent musical numbers"; looked at in this way, the plotline would correspond to the libretto, which provides the framework for the connective recitatives. The fairytale plot is certainly much more than a libretto. And the motifs themselves are also more than relatively unimportant building blocks which can be easily replaced by others and which merit the interest of the scholar only from the point of view of their role in the complete work.[327] The interest of the twentieth century in the whole, something which as such is important and essential, needs to be supplemented by an interest in the individual part, the separable entity, which is not just a building block but, at the same time, itself a whole in miniature.

The purpose of works of art is not fulfilled when they become rigid and are passively taken in by observers or listeners. However legitimate it may be for the whole to be harmonious—something which does not have to be an idle substitute for an inharmonious reality, but which can be a helpful model in the sense of Schiller's notion of "esthetic education" (*ästhetische Erziehung*)—it is just as legitimate that the lively spores bound up in it should liberate themselves and enter on a new life in another narrative, or in the memory hoard of the listener, where the individual motif can maintain its power of illumination, even increase it, when the whole has long since been forgotten. The individual motif has then been integrated into the imaginative ken, into the intellectual and spiritual life of the person involved. All life oscillates between freedom and constraint, and death takes part in the game.

Parts of motifs also have a life of their own, e.g., figures and objects. Where Stith Thompson includes as "motifs" not only *incidents* but also witches, fairies, the stepmother, the preferentially treated youngest, magical objects, and unusual beliefs and customs,[328] for us a motif is a plot kernel. In our view, figures—witches, dragons, and princes, just like fishermen or maids—are just content elements, irreducible building blocks similar to atoms, simple carriers of the action. But these carriers of the action have their own special significance. It is not only motifs, incidents in a narrative sequence, that can free themselves from one plot and enter into a new one or even remain fixed as isolated entities in the memory, but figures and objects as well: a beautiful princess, an unhappy goose-girl, a wishing table, or a dragon. That the props of the fairytale, even of the farce fairytale, can liberate themselves from the narrative and become available as something belonging to the general culture can be directly demonstrated in the instance of the wishing table. In 1971, when the former president of the Federal Republic of Germany, Gustav Heinemann, appealed over television for donations to relieve hunger in the world, he made reference to "our wishing-table existence" ("Tischleindeckdichdasein"). He could not have used a more telling turn of phrase to bring out the point he wished to make. Whatever particular plot function the wishing table might have in various fairytale narratives is here of no importance. The prop has become independent; it has achieved importance in its own right and has entered into a significant, nonesthetic meaning context.

Motifs and parts of motifs are not just important in their respective (or even only in their hypothetically inferred original) contexts. What Stifter has his Hagestolz say about the individual person, "Jeder ist um sein selbst willen da" ("Everyone exists for his own sake"), is also true (*mutatis mutandis)* of motifs and content elements. If from one point of view they appear to be relatively easily replaceable elements in a plot sequence, from another point of view one might regard the plotline simply as a useful framework for presenting fascinating motifs and figures. A hoard of individual motifs and images would then be just waiting to be used. Neither point of view alone can do justice to the total phenomenon. The narrative elements as parts of an individual narrative are in syntagmatic relationship with one another, but at the same time, as parts of a standing motif and image hoard, they show broader paradigmatic relationships. They are thus doubly significant: They belong to various imaginative contexts, but have, in addition, their own profile, their own attractiveness. They are interchangeable as role fillers, as plot elements, but as representations of various possibilities of existence they have their own privileges of occurrence and are not mutually replaceable, neither anthropologically or esthetically. Falling back on only a few content elements and motifs, the reduction of the various fairytale types to a single type (see p. 144) would also be esthetic impoverishment. *Aisthesis,* sensory perception: The senses delighting in perception wish to be nourished. Even in the esthetic, nourishment cannot be monotonous; it must be various.

## THEMES, CONSTELLATIONS, AND ATTITUDES

There are themes which crop up time and again in the fairytale: readiness to help, die, or fight; the wish to do harm; the human world is not in order; dangers threaten from within the family, from within one's circle of friends, even from within oneself; there is nothing impossible, no problem is unsolvable; essential help comes from otherworldly (or unknown) powers; the small and the weak can triumph over the large and the strong; justice prevails; appearances are deceptive. Other themes are encountered less frequently: poverty perverts (the parents of Hansel and Gretel—more often the theme is "wealth corrupts": the rich vs. the poor brother or neighbor, the rich vs. the poor sister, etc.); justice should be tempered with mercy; destiny is inevitable.

The selection of themes from the total number of possibilities and the frequency with which they appear contribute to the constitution of the fairytale as genre—and to the determination of the world and the portrait of man which appear in it. They are at the same time of esthetic significance: Their numerous modifications offer variety, and the predominance, the ubiquity, of certain larger themes helps to give both individual narratives and the entire genre a certain measure of uniformity.

Among all the themes mentioned, it is the conflict between *appearance and reality* which stands in first place in the fairytale. Setting aside the introductory formulas that play with appearance and reality, one can see the theme represented first purely in terms of surface features: The underestimated youngest, the neglected stepdaughter, the scald-head (who in reality has golden hair), the kitchen maid, and similar "dark figures" are among the favorite and most common fairytale heroes and heroines. The term *unpromising hero* is found in the Anglo-Saxon context. In addition to these "unpromising heroes" and heroines, who all have more to them than meets the eye, there are *unpromising helpers* (unprepossessing old men and women, little gray men, and animals, including those apparently powerless like the ant mentioned in the last section: "Canst thou, poor Devil, give me whatsoever?"—see pp. 49) and *unpromising things*. There are also *apparently* unaccomplishable tasks, not only those which are insoluble given realistic expectations and which with the help of magic are accomplished in the twinkling of an eye (see pp. 146–147, playing with time: That which takes a long time to ripen, from the planting to the harvest, is made to do so at breakneck speed), but also the commissions that are intended to bring about the death of the hero ("Uriah letter") and, contrary to expectation, bring him good fortune (the irony associated with the child of fortune); the dangerous demons and animals and revolting things which, in contradiction to all appearances, become helpers, etc. The situation is similar yet different with helper figures of the Faithful John sort: They appear suddenly to be unfaithful or treacherous, but precisely that which appears to be cruel faithlessness is the essence of true loyalty. Female sufferers on the Patient Griselda model, like the sister of the six swans, who carries out the difficult task which leads to the disenchantment of her brothers (KHM 49, AT 451: *brothers transformed into animals*), and even self-confident, more egocentric figures like those of the obstinate *Our Lady's child* variety (for example, the heroine of our model fairytale, pp. 2–5), bravely acquiesce in appearing to have killed and even devoured their own children, and despite all the injustice which they, their children, and finally also their husbands suffer as a result, they remain adamant and accept the false appearance right to the last—the explanation here comes from some other source, while the Faithful John figure finally reveals everything himself. But there are also false appearances associated with figures represented negatively: Slanderers like Ferdinand the False (KHM 126, AT 531) pretend to the king that the hero has boasted about being able to achieve things that appear impossible; treacherous mothers or sisters who live in sin with monsters pretend to be sick in order to get rid of their son or brother, who then innocently sets off to bring the supposed remedy back from some deadly realm (AT 315: *The faithless sister,* 590: *The treacherous mother;* cf. 318:*The faithless wife*).[329] Appearances are also deceptive in the case of beautiful princesses who dance their shoes to pieces every night: They are, in contradiction to their beautiful exterior, bound up with monsters or demonic otherworldly beings—and such is the case with all the other beauties whose bodies are full of snakes, worms, or vermin (see pp. 6–7). But their being associated with evil is in a deeper sense also just appearance: Those who are bound to underworld demons can be released through the killing of the demon, those infested with worms can be cured by an operation; both can thus be returned to their true nature—the evil spell was just that, an evil spell. With Snow White's beautiful stepmother (or mother) and corresponding figures in other fairytales, the beauty is, in another sense, only appearance. The queen is not, as she thinks, the most beautiful in the land, she is only the second most beautiful; and thus, to her at least, her entire beauty has become worthless, pointless, only the appearance of beauty.[330]*

The latter are peripheral instances of the theme of appearance versus reality. But precisely because the theme is central to the fairytale, it has the most subtle ramifications. The portrayal of the conflict between appearance and reality is characteristic of the fairytale as genre. In no other genre of folk literature does it appear so frequently and in so many and various forms. This fact has not only esthetic but also anthropological significance: Since the central significance of the relationship between appearance and reality has been recognized or felt both in philosophy from the ancient Greeks up through Kant and into our own times and in individual literature *(Individualdichtung)* from Sophocles' *Oedipus Rex* up through manneristic and baroque literature and again into our own times, it is certainly noteworthy that this theme in particular is all-pervasive in the simple fairytale. Man, by his very nature, is confronted with the problem of appearance versus reality. "Allgemach beschlich es mich wie Grauen/Schein und Wesen so verwandt zu schauen" ("Gradually it filled me with dread to observe how similar are appearance and reality"), wrote Conrad Ferdinand Meyer on noticing how perfectly the flight of a gull was mirrored in the sea. "Und du selber, bist du echt beflügelt?/ Oder nur gemalt und abgespiegelt?" ("And you, are you really provided with wings? Or only painted and reflected?"). Meyer is a poet who sees death and life as neighboring, as confusable with one another. The ancient statue dug up in the garden which the girl takes to be a god of love is in reality the god of death. The theme of appearance/reality is even more universally present in the fairytale than in Meyer—but in the fairytale everything is set at a distance. Nonpathetically, without causing "dread," it presents an aspect of the basic condition *(Grundbefindlichkeit)* of man. *At a distance* also suggests the esthetic significance of the play of appearance versus reality. The unequivocalness which is peculiar to the fairytale—"black and white contrasts" *(Schwarzweißmalerei)*, extreme completeness of form, the partial equation of beautiful with good, on the one hand, and ugly with bad, on the other—is toned down by the multifarious playing off of appearance against reality, which, of course, is one of the basic principles of art and the esthetic in general. This playing off can enter in as early as the opening formula. Even the simple "Once upon a time" is ambiguous; behind the expression shimmers an opposite meaning: Oriental fairytales often begin with the formula "It was or not,"[331] while Hungarian ones enjoy beginning with "Where was it, where wasn't it"[332] plus a surrealistic place designation ("In back of the beyond"—in the middle of a white flea, see p. 52), by means of which, in the words of Gyula Ortutay, "the plot moves into the nonreal." A Rumanian fairytale may begin "Once upon a time as has never been, for if it hadn't happened, one wouldn't tell about it," or, even more direct, "When the poplar bore pears and the willow violets, when the bears fought each other using their tails. . . ."[333] The Gypsy opening, "It was, and it wasn't. If it hadn't been, one wouldn't tell about it"—"the standard phrase at the beginning of Taikon's fairytales"—is "perhaps . . . of Rumanian origin" (Tillhagen).[334] During the narration, Taikon time and again inserts "As it was and as it wasn't,"[335] and at the end in his stories, just as in those of many other tellers, formulas occur which declare it to have all been a "fairytale," that is, only appearance, a lie. Rumanian: "I jumped into the saddle . . . , I climbed onto a chicken and rode through the dung; I sat down on a scythe and told lies."[336] Mihai Pop emphasizes, certainly with justification, that the opening formulas are intended to lead one from the real into a nonreal world, the closing formulas from the nonreal back into the real.[337] The tendency of the fairytale of magic to establish such a frame is in accord with its inclination to clarity of form, to the classical, in the stylistic sense. But these formulas are, in addition, the overture and finale to a piece in which the theme of appearance versus reality rings throughout.

Other important themes—important in and of themselves and frequent in the fairytale—are closely related to the theme of appearance versus reality. Such is the case with the theme of the *victory of the weak over the strong* and that of the *reversal (Umschlag ins Gegenteil)*. The little man conquers the dragon or the giant, and the youngest (thus the weakest) and dumbest (he is generally only seemingly stupid, but he can also actually be stupid, especially in the farce fairytale) shows himself to be superior to his brothers, just as is the case with the mistreated youngest daughter or stepdaughter with respect to her better-treated siblings, and with unpromising things with respect to shiny ones. The apparently ordinary, small, weak, or ugly triumphs over the apparently—or even actually— big, strong, powerful, or beautiful. And here the possibility of reversal is already apparent: The advantaged change places with the disadvantaged. In animal tales, the smaller animal defeats the larger, thus the hedgehog defeats the rabbit, the crab the fox.[338] In many fairytales the poor boy becomes prince consort or king. The disgust or anxiety of the bride or husband of an animal mate turns into love. The helper turns into an opponent, hence the devil who aids the poor man to gain wealth but then takes away his child, or Rumpelstiltskin, who helps the heroine in time of need but then also wishes to have her child, or even her, for himself.[339] On the other hand, the opponent or apparent opponent can become a helper or a beloved mate: directly, as with the animal bridegroom or the robbers who rewrite the Uriah letter, or indirectly, as with every antagonist who intends to harm the hero or heroine but ends up helping in the attempt. Situations can also be subject to reversal: The birthday celebration of Sleeping Beauty unexpectedly leads to harm instead of well-being; people turned to stone are revivified in a single stroke; the child of fortune who is supposedly sent to his death by the king or some rich man (the "Uriah letter") ends up instead married to the daughter of the king or rich man—and this rich man, who again tries to arrange the death of the hero, is himself pushed into the lime pit as a result of his order's being carried out; he has laid the groundwork for his own demise (AT 930). There is irony here, as in many of the other reversals mentioned.

*Irony* flashes in the opening and closing formulas of the fairytale and in several—partially traditional, partially improvised—incidental remarks of the narrator or individual fairytale figures. But far more important is the irony at work in *what happens* in the fairytale. One can speak of irony anyplace where what happens is the opposite of what those affected have strived for or expected. One speaks of tragic irony, where things are really worse than one believes: Goethe's Iphigenia, who, in exile among "barbarians," believes the members of her family to be honorably and happily united back in her "homeland"—yet it is there that her father has been done in through the machinations of her mother, and her mother, in turn, has been murdered by her own son, Iphigenia's brother, and she, Iphigenia, is the innocent cause of this horrible sequence of events. Such tragic irony can, however, be contrasted with another, more positive sort of irony, and often at the same moment and in the same meaning context: Iphigenia herself has experienced a much better fate than her family, and better than she imagines; she has not only been spared, she has also remained guiltless, and moreover she has been a source of blessings to her barbarian people, in a manner and to a degree that would not have been possible for her in her "homeland." Word irony, *rhetorical irony,* is mostly mocking, disillusioning, and negative; and sequential irony, *the irony of event,* is known to us mainly in the form of tragic irony, something thus also negative. Therefore, I prefer to call the rarer positive variety of irony *contrary irony (Konträrironie).* It occurs infrequently in literature, just as it does in life—but it is the predominant variety in the fairytale, as one might expect, given the cheery character of the genre.[340] Even in the fairytale, of course, it is clear that good, or what is intended to be good, can ironically lead to evil: The celebration after the birth of Sleeping Beauty, which is intended to bestow blessings on the child, leads to her enchantment; a father's intention of fulfilling the strange wish of his youngest daughter causes harm. But the fairytale often brings forth the opposite configuration. Evil leads to good (just as in both of the examples just mentioned everything turns out well after all). That has already become apparent in our presentation up to this point.[341] The irony of fate predestines that the messenger carrying a letter intended to bring about his death should not only be spared but advance in the world: He marries the daughter of the one who has commissioned the intended crime, and it is just as if the latter had arranged for it to happen. On the way, the boy quite superfluously also falls into the hands of robbers. But even here the letter that is intended to do away with him saves him: The robbers open it, it arouses their orneriness, and instead of killing the messenger who has been sentenced to death, as they would have done under normal circumstances, they rewrite the letter intended to bring about harm as a letter leading to benefits. The actual Uriah letter, which was written by King David and has lent its name to all subsequent examples (II Samuel 11.15), is not rewritten by anyone, and the death sentence is carried out. Hamlet, who is sent to England by his criminal uncle with a letter intended to bring about his death, rewrites it himself, not as a beneficial letter but as a letter leading to harm for others (*Hamlet*, V. ii. 17–53). In the fairytale, however, the irony of fate, true contrary irony, rules: The letter commissioning the murder works counterproductively; the robbers succumb to a sort of contrary suggestion; while the tired hero is sleeping peacefully in spite of the warning of the old housekeeper ("when they come home, then they'll kill you," KHM 29, AT 461), fate is working for him. Things turn out otherwise than as planned; the evil letter writer himself brings about exactly what he seeks to avoid—negative irony is directed against him. In the second part of the fairytale, he dashes headlong to his own destruction, sometimes as a result of unsuccessful imitation of his successful son-in-law, sometimes as a result of a new attempt to commission the murder, which then backfires on him (death in the lime pit). The situation of the boy sleeping unconcerned in the house of murderers is reminiscent of another with which we are already familiar: the fairytale hero who is assigned unaccomplishable tasks in the otherworld by an evil demon; for him, as well, they are accomplished while he is sleeping, ironically by the demon's own daughter. In the fairytale not only the same figures and situations turn up time and time again, but also the same models, though in many and various modifications. That a demon should kill his own children instead of the strangers he intends to kill (AT 317, Motif K 1611) is also irony. The negative irony in the fairytale is mainly directed against evil-doers: They meet their deaths in their own ovens, through their own tools, or through their own methods, or, as in Perrault's "Petit Poucet," they kill their own daughters or wives. Snow White, of course, thus a sympathetically drawn figure, also harms herself, bringing about her own death or apparent death—but it is just this "death" which then brings her the prince; and here contrary irony again comes into play: The clumsiness (stumbling) of the servants or, in other variants, their anger about the fact that they have to serve a dead maiden—one angrily strikes her[342]—causes the bit of apple which Snow

White has choked on to come back up, and the girl wakes from her death sleep. It is also a sort of irony when in certain variants of Cinderella the son of the house sets out to seek the beautiful girl, with no idea that he can—and finally will—find her at the place where he started, at home. Above all, however, one finds irony interwoven with the problem of appearance vs. reality: It is irony, even positive irony, that, contrary to all expectations and arrangements, the despised and the maltreated time and again end up emerging as winners, and that they finally outshine those in whose shadows they have stood. The dominance of such contrary irony in the fairytale is not accidental, and its effects are not random; it is an indispensable contributing factor to the view of the world and portrait of man which we encounter in the fairytale. It is certainly also no accident that we see the phenomenon of contrary irony clearly represented in individual literature in a work of the optimistic Enlightenment, Goethe's *Iphigenia*.[343]

Just as the phenomenon of *self-injury* and *self-destruction* belongs to the area of irony, so also does the phenomenon of *manipulation*. We have run into manipulations, clever uses of scene management by individual figures, a number of times already. Gretel maneuvers the man-eating witch into her own oven; she is able to only because—and herein lies the irony—the witch shows Gretel, who pretends to be stupid, how one can creep into the oven or get shoved inside. Manipulation is not the same as ordering something done; as with irony, it is a matter of indirectness. The behind-the-scenes manipulation turns others into puppets, but in such a way that—and again it is precisely herein that the irony lies—they think they are acting independently and of their own free will. In the Ölenberg manuscript, the witch says to Gretel, "Sit on the board, I'll shove you into the oven. See if the bread is about done." The girl, however, says to her: "I don't understand. You sit on it first and I'll shove you in." The old woman sits on it, and the little sister pushes her in, closes the door and the witch gets burned up.

The same mixture of action on the part of the manipulator and cooperation from the victim occurs in the Danish Ederland fairytale (AT 328). The man-eating troll wishes to kill Ederland and put her in the soup:

"Put your head on the block so I can chop it off!" "Sure, I'll do that," said Ederland, "but I don't really know how I should do it. You'll have to show me first." "Ah," said the old troll, "it's really pretty easy. You only have to do this," and with that he put his head on the block. In a flash Ederland had grabbed the ax, and in one blow she chopped his head off. Then she put the nightcap on the head and put it in the bed, and then she put the body in the soup kettle, which hung over the fireplace.

The troll's sons, who had commissioned their father to cook the girl Ederland for supper, eat him instead.[344]* The irony is magnified: The old troll allows himself to be manipulated so that what happens is the opposite of what is intended, and, in addition, the sons involuntarily bring about the death of their father; not only are they cheated out of the meal that was supposed to be made out of the young girl they despise, but they are unwittingly turned into cannibals who devour the tough flesh of their old father. The trick with the nightcap, a prototype already represented in ancient Greece, has become familiar especially through Perrault's "Petit Poucet": The tiny Thumbling puts the little golden crowns of the ogre's seven sleeping daughters on his own head and those of his brothers, and the caps of the boys on the sleeping daughters, in order to decoy the bloodthirsty father to his own (already bloodthirsty) children, so that he will cut their throats during the night instead of those of the seven boys, as is his real intention.[345]* In countless versions of "Bluebeard," the third sister manages to manipulate the murderer so that he carries the resurrected victims and finally her, as well, back home on his own back without knowing or wishing to do so.[346] Thus the themes of appearance versus reality and of self-injury intertwine in many and various ways with the model of manipulation and the phenomenon of irony. In the fairytale, one constantly runs into manipulations, into examples of scene management in which other figures are unknowingly turned into puppets, very much in accord with the frequency of this particular phenomenon in actual human relations. To this degree, the fairytale is "realistic." Animal fairytales, fables, and religious fairytales also display such realistic nonrealism: Small and weak animals manipulate the large and strong, since it is precisely the weak that have reason to use indirect control. The strong can achieve a great deal without using detours; of course, not everything—often they also use scene management, whether for demagogical or for pedagogical reasons, as in the case of Jesus, who, in the farcical religious fairytale, time and again has poor Peter get into embarrassing situations.[347]* There is a lot of high spirits and mischievousness in such scene management and manipulation—and for good reason: Man is by nature a manager and manipulator through and through; he manipulates others, he manipulates nature, and he even manipulates himself. And since he is one who is initially weak, in comparison with the powers of nature and of many who surrounded him, especially his parents, it is obvious that he should also generally attribute the successful manipulations in the world of his narratives to the disadvantaged. He identifies with them not only if he is himself socially, economically, or politically underprivileged, but simply because of his role as man; he fully enjoys the manipulations in the narratives in a playful and good-humored way. Scene management and manipulations are also assigned to the secondary figures in the fairytale, to the negatively represented antagonists, who can enjoy great success for a while but who in the end still fail. Slanderers do indeed succeed time and again in driving Ederland, the girl who tends the chickens (see pp. 131–132), the Norwegian ash-boy (see note 340), and the Lotharingian nephew of the King of England (AT 531, cf. pp. 32, 67–68, and 126–127) into dangerous situations, but the strings which the scene managers pull, completely contrary to their expectations, lead the manipulated not to destruction but to even greater successes. Thus the irony-oriented basic pattern that we have already seen in the child of fortune fairytale (AT 461, 930) again becomes apparent: The evil-doers, with all their machinations, end up achieving the opposite of what they want; their intrigues result in benefits for their victims, not harm, and they themselves go under as a result of their own maneuvers (the self-destructiveness of evil).

Just as in the case of motifs and content elements, we have limited ourselves to a selection of themes, constellations, and attitudes. But while we might equally or almost equally as well have examined a vast number of further motifs and features, we have here encountered the predominant themes which interact to give the fairytale its particular character. The cardinal theme of the conflict between appearance and reality is reflected in the change of situations, conditions of existence, and forms of appearance into radically different ones, changes presented in the form of sudden transformations, enchantments and disenchantments, and also in the rising and falling of personal fortunes, in the shift from poverty to riches, or from servant status to kingdom, and in many another. If sequences can be seen as a transposing of juxtapositions onto the time axis, then the change of one situation into its opposite, of a condition into one completely different, is a factoring of the appearance/reality complex, a translation of the contradictory simultaneity into a contrastive sequence. As in the case of manipulation (the scene manager/puppet model), both the conflict between appearance and reality and the change into something opposite or in some way different are tied up with irony, which itself belongs to the features characterizing the fairytale and which comes out especially clearly in the also-emphasized theme of self-injury, self-destruction. That evil-doers, without knowing it, have to pronounce their own death sentences is characteristic: They are the cause of their own destruction. And that the weak are able to triumph over the strong, the small over the large, is again an expression of the all-pervasive theme of appearance versus reality.

Conceptual themes, attitudes, and positions can be carried by very different motifs, just as one and the same motif can carry different themes.[348] It is not just the play of the variously presented, colorfully differentiated motifs that has artistic effect, but also that of the themes present under the surface, that occur on another level in the individual narratives, pervading them in different combinations and to different degrees. And the particular character of these themes contributes significantly to determining the conceptual contours of the fairytale.

# 5

## Portrait of Man

When we raise the question of whether someone who listens to or reads fairytales receives in the process a particular view of man and the world, we are not concerned with the special effect of particular fairytale types or individual versions, say, of the *Snow-White* type, the *Hansel and Gretel* type, or the *dragon-slayer* type, or of the Grimms' version or an accidentally recorded Rhaeto-romance variant of "Snow White"; we are concerned with the fairytale as such, especially the European fairytale familiar to us: In addition to the structural and stylistic similarities in the stories, is there a correspondence in content? Does the *genre* fairytale contain a portrait of man and the world which turns up somehow in all the individual stories, perhaps most clearly in what is, with striking unanimity, referred to as the "fairytale proper," the fairytale of magic, but also beyond the fairytale of magic in the groups designated as animal fairytales, novella fairytales, religious fairytales, and farce fairytales? Whoever intends to answer this question must look at the fairytale hero and his role, for the fairytale hero or heroine stands at the center of the stories; it is with them that the male and female listeners, readers, and narrators identify, even given a certain distance. It has been established by the observations of field researchers that women like to tell fairytales that have heroines, that soldiers often make their heroes soldiers, and, turning the situation around, that a shoemaker, for example, makes the villain a tailor.[349] Our question is concerned with the general. We are essentially concerned with the portrait of man, and only incidentally with the variable pictures of men and women that turn up in fairytales. We are concerned with the features which hero and heroine have in common, only secondarily with those which differentiate them. What they have in common seems to stand out more strongly and clearly than what differentiates them.[350]

Hero and heroine are the dominating central figures. All others are defined with reference to them; they are either their adversaries (dragon, serpent, witch, ogre, giant, older siblings, stepsisters, stepmothers, traveling companions, usurpers of whatever variety, etc.), their helpers (grateful animals, grateful dead, heavenly bodies and winds, old women, little men, and, again, siblings or traveling companions), their partners (bride or bridegroom), or simply contrast figures (older brothers or sisters—who do not necessarily have to actively play the role of adversary).

The fact that the interest both of the fairytale narrator and of his listener is focused on what happens to the hero, who, whether masculine or feminine, is generally human (leaving aside the special group of animal fairytales) has led individual scholars to call the fairytale a humanistic genre.[351]* In the *local legend,* at least in the central group of so-called demonological legends, the intrusion of something "completely different" *(Ganz Anderes)* is central. Narrator and listener, to say nothing of the legend figures themselves, stare spellbound at otherworldly beings, at demons, ghosts, or some incomprehensible "it," and wonder why it has taken a hand in something or even appeared—it is exactly this attitude that is responsible for the fact that local legends so often contain only a single episode, while the fairytale, which distances itself from the "otherworldly" and is freer in its dealings with it, does not allow itself to be fettered to a single incident that would inhibit the unfolding of the plot, and thus episode follows episode. In the myth it is not even necessary for humans to appear—the dramatis personae can be limited to gods and demigods; where man does appear, he is mainly relegated to a secondary role, quite the opposite of the situation in the fairytale. And in the myth-like narratives of so-called primitive peoples *(Naturvölker),* it is often the animal that is prominent. It is in this sense, then, that the European/ oriental fairytale can actually be called "humanistic." When we refer to the fairytale hero in the following discussion, we also include the fairytale heroine, even when it is not explicitly so stated. We will take hero and heroine to be the most characteristic representatives of man in the fairytale; secondary figures will be discussed briefly in the second segment of the chapter.

## THE FAIRYTALE HERO

The first thing that is apparent in the fairytale, in contrast to the local legend, is that it portrays its hero as *isolated.* He is often an only child. The phrase "They had no children" is familiar to every fairytale listener. When the couple then finally do have a child, whether they are king and queen or poor people, this child is often set apart from its surroundings by some more or less obvious peculiarity—it is born as the result of some magical conception, for example, because the mother has eaten a magic apple or a magic fish, or it comes into the world in animal form, as a snake, a hedgehog, or a "little donkey" (KHM 144); instead of an "animal child" (the common term in fairytale scholarship), it may also be a Thumbling or in some other way a "half" or unpromising human, in the farce fairytale even one that is deformed, or perhaps also a lazybones who has the gift of being able to "wish" for what he wants (he then conjures up a child for the princess, AT 675, KHM 54 A).

Even more often than an only child, the fairytale hero or heroine is the youngest child or a stepchild. In real, biological terms, the youngest, smallest child is also the weakest, but in the fairytale, a genre only partially constrained by considerations of realism, no scuffles between brothers or sisters are presented; the youngest is isolated by other means. He appears as a dumbbell or a (male or female) Cinderella, as underestimated, despised, or disadvantaged (the last is also true of the stepchild). The special status of the hero is also brought out through the use of the technical and esthetic principle of emphasis on the last element, of qualified intensification, which is also noticeable in the sequencing of tasks and in encounters with opponents (dragons) or partners (princesses): The last link in the chain is the decisive one. In this way, the technical, the esthetic, and the anthropological are interwoven, and the theme of appearance versus reality plays its part, too. Stylistic and structural elements virtually lead in and of themselves to a particular pronouncement.

Youngest children and stepchildren are the most peripheral members of the family; thus, looked at from the point of view of the structure of the system and also from a practical narrative point of view, they are easily detachable. The fairytale heroes are generally also the most peripheral members of society, children of those at the top or else of the very poor; they are prince and princess or swine-herd and goose-girl. From the point of view of both the family and society, the fairytale hero is in an extreme position, an outside position, thus isolated or easily isolatable and therefore relatively easy to draw into a central or an extreme opposite position.

The fairytale hero is also easily detachable in another sense: He departs from home. While the individuals in the local legend have their encounters mainly in their own village or city or in the environs, the fairytale hero generally leaves home, for one reason or another—often because of a family conflict,[352]* at other times in order to fulfill a task, to bring about a disenchantment, or simply "to see the world." It may also happen that the hero returns home, but that is something relatively unimportant, failing to occur in many instances. The fairytale hero is not one who returns to his point of origin, like the title figures of epics, epic songs, ballads, and war-end narratives from the Odyssey up through the modern novels about returning home, but one who by nature leaves home to wander out into the world, in a sense out into the void. He does not know the world which he goes out into; at first he also does not know what means exist to enable him to accomplish the task he has been set—sometimes he does not even know what his goals are. The real fairytale hero is no Lucky Hans who comes back home to mother—"Lucky Hans" is a farce fairytale, in a certain sense an anti-fairytale: The hero fails in the face of every difficulty, avoids everything requiring any effort, and always takes the easiest way out; he moves backward, not forward; he regresses. Lucky Hans is presented to us as one who returns, but the real fairytale hero is one who departs. And while that is primarily true for the masculine hero, it is an appropriate characterization of many heroines, as well, whether directly, as in the case of the sister of the seven ravens and of the very independent beauty in our model fairytale (pp. 2–5), or indirectly: Whoever succeeds in marrying a prince automatically enters a new world.

One feature to which we have just called attention, the fact that the fairytale hero does not know what means he can use to overcome the difficulties which he encounters, turns out to be a further significant characteristic of what we have designated the fundamentally "isolated" fairytale hero: The fairytale hero, even if he is a dragon-slayer, is time and again shown as one in need of help, often as one who is helpless, who sits down on the ground and weeps because he has no idea what to do. The fairytale hero is a deficient creature. He has no specific abilities; unlike the animals, which have inborn instincts, he is not equipped by nature for special tasks. The fairytale hero is in this way, just as in so many others, a general reflection of man, a being that has in fact been described by contemporary biologists and anthropologists as a deficient creature without specific abilities[353]*—an essentially correct description, despite objections that might be raised to it. There are animals that swim better and run faster than man, and still others that can fly, something that man cannot do at all without technical aid—but in a roundabout way, indirectly, he achieves more than all the animals; thanks to the technical means that he (in concrete terms, other men) has invented and built, he can cover greater distances and faster than any animal, on land, in water, and in the air. Prince, princess, and king are especially good representatives of man. They have no special trade; they have no special training, and yet they can do everything. But even those with a special trade do not accomplish the decisive tasks by using their professional knowledge. "The miller's helper does not rise to prince consort on the basis of his milling, nor the brave little tailor on the basis of his sewing," observes Volker Klotz.[354] Fairytale figures are neither character nor professional types, but just figures, carriers of the action, which means that they are open to the most diverse possibilities, like man as man, not really restricted by a particular character, background, or occupation.

The fairytale hero's fundamental isolation entails something further, however: Specifically because he is isolated and can easily detach himself, he is also capable of entering into new constellations. He is not just dependent on helpers and help, he actually receives such help—helpers pop up. Differing from his siblings, the fairytale hero is capable of making contact with helpers, of accepting their gifts and advice. The fairytale hero is *the receiver (der Begabte)* par excellence.

The helpers are largely otherworldly beings, i.e., beings that belong to some other world (though they differ from the otherworldly beings of the local legend in lacking the terrifying or confounding aura associated with the "completely different"): a little old gray man, an old woman, an unfamiliar wanderer (who can later turn out to be one of the grateful dead), the dead mother, the dead father, or the daughter of the demon or the ogre (who accomplishes the apparently insoluble "impossible" tasks for the hero and runs away with him). Then there are the magical animals, the animal bride (a toad, for example) or bridegroom (a lion or simply a monster), who have been enchanted and who later, after being disenchanted and freed from their alien form, turn back into human beings. There are grateful animals with magic powers: an ant, a raven, a wolf, an eagle (see p. 14). Grateful dead in animal form (e.g., a fox) and animal brothers-in-law that stand by the hero in the fight with the dragon or bull, as in the case of the dogs that can snap steel or iron or other helpful animals like those that aid the dragon-slayer in the *two brothers* fairytale, belong to the same category. There can also be heavenly bodies—the sun, the moon, the stars—or winds, which show the hero or heroine the way or provide the indispensable gift, the golden spinning wheel or magnificent costume that leads to a reunion with the long-lost mate. Less often the helper appears in human form, as a faithful servant, the dragon-slayer's brother, or the faithful sister (when the brothers have been turned into some alien form or have fallen under the power of a witch). Even underworld beings can turn out to be helpful, like Frau Holle or the devil's grandmother, who functionally plays the same role as the robbers' housekeeper, or the beautiful daughter of the task-setting demon.

The fairytale hero, being isolated, thus enters, one might say, effortlessly into fruitful contact with distant worlds, with worlds above and below, with nature and with individual figures of our world. Isolated does not mean exposed or lonely; on the contrary, such isolation is the prerequisite for a fundamentally universal ability to enter into new constellations—it frees man to enter into any relationship that is somehow important, one which can just as easily be broken off again as soon as it is no longer important: Magical gifts are used only in situations of emergency; both before and after, the hero does not even think about them (except perhaps in the farce fairytale), and otherworldly beings fade from sight as soon as they have played their part. Nevertheless, the relationship with figures in animal form can be of remarkable duration and intensity: Animal helpers accompany many fairytale heroes over long stretches of their way. The hero never receives as a gift the ability to turn himself into a fairy or a helpful old man, but he can be given the ability to take on the form of a helpful animal (see pp. 14–15). The helpful animals are also not just donors of gifts, like other helpful figures, but may intervene directly and stand by the hero during the action. On the other hand, such animal helpers, again in contrast to other figures of the otherworldly sort in the fairytale, can be dependent on the aid of mortals: They wish to be disenchanted, to leave behind their animal form and return to being human, whether it would result from the hero's chopping off their animal head or the heroine's slamming them against the wall or deciding to marry them. Thus even the relatively close relationship between human and animal helper or animal partner does not lack that moment of freedom, of change. The hero is capable of taking on the animal form; the beast, on the other hand, leaves behind his alien form and transforms back into a human. Fairytale heroes, being isolated and thus having no family or community ties, being neither tied down by personal characteristics nor limited by specific talents or training, are potentially always open to entering into new relationships *(allverbunden).*

Man has been designated by modern anthropologists as not only a creature of deficiencies but also a *creature of detours.*[355]\* The fairytale hero is as little the master of his own fate as is man in general. His dependence on help from without, especially from otherworldly sources, is parallel to what is referred to in theology as grace. To this degree, one can speak of a religious touch in the fairytale portrait of man. The fact that the fairytale hero is usually unable to reach his goals on the basis of his strength alone—here again we must look upon the farce fairytale as an exception—entails not only that he is dependent (in the religious sense) but also that he is one who makes detours. This characteristic is shown more clearly where he ignores advice and disregards commandments or interdictions. The tendency to make detours is beautifully illustrated in the Grimms' fairytale about the golden bird (KHM 57); it is a good representative of the entire story type (AT 550): The helpful fox, who puts all three brothers to the test and judges only the youngest to be worthy of his help, warns the boy not to take the golden bird, which he is to steal, out of the wooden cage and put it into the golden one. The boy does it anyway and is forced to undertake a second expedition: He now has to deliver the golden horse. Against the advice of the fox, he puts the golden saddle on it and is again caught in the act, and his life will be spared only if he kidnaps "the beautiful princess of the golden castle." Despite the warning of the fox, the boy allows her to take leave of her parents (in doing so he violates the interdiction against being moved to pity, an interdiction appearing in other fairytales as well), and now he must accomplish an absurd task (to carry away a whole mountain within eight days), something which, after seven of the days have elapsed (the embedding of a detour in a detour), the fox takes care of for him ("just lie down here and go to sleep.

I'll do the work for you"). In the end, all of the detours turn out to be good luck for the hero, for he gains in this manner progressively greater prizes, not only the golden bird (plus golden cage) and the golden horse (plus golden saddle), but the beautiful princess, as well, after he deceives each of the respective task setters in turn, again on the basis of the guidance of the fox. And in the second part of the fairytale a detour is again taken— the hero, against the advice of the fox, bails out his older brothers, who have been condemned to hang (again a violation of the interdiction against being moved to pity), and subsequently is robbed by them of his acquired prizes and pushed down a well. In light of all these detours, the well-known tendency of the fairytale to first allow the two older brothers to fail would also appear to be a detour. Thus just as in the case where the hero himself at first fails but finally reaches his goal, the fairytale, true to the technique of juxtaposition in place and in time, first presents two unsuccessful contenders and then brings the hero into the act after the second unsuccessful attempt, after this detour. Here again the narrative technique, the tendency to factoring, repetition, and variation, proves to be the basis not only of an esthetic effect but also of an anthropological statement: Man is a creature of detours. In the symbolic interpretation of C. G. Jung and his school, the various fairytale figures are seen to represent aspects of one and the same personality. From this point of view, the failure of the two older brothers would be a failure of the hero himself; their paths would be even more clearly recognizable as detours. Since these unsuccessful "premitations" (see pp. 104–105) are a component of countless fairytales, to the degree that one accepts the Jungian interpretation, man shows himself in the fairytale to be yet more completely a creature of detours (in this regard, see pp. 160–162). (He would be seen as such in any case purely on the basis of the many detours that become necessary as a result of the breaking of taboos.) In the fairytale about the golden bird, the detour of the sort taken by brother figures is even illustrated twice: The older brothers in turn first unsuccessfully guard the tree with the golden apples; then they set off, again in turn, on an unsuccessful quest of the golden bird. In both instances the task is accomplished only on the third try, by the youngest brother, who himself then makes several tries.

Our fairytale has at the same time used the detours to make progressive escalations visible: Each detour brings the hero one step higher. There are numerous parallels—the tasks or battles become ever more difficult; the path leads to ever more dangerous witches, to ever more distant and more powerful heavenly bodies or winds, to ever wiser givers of advice, or to ever more beautiful princesses. In actual popular versions of "Rapunzel"—not in the Grimms'—Rapunzel learns something from the witch, namely, useful magical arts; she moves out of the world of every day into the realm of the witch, and then on to a kingdom. If one, even with reservations, recognizes the "biographical" character of this fairytale, it is a matter of "biography advancing progressively upward"; psychologists speak of a "fairytale of development" *(Entwicklungsmärchen)*.[356] In light of the fact that fairytale figures are drawn just as figures, not as living persons or individuals, this designation can be accepted only with reservation. It is more a case of step-stair progression than of development, just as one cannot really speak of change, though one can of transformation. One can speak of change, of fairytales of maturation or development, only with respect to their symbolic significance. But since the fairytale has the tendency to project everything that is within outward, one is correspondingly justified in looking at what has been projected outward as symbolic of what is within, at transformations as representations of inner change—step-stair progressions, movement from station to station, as an indication of development or of maturation. In this sense, the fairytales show their heroes—and, through them, man in general—not only as takers of detours, as ones who achieve their goals indirectly, but as ones who *develop,* who *change.* It is obvious that the fairytale hero is also one who *transgresses boundaries,* since he violates interdictions, and especially since he opens forbidden doors. The same is true for the hero who penetrates into distant realms, whether into the world above, the world below, or only into a kingdom on the other side of the "Operenzer Sea."[357] The manipulating types of fairytale hero, which we discussed earlier (pp. 100–101, 131–133), are also creatures of detour in another sense.

The fairytale hero is a *traveler,* a *doer.* He is not a ponderer, an investigator, or a philosopher. It never occurs to him to try to find out what context his magical helpers belong to; he does not ask about the sources of their power. He explores neither the world within nor the world around him. He wanders through the world and acts. He runs into the most various figures and enters into relationships with them, as adversary, disenchanter, or suitor. He does what is right, without thinking much about it and often without realizing. Even when he sits down helplessly and weeps, he is acting properly: It is exactly his weeping which summons the helper. When the defiant little princess slams the frog against the wall, this act, though she does not know it, is exactly what must be done to fulfill the conditions for disenchantment. Antiheroes and antiheroines exist for the purpose of contrast: They do what is false; they do not press the right lever. In the Jungian sense, one must again consider that these contrastive figures may be looked upon not only as figures in their own right but also as the other side of the hero. Whether the fairytale—which for reasons of narrative technique enjoys factoring complexes into their elements—has the hero himself do what is false or shows the possibility of failure through the actions of contrast figures, would, from the Jungian point of view, be basically the same thing. What is obvious, however, is that the older brothers, the antiheroes, do what is false with the same self-confidence that the hero shows in doing what is right. They are also not ponderers, but doers.

The hero and heroine of the fairytale of magic, in particular, stand in the middle of a heavily charged tension field, as is apparent from the frequent occurrence of engagement or marriage to an animal partner. But the figure who has been changed into a beast, whether animal child, animal bridegroom, or animal bride, and is in need of disenchantment, is also a *carrier of extreme tension*. True to the style of the fairytale, this tension is again revealed mainly through action—one is told only of the immediate flight of the animal bridegroom when light falls upon him or when his animal pelt has been burnt up and of the abandoned bride's subsequent tireless wandering search, the strenuousness of which is again indicated by a concrete sign: Three pairs of iron shoes must be worn out. (That the fairytale may be open to humor at such a point, that it can lean toward the farcical, is shown by the—well-meaning and appropriate— advice of an "old woman" to the heroine that she should step into a warm cow pie with the shoes so that they will wear out more quickly).[358]* The ability to endure such long-term tension is revealed not only in the wandering search—in individual cases the pregnant heroine goes along for years without being able to bear her child—but just as impressively in stubbornly remaining silent or persisting in a denial, something which can also continue for years (*The seven ravens* and *Our Lady's child* types respectively). We can see the same thing, though more weakly represented, in the patience of *Griselda* figures, whether they are slandered wives or tormented stepdaughters, underrated youngest children, Cinderellas, scald-heads (the golden-haired/scald-headed figure has been called a "male Cinderella"),[359] or goose-girls who do not reveal who they really are, who at most reveal their sufferings to a stove or who are allowed to complain to a "whetstone of patience."[360]

It is, however, exactly the patient heroes and heroines who gather the strength and power unto themselves which allows them to be transformed into helpers, rescuers, and *disenchanters*. Significantly, it is precisely while in the alien form or circumstances that they acquire supernatural powers. And just as eyes that have been gouged out see seven times more sharply after they have been restored than they did previously, and a beautiful maiden who has been maliciously left hanging in a chimney for three years "has been made by the smoke much more beautiful than she was before,"[361] it is also the case that Little Parsley or Little Fennel (common names for the *Rapunzel* figure)[362] does not pine away in the witch's tower, but learns there the arts of magic with which she then saves not only herself but her lover, as well. The maiden who has to go about in the form of a swine up to the time of her wedding (AT 409 A, *animal child*) is, after she has laid aside the swine's skin, so beautiful that the people "thought they were looking upon the Virgin Mary," and they "all fell on their knees." The pastor who performs the marriage ceremony cannot "bring himself to move from the spot. It got on to six o'clock, and time for him to read the mass, but he still cannot bring himself to move from the spot; he just sits there and looks at the bride."[363] If here heavenly beauty is the result of years in the shadows, in other instances humans that have been changed into animals have the power to become magical helpers precisely when they are in alien form, during the period of their enchantment, and only during this time. As enchanted beings and only as such are they in a position to exercise extraordinary powers in the mastering of extraordinary situations. Whether that says something of anthropological significance with respect to the nature of suffering, we will leave open. It is dependent upon one's interpretation, on the explanation or the experiencing of the fairytale in symbolic terms. We will content ourselves with pointing out what is directly apparent—the fact that in the fairytale it is precisely the unpromising and the handicapped that can become rescuers and disenchanters, whether it is a case of underestimated central figures, grateful animals ("What will you ever be able to do for me, . . . poor little animal?"),[364] or humans in animal form.

Certain fairytales are referred to as disenchantment fairytales (*Erlösungsmärchen*). In a broader sense, all fairytales of magic are somehow concerned with disenchantment. This conclusion follows not only from the large variety of forms that helpers take, but from the fact that the figures at the center of the action are often disenchanters or ones waiting to be disenchanted. Released from enchantment are animal children, animal brides, animal husbands, and those turned to stone or immersed in a magical sleep, at times their whole surroundings with them—the whole court, all their followers, a city, a kingdom, etc. Again it must remain an open question whether the inclusion of the surroundings in the enchantment should be interpreted as an indication that the shadow of evil can also fall across the lives of persons merely associated with those directly involved. In any case, collective disenchantments of this sort demonstrate the significance of the phenomenon of disenchantment in the fairytale, and the fact that it affects not only the individual but the group, as well. The reason for the enchantment is not always revealed. The emphasis lies clearly not on the enchantment but on the disenchantment; the source of the enchantment, where the responsibilities lie, is of less interest to the fairytale than the actual need for disenchantment. That man is a creature in need of deliverance is one of the pronouncements of the fairytale recognizable in many forms. In this regard, the fairytale comes close to the religious position.[365]

Help, rescue, and disenchantment can come from unfamiliar powers, but also from humans. The maiden kidnapped by demons or at the mercy of a dragon is rescued and delivered by the hero. Those carried off to the glass mountain and transformed into animals are rescued by their own sister. Those faced with insoluble tasks are aided either by some figure belonging to the magical realm (in the *Amor and Psyche* type, by the vanished husband himself)[366] or by a human in animal form. Deliverance consists not only in being released from some animal form (one speaks of mutual deliverance: the enchanted figure helps the hero, and the hero frees the enchanted figure from the alien form), but also in the deliverance of hero or heroine from a "shadowy state" (*Dunkelgestalt*),[367] in their being allowed to emerge from the condition of being underestimated, or in the revelation of the magnificent reality hidden under the false appearance—the ugly kitchen maid in the wooden dress: "She cast aside the wooden skirt and stood there in full splendor in her golden dress."[368] Whether the maiden's wooden skirt is a sign of the otherworldly suggesting a coffin is both esthetically and anthropologically unimportant. In the framework of the fairytale, the wooden skirt would not in and of itself lead one not otherwise conditioned to be reminded of a coffin. What is apparent is that she is released from her clattering dress and returned to her true being; in place of dark ugliness appears radiant beauty.

Propp considers the dragon-slayer fairytale to be the general prototype of all fairytales of magic. And all fairytale heroes and heroines are in fact somehow or other dragon-slayers, rescuers, disenchanters, or victims of "dragons," those rescued and freed.

## SECONDARY FIGURES AND PROPS

From the discussion in the preceding section, it is already apparent that secondary figures have something in common with the main figures, that in many cases they also can be rescuers, disenchanters, or those in need of deliverance. Everyone who listens to or reads fairytales comes unconsciously to recognize that the presence of the many helpers, givers of advice, and providers of gifts likewise does its part in developing the picture of man. In the fairytale, man appears as one dependent upon helpers, of the normal and the otherworldly sort. In order to develop, however, he also requires adversaries or antagonists of some sort; every fairytale has human or nonhuman figures that threaten the hero or assign him tasks, set commissions, pronounce interdictions, formulate conditions, or issue orders. But it would not be appropriate to then conclude that man appears in the fairytale as someone directed from without. To begin with, both the hero and the secondary figures still display a goodly amount of individual initiative. The hero decides to rescue the maiden at the mercy of the dragon, but afterwards he sets off to travel around for a year before undertaking to expose the usurper. Or the youngest, after his two older brothers have not returned, still manages, despite the opposition of his parents, also to gain permission to set out. Secondary figures, on their own initiative, plot against the hero, malign him or usurp his place. The direction from without is thus anything but universal; fairytale figures, both central and otherwise, also set goals for themselves. And one should remember as well that it is the way of the fairytale to dramatize the action, and thus to present it outwardly—one may say, along with Carl Spitteler, Axel Olrik, and other theoreticians of the epic: Everything internal is so far as possible translated into something external.[369]* This formulation allows one to conclude the converse, as do the psychological interpreters of the fairytale, and see everything external as a representation of the internal. For C. G. Jung and his students, as has already been indicated (see pp. 11, 97, 140–141, and 142), the various figures in the fairytale are aspects of one and the same personality. According to such an interpretation, when the hero is linked with the false bride, it means that a destructive force in his soul has temporarily pushed to the forefront; when he tricks giants out of their magical objects and adapts them to his own purposes, it would be an indication that he takes valuable powers away from indefinite forces within him and quite legitimately places them at the disposal of his conscious ego. In this way, what appears to be immoral in the fairytale allows itself to be rather convincingly neutralized and rationalized. It would, however, be a mistake (and the Jungian school does not do so) to assume that the external in fairytale literature is *only* a representation of the internal. Everything external, not just in literature but also in reality, can be or become a symbol. It is, however, still itself, as well, not only in reality but also in literature. It is significant that over against the hero in the fairytale one finds partners, helpers, those in need of help, rivals, adversaries, enemies, and task setters, figures either on his side or working against him.

It is just as significant that the fairytale hero interacts not only with human figures but with nonhuman, as well, with animals and monsters, with figures on the other side of everyday reality—and also with objects. The prop, the object, plays a larger role in the fairytale than in the local legend, the farce, or the fable first of all because the fairytale is a longer narrative of several episodes. But that is scarcely the only reason. The focus of the local legend is on the extraordinary; the farce shows individual situations; and the fable is intended to instruct—but the fairytale places man in a complete context, and objects belong to this context just as do heavenly bodies and winds, forest and sea, animals, and creatures born of belief or fantasy.

The *object*, like everything else in the fairytale, is first of all a carrier and mover of the action. Magical objects, especially, are, so to speak, predestined to be movers of the action—that magic plays such an important role in the fairytale is a direct result. But just as with other fairytale elements, the magical object has a life of its own above and beyond its plot function—within the narrative, of course, but even more so in the later recollection of the listener: the wishing table, the cudgel in the sack, and the seven-league boots, as well as the ship that travels over both land and water, the ring that fulfills every wish or summons helpful otherworldly beings, the magic pipe that forces everyone to dance, or the water of life or the herb that restores the dead.[370]* Props also play a certain role in the fable—in the Carolingian version of the fable of the sick lion and his court (AT 50), the fox that comes late to visit the ailing lion hangs a bunch of worn-out shoes over his shoulder, which are intended to demonstrate how widely he has traveled in search of the proper remedy.[371] Fables can involve interaction purely between animals, between humans and animals, or even between objects; in the last case, however, they are not props but personified main carriers of the plot. The object as prop has very much less significance in the fable than in the fairytale, where magical objects are lost and only with great effort recovered (AT 560), but where nonmagical things also have significant functions: as signs of recognition, as provisions—whether for use in case of the hero's own hunger, for use in appeasing, distracting, or restoring dangerous or helpful otherworldly beings, or as the basis of a test (the older brothers keep their cake for themselves, the youngest shares his with a beggar), as worthless (e.g., glass) tools, and as precious items which are either to be used (magnificent clothing or armor for appearing in public, objects of gold for manipulating a princess or the second wife of the lost husband) or to be sought and brought back—for example, the most beautiful fabric (KHM 63, AT 402) or the giant's magnificent bed coverlet (AT 328).[372]

"If I just had three drops of blood, I'd show you a thing or two!" shouts the dragon in the heated battle with the boy who has turned himself into a lion. The boy picks up the phrase and shouts, "If I just had a half of wine and a roasted joint . . .!" The dragon has to do without his restoring drops of blood, but the boy's servant instantly brings him a half of wine and a roasted turkey hen.[373] In other cases a bit of bread is sufficient, or, instead of food, a kiss; the two can also be combined. "Ah," laments the exhausted wild sow, "if I could only return to the mudhole to wallow. When I came out, I would tear you to pieces." The princely contender then says, "Ah, if I just had the priest's little daughter here, she would hand me a glass of wine, and I could kiss her on both cheeks, and then I would dismember you like a fish!" While the wild pig wallows in the mudhole, the prince consumes the pita cake and the wine, kisses the priest's little daughter, and then rushes at the monster and kills it.[374] Time and again in the fairytale there is talk of eating, of food in general. This eating does not always have a plot function, but it is mentioned nonetheless. Instead of the helper's telling the hero faced with carrying out an impossible task that he can lie down and go to sleep, we read in the Breton fairytale, which in general speaks happily of food, "You don't have to do anything but eat and drink," and before the boy has finished eating, the magically gifted daughter of the task setter, who brought the hero his lunch, has cut down the forest for him, something he was supposed to accomplish with a wooden ax.[375] The Rhaeto-romance narrator of a version of *Faithful John* does not miss the opportunity to mention breakfast (which is of no significance for the plot): "In the morning, after they had had breakfast . . ., all three of them departed." Later: "One day, he took his horse and something to eat" and rode to the wise "black ladies." When the faithful Giovan asks the oldest of the black ladies what he should do to disenchant her and her sisters, she answers, "First build yourself up again and take a vacation of a week to a fortnight. Eat and drink well, and then, when you're able to hold out for three nights. . . ." Then, after the *ferias*, when the three gruesome nights are to begin, the story continues: "After supper, he went upstairs and into that hall," and so it goes before the second and the third night as well ("After he was well rested and had eaten his fill. . . .").[376]

Eating and drinking are among the most common everyday activities of man, food and drink among the indispensable and daily realities of life. It is notable that in the fairytale everyday reality is omnipresent, and quite apart from its relevance to the plot. Objects belong to the world of man. In real life, the things made by man himself—even if they are not actually made by the one who uses them— appear in diverse forms and have an importance which can scarcely be overestimated. They offer us protection and support. We can make use of them, but we can also fall under their influence: They can enslave or threaten us. The American psychiatrist Harold F. Searles demonstrates in his book *The Nonhuman Environment* (New York, 1960) that our nonhuman surroundings, especially inanimate objects, help to create and maintain our feelings of identity by permitting us to define ourselves with respect to them; we neither stand in empty rooms nor are we exposed to contant change. Searles, like so many others before him, sees more a quantitative than a qualitative distinction between the healthy and the mentally ill; and he attributes to the "primitive," to man of the Middle Ages, and to the child a relatively natural relationship to the nonhuman environment (that produced by man as well as that of nature), but to our own times an "unhealthy" alienation from it *(an unhealthy psychological estrangement from the nonhuman environment)*. He believes that the schizophrenic, with his attachment to an old shirt or his old wallet, indeed overvalues the importance of things, but that the "normal person," who changes automobiles and houses for reasons of prestige, actually undervalues them (pp. 386–389).[377]

One can also call natural the way the fairytale hero deals with things. They are there for him to use, but he does not become a slave to them. He can forget magical gifts that he has received as long as he does not need them, but he has kept them with him; they are at hand as soon as they are needed. He is not weighed down by them; he handles them easily, and his relationship to them in general mirrors his basic isolation and ability to enter into any given constellation. Being chained to the possession of things as a pseudoguarantee of identity is not one of his characteristics; but that even everyday things may be helpful is something obvious to him, as is most clearly illustrated by his attitude toward food and drink, which was briefly described earlier. And the general convention of the fairytale that recognition markers (a ring knotted in the hair of the hero, a handkerchief, or a slipper) are more important for identification than the person himself, that a golden dress makes possible the revelation of the actual being of its wearer, reflects the importance of things, of props, in the spiritual organization of man. The possibility of using props for the purposes of self-identification and self-justification is shown especially clearly in the already-mentioned forms of confession to a stove (KHM 89, "The Goose-girl") and talking to the stone of patience, as we encounter it in Greek narratives: The heroine requests as little presents a murder knife, a (hangman's) noose, and the stone (or whetstone) of patience (AT 425 G, 437). Unappreciated and forced out of her legitimate place, she asks the knife, "Shall I kill myself?" and the noose, "Shall I hang myself?" "Kill yourself," "Hang yourself," are the answers. But finally (emphasis on the final element!) she asks the stone. It answers, "Have patience"—and everything turns out well, for the eavesdropping prince has now found out the truth (cf. pp. 59–60, 142).

The danger of becoming a slave to things is, for example, demonstrated in the fairytale in the uncontrollable desire of the second wife or the bride-to-be-won for beautiful objects of gold (see pp. 14–15). Whether one should look upon transformations into objects—into an iron stove (KHM 127); into a white stick, which is cast into the sea;[378] into a block of wood, which is tossed on the fire (KHM 43, "Frau Trude," similar to the local legend); or into a toothpick or a hassock (similar to the farce, see p. 117)—as a reflection of abnormal deanimation impulses must remain an open question. The fairytale certainly also reflects psychological conflicts and abnormalities—the inflexible princess in the farce fairytale about King Thrushbeard (KHM 52, AT 900), who makes fun of "everybody" and especially of her suitors, and who is not really good for any sort of work, has been diagnosed by Hildegard Buder as a hysteric;[379] it is certainly no accident that her husband makes use of objects to demonstrate to her her lack of finesse (the willow switches make her hands raw, the spinning thread cuts her fingers till they bleed, and her pots get broken: "I can well see that you're not good for any proper work"). The uselessness of glass or wooden tools may shed some light on the psychological state of the hero. And the story of Frau Trude, in which an ungovernable girl is transformed into a block of wood by the witch and burned on the fire, can be directly interpreted as a psychogram. On the other hand, self-transformation into objects—into a ring or a needle in the magic contest, into a church or a skiff during the magical flight—attests rather to the close ties between man and object. (We have also interpreted the ability of the fairytale hero to take on the form of the animal helper as an expression of an especially close relationship to it. See pp. 138–139.) The transformation of a girl into a rose (AT 408; see p. 122) certainly need not represent an abnormal condition.

Every explanation of a symbolic or allegorical sort moves into the uncertain area of speculation. This much, however, can be stated with certainty: The everyday and the magical objects that are present in the fairytale stand for the everyday world and the supernatural world in general; the human figures in the fairytale have a relationship to both and stand in the tension field of both. By means of objects, contacts are made concrete; by means of props, relationships become visible. These functions are just as important as the role objects have as catalysts, as carriers of the action. The clarity of line of fairytale objects (a castle, a staircase, or a little box that can hold an entire city) shows plainly the power of the world of things to provide firmness and consistency, just as the availability of magical objects reveals a relaxed relationship to substances and powers, without there being any obsession with them. The broad range of everyday objects and happenings is the counterbalance to the (less frequent, but thus more noticeable) magical or supernatural happenings, just as the reverse, a small bit of realism in the midst of a surrealistic happening, is one of the particularly attractive features of the fairytale (see pp. 105–107). The real in the fairytale is not just esthetically important, as contrast and countercontrast, but anthropologically so, as well. The real, the common, the everyday things and happenings, reflect the world-incorporating character, the universalism, of the fairytale, which shows its figures in their relationship to the real as well as to the nonreal. Without them, the narrative would degenerate into the fantastic; its human figures, like many of the fable figures mounted for didactic purposes, would hang in a void. Everyday objects and magical objects (the stove to which a human confides her sorrow, the question-answering stone of patience, recognition markers, and the magnificent clothing deriving from otherworldly sources) aid in the achievement, recovery, or mani festation of identity; they speak especially clearly and representatively for the importance of the nonliving environment for man.


## PROBLEMS

What about the effect of the portrait of man and the world which fairytale listeners or readers unconsciously take over? Is it beneficial for the most impressionable of today's fairytale listeners, the children; are fairytales proper fare for children, or must they be looked upon as dangerous, as harmful? I would like to take a position on this question on the basis of what has been heretofore demonstrated and of some further considerations.

If the portrait of man which is presented to the listeners and readers of fairytales—to those who know not just a few individual stories but a larger number of fairytale narratives—really looks like what we have characterized in this chapter, then it is a *true* portrait of man. Man as man, in comparison to other forms of life, is actually relatively easily separated from his environment and therefore capable of entering into any number of relationships; he is dependent upon help and helpers, and normally such help is also available to him: Helpers stand by him from the cradle to the grave. Man is highly vulnerable but at the same time capable of reaching distant, high-set goals. He is a doer; he is able to withstand great tensions and tensings; he often reaches his goals indirectly, via detours; he is capable of transformation and development; he can be successful and he can fail; he can be the savior or the destroyer of others, and he must allow himself to be saved and to be harmed by others. He can be rescuer and he can be rescued.

This portrait of man has truth value. It seems to me to have validity independent of time and place, and it is made doubly impressive by the fact that it is presented not realistically but with marvelous alienation. But the fairytale does not show man completely; it needs to be supplemented. And it is supplemented—other genres of folk literature, preeminently local legends and farces, run parallel to the fairytale, having been told alongside it for hundreds of years. Despite numerous mixed forms the genres have remained clearly and recognizably distinct. Today, in addition to fairytales, children also get to know farce fairytales and, later, local legends.

The *local legend* shows man from quite a different side than does the fairytale. In it man appears less a doer than a being subject to fate and history.[380]* In contrast to the flatly drawn fairytale figures, humans in the local legend are shown to be capable of being shaken. What they experience works into the depths of their souls, making them sick, and not infrequently it is a sickness unto death. Occasionally, they fall victim to madness—something which as good as never occurs in the fairytale. The sicknesses of the fairytale are either feigned (*The treacherous mother,* AT 590, cf. 315) or have some plot function (the sickness of the king or the father is the reason for seeking the healing waters, or the sickness of the princess offers the hero the opportunity to cure and then marry her). The sickness of the heroes or heroines themselves is lovesickness, and it likewise becomes a propellant of the plot, whereas in the local legend, after an encounter with a weird being (apparently one from another world, for example a being belonging to the world of the dead), humans frequently waste away, without its being an impetus to further action. Humans in the local legend are exposed to anxiety. Fairytale figures can also be afraid, of wild beasts, dragons, witches, and monsters of every sort, but they are afraid of *concrete dangers;* anxiety in the face of the numinous, the uncertain, or the weird is alien to them. And yet anxiety still belongs fundamentally to man. The local legend looks at man from this perspective. The individual portrayed as experiencer becomes a ponderer. He seeks the nature and source of the powers which move him, astound him, and cause him anxiety; he looks for explanations for the unexplained, and in so doing is not buoyed up like the figures in the saint's legend by the certainty of religious faith or even by dogmas. Differing from figures in the fairytale and the saint's legend, individuals in the local legend are largely questioners. In this respect, they are even more active than the fairytale figures; more self-reliant, they come, despite being entangled in traditional ways of looking at things (from which no one is entirely free), closer to Schopenhauer's ideal of the "independent thinker" *(Selbstdenker)* than do fairytale figures. The often-mentioned "curiosity" of the fairytale hero can only with reservation be referred to as such. It is more the temptation offered by the interdiction which causes a fairytale figure to open the forbidden door. The hero of a fairytale of magic seldom shows any inclination to try out a magical gift he has received; only farce fairytales go in for such things. It is not as thinker, investigator, or experimenter that the fairytale hero transgresses boundaries, but as doer. To put it another way, even what he perceives is displayed in the form of some action.

When Ernst Bloch and Christa Bürger speak of "the spell of the local legend,"[381] which is supposed to hold the listener "within the close confines set by the ruling powers by generating fear of the clutches of numinous powers,"[382] theirs is a one-sided view. "The local legend teaches that man is master neither of himself nor of nature," one reads in Christa Bürger. Yes, but is it not then true that man is only partially master of himself? And the consequences of our thinking that we are legitimately and without limitation the masters of nature stand today before our eyes in all their horror, and not just before our eyes. The local legend shows as little all the sides of man as does the fairytale or any other narrative genre. But like the fairytale, it brings out important characteristics of the world of man, only different ones. The fairytale and the local legend complement one another. In the fairytale, man appears principally (though not only!) as doer *(Täter)*, in the local legend principally (though not exclusively) as experiencer *(Erlebender)*, one capable of being shaken, as one who feels, and as investigator, ponderer, and thinker. One of the foremost experts on the local legend, Friedrich Ranke, refers to the local legend as "primitive science."[383]

It is revealing and certainly sensible that the child's pleasure in the fairytale appears earlier than his interest in the local legend. The fairytale fills the child with trust; the local legend engenders uncertainty. In order to develop, a child first of all needs trust, self-confidence, and confidence in the world which he grows into and which supports him. That man and the world are questionable, and questionable in more than one sense, is something that he should and will learn later. One form of uncertainty will be brought home to the child in the form of the local legend. The opposite pole is represented not only by the fairytale but, on the other side, by the *farce,* and also by farce fairytales of the "Brave Little Tailor" (KHM 20) or "Clever Gretel" (KHM 77) sort. It is indicative of the pedagogical wisdom of the Brothers Grimm that they included in their fairytale collection stories of both the farce and the local legend variety. If the fairytale of magic generally shows the hero dependent on help from outside, the brave little tailor and other heroes of farce fairytales are really masters of their own fate, as is also the case in "Strong Hans," the "Young Giant" (KHM 90), or "Thumbling's Travels" ("He had courage in his heart," KHM 45, cf. 37, "Thumbling"). On the other hand, farces can also portray man as a fool, a dupe—*also* a human possibility. This role is something which in life is not assigned only to special figures. Every individual must play it from time to time, suddenly standing before others or before himself as an unmitigated blockhead. Fairytales of magic and farce fairy-tales complement one another, just as the fairytale and the local legend complement one another, only in a different way. There is among the genres something a bit like division of labor.[384]

Does the fairytale accustom its hearers—today primarily children—to cruelty and sadism, to thinking in terms of black and white, in the sense of demonizing adversaries and enemies; does it foster aggression and sadism; does it bring children up to "think conservatively," to accept a hierarchical, patriarchical form of society; does it have repressive effects insofar as it glorifies obedience, humility, and subordination; is it "the opium of the people" or even the opium for the people? Such reproaches are widely heard and bear thinking about. Briefly, I would like to say the following in this regard: Instances of cruelty often appear in the fairytale, principally in the form of cruel punishments. That is a consequence of the particular stylistic tendency of the fairytale toward the extreme. A princely reward or a sentence of death is but one of the many contrasts used in the fairytale (see p. 95). Almost everything in the fairytale is sharply stylized. And for just this reason, the cruel punishments (head chopped off, body pulled apart by four horses, etc.) are also not really seen in the same light as they would be in a realistic narrative. The extremeness in form is accepted as a matter of course; it is a sort of rule of the game, a tacitly accepted agreement. It does not prevent forgiveness from coming in at times—whether as a result of the Christian persuasion of the narrator or because it is somehow in accord with the spirit of the times.

If severe and unmistakable punishment were to be completely eliminated from the fairytale, however, it would be a stylistic and esthetic loss;
the conciseness of the representation would be compromised. Is it
pedagogically dangerous? With very sensitive or psychologically unstable
children, it is wise to exercise discretion, both in the choice of fairytale
and in the way that it is presented. Even for healthy children one would
not choose fairytales in which clear-cut examples of cruelty are piled one
on another. In those fairytales told among circles of adults, such a piling
up—for example, of the evil deeds of ogres or witches—could occur;[385] in
the Grimms' Fairytales, one does not encounter them. Anyone who is put
off by the fact that Cinderella does not open her mouth when her sweet
little doves peck out the eyes of each of the older sisters, one after the
other and in a most systematic manner (KHM 21), should reach for the
first edition of the Grimms' tales (1812; subsequent printings: Panzer
1913, 1948, etc.; Rölleke 1975). There the narration closes with the
verses: "Der Schuck [Schuh] ist nicht zu klein, die rechte Braut, die führt
er heim" ("The shoe is not too small, the proper bride he's taking home").
No eyes are pecked out; this feature is brought in only in the second
edition (1819), following another version of the story from Hesse—it did
not disturb the Brothers Grimm to use several versions of the same
fairytale to supplement one another. Their versions, therefore, need not
be considered sacrosanct by narrators today. The cruel ending of the
Cinderella fairytale does, however, remain true to one of the peculiar
characteristics of the fairytale style: The cruelty is not elaborated on; no
cry of pain is uttered; nothing is said about any attempt by the sisters to
protect themselves—the two sisters, who had such an unpleasant experience on the way into the church, after the wedding ceremony, and again
at the side of the bride and groom, go out through the portals as if nothing
had happened, and each now also offers the other eye to the two doves,
just like figures of cardboard or papier-maché. That is what they are—
play figures, not living persons. No blood flows; one hears nothing about
whether the eyeball protrudes or its liquid flows out—nor does one imagine the situation in these terms. Neither the fairytale narrator nor the
more or less healthy listener elaborates such things; there is no exalting in
cruelty. The instances of cruelty in the fairytale—in contrast to certain
fairytale films—are not realistically described; in tune with the overall
style of the fairytale, there is no sign of taking pleasure in going into detail
about pain and torture, in dwelling on what is reported. Thus one cannot
really speak of sadism. Anyone who does, misunderstands the nature of
the fairytale. It can be cruel, but it is not sadistic.

In addition, one can look upon the negatively portrayed figures of the
fairytale, especially dragons, monsters, and witches, as representatives of
evil itself—for the child they are personifications of evil. And evil must be
combatted and defeated, a notion in accord with the ethics of not just the

child. The child still identifies person and attitude. To hate the evil and love the evil-doer (in Christian terms to hate the sin but love the sinner) is something he is still too young for. The model which he is offered in the fairytale is appropriate for his stage of development. The sharp distinction between friend and foe is one of the rules of children's games as much as of the fairytale. But even the child is seldom tempted to confuse play and reality. Games and fairytales strengthen and exercise the child's ability to set values, precisely as a result of the process of abstracting in black and white. He will learn later to distinguish between person and value; the early experiences with games and fairytales will not prevent the realization that one should not view an adversary as the representation of evil. Psychologists and psychiatrists consider a fantasy-level confrontation with dangers to be necessary. "Children who have not been exposed to fairytales are unprepared for the cruelty in life when they encounter it."[386] This statement of psychiatrist Graf Wittgenstein seems too absolute to me, too exclusionary—there are other possibilities of preparation than the fairytale—but it shows that an important positive role can be attributed even to the cruelty in the fairytale.

Aggression is a part of man just as it is of every other living creature. It is there, and scarcely in need of reinforcement, though perhaps it is in need of shaping. In the mature person it should take on humane forms. The dragons with which man must do battle as man—i.e., as opposed to all other living creatures—are his problems. He must take hold of and master them like the hero of the dragon-slayer fairytale with his three helpful dogs, one of which can be called "Snap-Steel-and-Iron." This motif of the helpful animals, which occurs so frequently, shows also that the fairytale does not exclusively show aggressive behavior. Even a wild animal can turn out to be the friend and helper of the fairytale hero when the latter, for his part, helps or protects it instead of killing it ("Dear hunter, let me live and I will give you two of my young," KHM 60). The lion out of whose paw Androcles pulls a thorn, and the lion which is aided by Ywain in the battle with the dragon, are well-known examples from outside of the fairytale. "Der wurm was starc unde grôz/daz viur im ûz dem munde schôz" ("The dragon was strong and huge; the fire shot out of its mouth"), we read in Hartmann von Aue. In the fairytale, too, the dragon is an imaginary monster, the epitome of the will to destroy; it is his nature to attack. The aggression of the fairytale hero is specifically directed against the dragon, not against real wild animals. Real animals, when one exhibits a willingness to be friendly to them, can turn not only into helpers but even into human beings: "Die Verwandlung des Bären in einen Prinzen in dem Augenblicke, als der Bär geliebt wurde—vielleicht geschähe eine ähnliche Verwandlung, wenn der Mensch das Übel in der Welt liebgewönne" ("The transformation of the bear into a prince at that moment when the bear felt loved—perhaps a similar transformation would occur if man came to love the evil in the world").[387] The contrast figures, the antiheroes of the fairytale, the older brothers and stepsisters, are often unfriendly or provocatively aggressive; the fairytale hero and heroine, however, have many more positive than negative contacts. Even without waiting for statistical support (which would in any case present problems using children), one might justifiably say that the fairytale scarcely engenders any undesirable aggressions.

The other large group of objections to having the fairytale in the nursery can be included under the rubric "repression." It is the same Ernst Bloch and Christa Bürger who condemn the local legend for belittling the advancement of man's control of nature and for justifying "the existing social order"[388] that attribute to the fairytale an "emancipatory," "rebellious," "animating character"[389] and take issue with the assertion that it has only a surrogate function, that it belongs among the opiates of the people: "The fairytale does not present itself . . . as a substitute for doing."[390] But we are still not relieved of the responsibility of taking seriously the reservations mentioned earlier (see p. 152), especially since Bloch and Bürger use farce fairytales to support their argument. One has to concede immediately that the social order dominant in the fairytale is a hierarchical one. It need not, for all that, be judged negatively. In every group, even in heavily democratic large, medium, and small groups, a stratification, i.e., a "hierarchical" order, prevails in some way; and in every theory there is a hierarchy of values—in practice, one prefers today to speak of "priorities." Man, more than any other living creature, is granted freedom, but his range of freedom is also limited, not only by nature and through internal or external compulsion, but also because of the necessity for him to take his place in some larger whole. He has to be able both to obey and to give orders, and moreover to have the (internal and external) possibility of relatively free self-expression—relatively free, since absolute freedom and autonomy are neither suitable nor possible for man. The fairytale hero and heroine display both: obedience, humility, and modesty—and willfulness and independent initiative. Cinderella, of course, does the work she is told to do, but secretly she still attends the ball. Interdictions are not just violated sporadically, but precisely as a matter of course. The fairytale hero is one who sets out, one who goes off into the unknown. And he can go from the very bottom to the very top, just as, the other way round, the reigning king can be deposed. It is true that the power structure as such remains intact; the fairytale is not democratic (with the exception of peripheral forms: In Grisons the dwarfs take a vote to determine if they should punish the disobedient Snow White by frying her in the frying pan or if they want to let her live).[391] The social order remains, but it is permeable. That the kingdom is generally passed on not to the son but to the son-in-law (who is not infrequently originally as poor as a churchmouse), as a result of his receiving the hand of the princess, may still refer back to a matriarchical social order, but in any case it attributes an important role to the woman, and there are also among these princesses rather resolute task setters and riddle posers—in the farce fairytale, figures of the Clever Gretel sort (KHM 77)—who are head and shoulders above their male partners. But it is true in general that fairytale heroes are more often the doers, and the heroines more often those who endure with patience. The dragon-slayer accomplishes heroic deeds, even if it is notably the case in the fairytale that he is generally assisted by animals, but the maligned woman stands the test by patiently carrying the burdens of her suffering.[392] It is debatable whether such role assignments are to some degree in accord with the different natures of man and woman or whether they simply reflect the conditions of a particular epoch and society—the debate is unresolved. The fairytale can be accused of a certain amount of injustice with respect to woman: She appears very often as a witch or wicked stepmother. But the main thrust of the fairytale is certainly not toward the repression of woman, who, in the form of the beautiful princess, so often appears as the embodiment of something of the highest value, while, conversely, the ogres, man-eaters, maligners, and usurpers balance out the female figures that are represented negatively, from the point of view of numbers, even more clearly in the non-German fairytales than in the Grimms' collection. It is proof of the fact that the fairytale does not assign its roles in the one-sided way that many believe that in fairytales involving brothers and sisters it is often the girl who plays a more active role than her brother(s) (in Grimm: "The Seven Ravens," "Little Brother and Little Sister," "Hansel and Gretel"); that in the magical flight it is the bride who does what is decisive, not the bridegroom, just as is the case in the accomplishment of "impossible" tasks which the hero has been assigned by some otherworldly demon; and, further, that active male and female villains are equally represented.

The princess is a symbol of something of the highest value. Prince and king are also symbols. No one is likely to become a monarchist when he grows up simply because he listened to fairytales as a child. When one accuses fairytales of perpetuating a power structure which has been superceded and no longer represents the reality of Western Europe today, it can be said that it is precisely for this reason that they have a stronger symbolic effect.[393]* Just as gold, which is of relatively little practical worth, has a greater symbolic value than all the metals that one turns into tools, and just as the most important metal of a past culture may take on sacred properties in a later one in which it is hardly used, the princes and princesses in the fairytale, who as such do not exist in reality, also have a special symbolic force precisely because they do not exist. A king makes a better symbol than a president, a prime minister, or the presiding officer of an administrative council. Those who remove the kings and queens and princes and princesses and replace them with rural figures, as Otto Gmelin tried to do, destroy the fairytale in the process.[394] Princes and kings are appropriate to the fairytale not only because they are figures of the extreme and can easily function as representatives of the beautiful, but also because they are in accord with the universalist tendency of the fairytale. The king can ban all the spindles from his realm, but the knight only from his castle (see pp. 61–62). The king is representative of the whole. Fairytale figures are fundamentally representatives. If the "group" plays a smaller role than the individual in the fairytale, it is again a consequence of the linear style. Precisely because of this style, however, the figures do not appear as individualities but as carriers of the action, as fillers of roles and carriers of meanings, as symbols—for both the intrapsychological and the supraindividual.

Wars are mentioned frequently in the fairytale; it is for the fairytale something self-evident that they occur. But battlefield descriptions are lacking. Wars serve the purpose of motivating the absence of the king or prince—during which time his wife is exposed to wicked intrigues. Or they offer the underestimated son-in-law or future son-in-law, the scald-headed/golden-haired boy (KHM 136, AT 314, 502), the opportunity to prove his ability: "Like a cloud he rode past the others, used his saber to issue the orders, and drove back the enemies so swiftly that the war could soon be called off."[395] That is sufficient; the events on the battlefield are of no further interest. Revolts and revolutions, on the other hand, simply do not appear in the European fairytale—the elimination of the king not acceptable to the bride, of the wicked task setter, or of the evil queen does not have the character of a revolt, to say nothing of a revolution. To bring such things into the fairytale would be just as false as removing the kings and princesses. Wars have a stronger symbolic potential than revolts or revolutions, and they will retain this potential when one day there are no more wars. War is the embodiment of conflict, of struggle in general. It cannot be excluded from the world-encompassing fairytale. Revolts and revolutions are more special phenomena.

Fairytales may have various effects on listeners or readers, depending on personality and mood and on position and situation. In individual instances, they may either arouse anxiety or provide an introduction to how one deals with anxiety, and thus also open up ways to overcome it. They can awaken wishes and dreams or, as escape literature, as compensation literature, they can nourish and satisfy already extant wishes through the imagination, i.e., offer a substitute for real fulfillment. They can function as the "opium of the people" or also, as Ernst Bloch believes, as a utopian model "inciting to . . . good fortune" (*Glück*), their plots "sharply oriented toward good fortune, always putting good fortune on display," demonstrating to listeners: "No one is born to serfdom, no one to the status in which he finds himself and which has been dictated to him in a thousand myths of the masters."[396] The effects that the same fairytale can produce in different individuals at different times and in different classes are as various as the opinions of those who pronounce judgment on the fairytale.[397] It seems to me, however, that the main effect is not at all sociopolitical, however the term is interpreted, but psychohygienic, perhaps also psychotherapeutic. The interest in the fairytale is not primarily focused on the group but on the hero and his path, on the heroine and her fate. Someone who looks upon individual psychohygiene and psychotherapy as an undesirable method of relieving symptoms, one that distracts from the necessity of removing the social, system-dependent deficiencies which are at the root of the symptoms, may think very little of the primary effect of the fairytale. Someone, however, who believes that individual instances of both improper development and relatively ideal self-expression exist in *every* social system will welcome aids to development which foster a healthy and as rich as possible an expression of the self and which relieve or heal injuries. The fairytale is such an aid, not only because it brings across in countless variants—today to children, in the past to adults—a portrait of man which has model character because of its inner truth and its manner of presentation, but also because its clarity of style and its sublimating mode of narration can have both a personality-forming and a cathartic effect. "Man is only in part a political being" (Friedrich Dürrenmatt in his speech on receiving the Schiller Prize of the city of Mannheim).[398] However justified the warning of social critics may be that it is necessary to remove the causes behind improper development, one should still not overlook the fact that there are various "causes" working together, and that psychohygienic and psychotherapeutic help is not simply the treatment of symptoms, but help for actual people.

The purpose of the present book is not to polemicize, but rather to discuss the nature of the fairytale, above all to discuss the common features of the great majority of fairytales of magic that are told, listened to, and read in our regions and which stem from oral tradition. Nonetheless, an examination of critical opinions could not be avoided, specifically because we take them seriously and are convinced that in the case of many critics they are the result of sincere pedagogical and political concern. Along with the fairytale itself, the methods and goals of fairytale scholarship have also been the subject of discussion, examination, and attack. Is it legitimate to speak of *the* portrait of man in the fairytale? Is this portrait, quite apart from the fact that it is different from narrative to narrative and still more from one fairytale type to another, not also something different from epoch to epoch and from region to region? When one investigates the portrait of man in the fairytale, does one not run the risk of taking what is historically dependent for something ahistorical, for something universal in human nature? And does that not encourage the tendency to cement present conditions, to accept them as valid because they somehow correspond to the nature of man, instead of examining them critically, recognizing them as something dependent on the times, and, where it appears necessary, progressively altering them?[399]

With respect to individual fairytales, fairytale types, and fairytale genres, it is obvious that as lively works of literature they should differ from one another and provide us, in nuance as well as in substance, with a variable portrait of man. In some stories laziness, disobedience, and lack of modesty are judged to be faults, in others to be virtues. In some, the hero and heroine show sympathy; in others, sympathy is forbidden. In one case there is harsh punishment for the evil-doers; in another, forgiveness and even promotion. Some fairytale heroes achieve success because they lie, trick those they encounter out of their property, or steal their magical objects from them; others, by contrast, because they stick to the truth or adjudicate in a controversy between those they meet along the way—see that each receives what belongs to him—heal the sick, aid an entire city whose wells have run dry to obtain water, and so on. We have already noted that man and woman are not looked upon in exactly the same way, and that they are thus assigned different roles. But over and above all these differences, there are traits which in the fairytale genre as a whole are made to stand out, especially clearly and with greater intensity in the fairytale of magic than in its other varieties. These traits belong to man as man and differentiate him from other living creatures, for example, the qualified possibility of his standing apart (individualization, isolation) and of his taking up many and various contacts (integration); his specific relationship to freedom—independence, on the one hand, and his reliance on help and protection, on the other; his readiness and ability to accomplish tasks and master difficult situations, whether alone or with outside help; and his focusing on distant goals. It is not only basic physical needs and abilities that are common to man at all times but also those mental and spiritual. The fairytale itself is not ahistorical; it is subject to the tastes of the times, if less strongly than the corresponding individual literature, but in addition to particular features which are dependent on the epoch, which vary from region to region, and which are tied to social class, it also displays important and characteristic elements which are timeless and independent of region or class. There is, of course, a real danger that by appealing to what are supposed to be eternally constant, basic characteristics, one can come to the overly hasty conclusion that man is unchanging, even looking upon conditions that have been created by man as natural or ordained by God. Shakespeare has revealed this danger to us in the person of Richard III, one who in striving for the crown represents to others the crimes which he himself has perpetrated as the unfortunate workings of fate, in the face of which he, like them, is powerless. We must face up to such a danger but not forget that it is incumbent upon man not only to create a society that is worthy of human beings but, simultaneously and inseparably, to explore to the widest degree possible the nature and particular quality of being human. The fairytale, in which a particular portrait of man crystallizes as if of its own accord, can be of help here. Fairytale heroes are neither philosophers nor investigators. But fairytale narrators and listeners are, to a certain degree. It is their intention to entertain and to be entertained respectively, but in the process they unconsciously work out a particular portrait of man. We believe that we have shown that it is a portrait representative of man, one especially helpful in a epoch treatened by sterotyping, nihilism, nationalism, and chauvinism.

Mircea Eliade, an expert on shamanism and the rites of so-called primitive peoples (*Naturvölker*), is thinking not only of the historical roots of the fairytale but also of its present effect when he writes that it possesses an unmistakable initiatory structure (*structure initiatique*), that it transposes the experiences of initiation onto the level of the imagination. The modern fairytale reader is said to profit from this "imaginative initiation" (*initiation imaginaire apportée par les contes*). The pattern of initiation which is reflected in the fairytale—not only in the many tests which it contains, in the battles with monsters, in the apparently insuperable obstacles and apparently insoluble tasks, but also in the process of death and resuscitation, in the journeys to hell and to heaven—points to a very serious reality, which has validity not just for primitive peoples. "One has begun today to take into account that what has been referred to as initiation belongs to the human condition (*coexiste à la condition humaine*), that being human consists of an uninterrupted sequence of tests, of death and resurrection—whatever terms one uses today to translate these (originally religious) experiences into language." The *scénario initiatique* of the fairytale is said to have preserved for modern man timeless archetypal elements, so that these still have an effect on the psyche and can engender mutations in it: "Dans la psyché profonde, les scénarios initiatiques conservent leur gravité et continuent à transmettre leur message, à opérer des mutations."[400]

By using the words *archétypal* and *antihistorique,* Eliade leaves himself open to the accusation of being a standard-bearer for the ahistorical point of view, like C. G. Jung, who was the first to speak of archetypes in the sense of unconscious dispositions (psychological *Anordner*).[401] He and a series of his students have concerned themselves especially intensively with the meaning of fairytales. While we have sought to read from the wealth of the fairytale what is directly evident, the Jungian school offers a "symbolism of the fairytale," an "attempt at interpretation," which in places approaches a rather questionable allegorization ("a bird, thus a fortunate idea," "birds of prey, i.e., greedy plans," Thrushbeard "can be equated with Woden"), but which is remarkable in its basic conception, and it seems to me to lead in individual cases to interesting assumptions and surprising insights. Jung and his students see in the fairytale representations of intrapsychological processes, of happenings in the unconscious, or of clashes between the conscious and the unconscious, and they attribute the fairytale's power of fascination to these representations. The different figures are, in general, looked upon as aspects of one and the same personality; within this interpretation, the abstract style offers proof that they could not represent complete, individual personalities. From this point of view, the temporary association with the false bride portrays the emergence of an inferior and dangerous side of the individual psyche, of a temporary dominance of a false outlook on life. Sympathy for the treacherous brothers or for the raven nailed to the wall is wrong, for the former represent false conscious attitudes, and freeing the raven languishing from thirst, i.e., the unconscious thirsting to be a part of the conscious, releases the demonic (*Dämonie*) in the unconscious. The hero may with good conscience trick quarreling giants out of their magical objects, for the battlers represent "an unconscious shadow form (*Vorform*) of the hero himself"; he has to appropriate their treasures for himself, i.e., bring them up into the light of the conscious. In this way what appears to be immoral finds its justification. But since the representatives of the Jungian school admit that the fairytale does in fact reflect external as well as internal happenings (only that the latter are much more important, that they are really what is significant in the fairytale), these seemingly amoral or even immoral features are thus not finally disposed of.[402]*

The magical flight, from such a point of view, is a flight up into the world of the conscious, a process which is not always accomplished without sacrifices (*obstacle flight*, AT 313, III). Enchantment means being bound in the state of the unconscious, mostly as a result of an overly strong father or mother binding, which evokes in the fairytale the portrait of the magician or the witch (of the "terrible mother," of the devouring unconscious). In psychological terms, a curse would signify being dominated by a complex; the forbidden room would represent the encapsulating of dangerous contents of the psyche; the absence of the king or prince who has gone off to war would indicate the paralysis of the conscious. The fairytale hero is essentially the *Son*, which would represent the emerging conscious, stemming from the darkness (the ash-sitter, the lazybones) but leading into the future. Thus the European fairytale would portray processes that take place at the midpoint in life of man within the framework of our western culture, where feeling (represented by the hero or heroine in the fairytale) plays a lesser role than reason, but where man, at the midpoint of his life, seeks or should seek to reestablish the lost or blocked access to the unconscious. Many stories of primitive peoples, on the other hand, would reflect either a striving for the conscious or a resigned sliding back into the unconscious. Some myths of so-called primitive peoples could be looked upon as a sort of antecedent of the later fairytale.[403]

The last statement shows that the Jungian school in no way proceeds completely ahistorically, no more than do Propp and the structuralists, who clearly also relate folktales to particular stages of culture. Both approaches, however, seek to identify constants in the narratives, which in turn point to constants in human existence.

Our own attempts at interpretation follow the texts more closely than do those of the psychologists, and in general avoid daring speculations. If we examine the character and role of evil in the fairytale, we can establish immediately that the distinction between good and evil as such is one of the essential features of the fairytale. For both fairytale listeners and narrators, it goes without saying that man establishes values, not only esthetic values but ethical ones, as well. The sharp distinction between figures seen negatively and those seen positively reflects a basic human characteristic which is not limited to any particular epoch or place: Man consciously says yes or no; in contrast to animals, which are directed by instincts, he is relatively free to accept or reject; he is, as man, forced as well as free to evaluate. In terms of content, the values of various cultures and situations are different. Those differences are reflected in the fairytale, as well, which in one instance shows laziness as a vice (Pechmarie), in another as a mark of distinction (the hero as lazybones). Fairytale interpreters of the Jungian variety take it a step farther and explain the laziness of Pechmarie (KHM 24, AT 480) as remaining in the unconscious, as "being enslaved by matter," the "unwillingness to give form to the 'materia',"[404] while the initial laziness of the oven-sitter or the ash-sitter, or the hero of any lazybones fairytale, just as in the case of lack of promise, dirty clothes, and real or only apparent dullness (in the dumbbell fairytale), is explained as a necessary, fruitful state of being rooted in the unconscious.[405] Helpful mother figures, who, as in the *Cinderella* type, can also appear in animal form (cow, goat, sheep, little earth cow, etc.), represent the positive aspect, the nourishing power, of the unconscious, of the "maternal basis" (*mütterlicher Urgrund*);[406] witches and wicked stepmothers represent the negative aspect, the danger of being swallowed up. The varying interpretations of the same phenomenon in different narratives (of dullness, laziness, trickiness, cunning, lying, robbery, cruelty, sympathy, etc.), at times even in the same narrative (Rumpelstiltskin, who shifts from helper to adversary; the treacherous mother, etc.), would reflect the double-faced character, the ambivalence, of the powers of the unconscious and of one's relationships to them. Such interpretations are worth considering, but they remain interpretations, theories, while in the present book we have stayed as close as possible to what can actually be demonstrated. It can be demonstrated quite clearly that the fairytale sets values, that it sees and represents one set of figures positively, the other negatively. It demonstrates—to this degree we might also take the risk of theorizing—that conscious evaluation is a fundamental attitude of man as man. From the point of view of content, the values are not spelled out precisely. The fairytale provides as little an inflexible specification of the good as it allows itself to be bound by a precise definition of the beautiful. The outlines of beautiful and good can be filled in with variable coloring. In one case obedience proves to be appropriate, in another, disobedience; here honesty, there trickery. Nonetheless, it is at least possible to say that in the European fairytale, readiness to help generally appears as a positive value (as is also reflected in the readiness to help nonhuman creatures, and the reverse, where such creatures show a readiness to help man); an unprovoked inclination to do harm, on the other hand, appears as a negative one. With human figures such harmful intentions are associated primarily with the maligner (*Ferdinand the False* type, KHM 126, AT 531); with nonhuman figures, with the dragon, the man-eater (the ogre), and the witch. From this list it is also apparent that the term *unprovoked* must be modified, perhaps to *externally unprovoked*. For the envier, the maligner, is indeed provoked psychologically, from within himself. But the fairytale does not psychologize; its figures have, strictly speaking, nothing within. Dragons and man-eating ogres are also "provoked" to do their evil deeds by their very nature—they are in the business of eating humans—but not from without, not, or in any case not primarily, by the behavior of their victims. Since the fairytale is anthropocentric and sees everything from a human point of view, especially from the point of view of the hero or heroine, it evaluates positively action taken against forces threatening humans; it approves of the destruction of the dragon or witch just as it does of the killing of the children of the ogre. It abhors man-eating ogres (male and female) as such. Antagonists of the hero or heroine (for the fairytale, the central representatives of man) that come from this world are in most cases punished. This outlook contains a goodly portion of childlike naive evaluation: What is useful to me is good, what harms me is bad. "Ants, good ants, come all of you to my aid," calls out the hero of a southern French fairytale. "Sort out the grain from the rice for me!" And when he is supposed to make a mountain disappear within a single night: "Rats, good rats, come all of you to my aid! . . . carry this mountain away for me!" (AT 531).[407] In a version of the ring tale *(Ringerzählung)* about what things are strongest (AT 2031), also from the south of France, the little ant says upon breaking its leg on the ice, "Ah, you really are bad, ice!" The ice, however, finds that the sun is "still much worse; it heats me up and makes me melt"; the sun: "The cloud is still much worse; it covers me up"; the cloud: "The wind is still much worse; it blows me to pieces and chases me off"; the wind: "The wall is still much worse; it causes me to tarry here"; and the wall: "The rat is still much worse; it gnaws on me and digs holes through me."[408] Such formulations express the reaction that has been familiar to us since childhood: What causes me pain, hurts me, or even destroys me is bad. The fairytale does indeed have its childlike, naive side. But since its central figures are not just representatives of an ego that identifies itself with them, but stylized portraits of man in general, connections to a loftier ethic easily suggest themselves: "Handle so, daß du die Menschheit sowohl in deiner Person als in der Person eines jeden andern jederzeit zugleich als Zweck, niemals bloß als Mittel brauchst" ("Always operate as if you needed the humanity both in yourself and in every other person, also, as an end in and of itself and never simply as a means").[409] Ferdinand the False and other figures that are clearly represented in a negative manner treat their fellow beings "simply as a means"; the hero, on the other hand, mainly does so only with nonhuman creatures. Moreover, the readiness to help which is prominently represented in the fairytale, and which turns up in many and various forms, is reminiscent not only of common or garden moral values but also of those of the world religions, e.g., of Christianity.

The observation of the effect and function of harmful behavior in the fairytale leads still one step farther. Seen purely from the point of view of narrative technique, the "harm-doers," the antagonists, the adversaries of the hero, are plot movers. From a human point of view, enviers and maligners, evil-intentioned task setters, and witchlike stepmothers and mothers-in-law set sequences of action in motion, which, contrary to their expectations, end up working out to the advantage of the hero and heroine—leading them, for example, on to a kingdom or to the winning of treasures (easily interpreted symbolically), to the finding of an ideal marriage partner, or, instead of destroying them, quite the opposite, making them more beautiful (see p. 142). Seen in this light, the bad in the fairytale has the function which Goethe describes through the words of his Mephistopheles: "Ich bin der Geist, der stets verneint [. . . der] stets das Böse will und stets das Gute schafft" ("I am the Spirit that Denies [. . . that] always wills the Bad, and always works the Good")—verses 1338, 1336—and which "the Lord" in the prolog in heaven emphasizes:

> Des Menschen Tätigkeit kann allzuleicht erschlaffen,
> Er liebt sich bald die unbedingte Ruh;
> Drum geb ich gern ihm den Gesellen zu,
> Der reizt und wirkt und muß als Teufel schaffen.

> Man's active nature, flagging, seeks too soon the level;
> Unqualified repose he learns to crave;
> Whence willingly, the comrade him I gave,
> Who works, excites, and must create, as Devil.

—Verses 340–343 (translated by Bayard Taylor)

The bad in the fairytale, from the narrative point of view leaven for the plot, is anthropologically leaven for development, self-realization, and the actualization of possibilities: *diabolodizee* and *theodizee* at the same time. If we thus look upon the bad as something meaningful in the framework of the fairytale plot, then the interpretation of the fairytale along Jungian lines goes still farther. Since this interpretation, and not without justification, sees the various plot carriers represented as figures in the fairytale as aspects of man or of a single individual—one is after all accustomed to seeing in Faust and Mephistopheles two sides of one and the same person—it looks upon evil as a necessary ingredient not only of the plot of the fairytale but also of man himself; it belongs to human "completeness" *(Ganzheit):* "Das Minderwertige und selbst das Verwerfliche gehört zu mir und gibt mir Wesenheit und Körper, es ist mein *Schatten.* . . . Auch das Dunkle gehört zu meiner Ganzheit. . . ." ("The inferior and even the worthless is a part of me and lends me reality and substance; it is my *shadow.* . . . The dark side also necessarily belongs to my completeness . . .)[410] Using this point of departure, Jung and his school call for the "integration of the bad" into the personality of the individual and into society. We will content ourselves with saying that in the fairytale the transformation of the wild or tame beast into a human (of the lion or bear into a human marriage partner or of the animal helper into a prince) and the cleansing or healing of princesses filled with serpents or possessed by the devil do indeed suggest that it is possible to transform the bad into good, just as the constant turning up of the benevolent and helpful daughter, wife, mother, or grandmother of dangerous and destructive otherworldly beings (of demons, the sun/moon/wind, or the devil) shows the good that is hidden in the bad; and like the doers of harm, these appear clearly as advancers not only of the plot of the fairytale but also of the career of the fairytale hero. Yet it is obvious that the fairytale, alongside its portrayal of the transformation of harm into benefit, of "bad" into "good," just as often and just as clearly portrays the final elimination of the doers of harm, often in the extreme form of annihilation. Both the transformation of the bad—stated in modern terms, the perverting of it into good—and the elimination of the representative of the principle of the bad, can be interpreted symbolically, and by many fairytale listeners and readers doubtlessly *are* instinctively taken as symbolic. In which particular cases transformation is possible, in which ones the destruction of the "bad"—of the principle interpreted as bad—is necessary, the fairytale does not tell us. It is really only in part something psychagogical and pedagogical, but in its entirety a mirror of human existence and human possibilities.

If the fairytale survived many centuries in oral tradition and has vigorously continued to live on for more than a hundred and fifty years in book form, the reason, it seems to me, is to no small degree to be sought in the freedom which it allows and offers to listeners, readers, and narrators. The bad, about which we have just been speaking, is presented only in outline, something not essentially different from the case of the beautiful, with which we began our discussion. The more precise specification—it can vary from person to person and from epoch to epoch—is left to the listener or reader. And the narrator is allowed the freedom to discover and realize new variations, new possibilities of development, and new narrative goals. He is reteller and model for other tellers, heir and innovator at the same time, just as man is the carrier of tradition but oriented toward the future, preserver and renewer in one, and the fairytale itself, in the form of repetitions and anticipations, of imitations and premitations, sets forth this basic condition of man. The portrait of man which we encounter in the fairytale is not just determined by content; even the inner form, the character and life of the fairytale, corresponds to that of man: Limitation and freedom, integration into the whole but preservation of the identity of the individual element, stability and dynamism, clarity and mystery, recollection and anticipation, and reality and utopia[411]* are bound up into its narrative form and the history of its transmission, just as they are into the nature of man himself.

# GLOSSARY

**animal fairytale** *(Tiermärchen)*. Fairytale in which the main figures are animals (AT 1-299, Animal Tales). In contrast to the fable, it need have no didactic purpose.

**anthropology.** The study of the nature of man, especially of that which differentiates man from other living creatures.

**anti-fairytale** *(Antimärchen)*. Narrative having fairytale structure but with unhappy ending. See pp. 54f. and note 159.

**Arabian Nights.** Common English designation for the *Thousand and One Nights*, a work best known in English from the nineteenth-century translation of Sir Richard Burton. See also Galland.

**Basile, Giambatista** (1575–1632). The author of *Il Pentamerone* [Tales of the five days], a set of tales in the Neapolitan dialect published posthumously in 1634/36. The tales show personal coloring and stylistic embellishment, but stem largely from oral tradition. Translations exist in Italian and many other languages, including English.

**Bechstein, Ludwig** (1801–1860). The editor of the *Deutsches Märchenbuch* (1845) and the *Neues Deutsches Märchenbuch* (1856). The first, from the twelfth edition (1853) on with illustrations by Ludwig Richter, enjoyed wide popularity. Both volumes have been edited by Walter Scherf (Munich, 1965).

**blind motif** *(blindes Motiv)*. A narrative element having no plot function, as opposed to a *blunted* (truncated) *motif (stumpfes Motiv)*, which is an element whose potential is not fully developed, which remains somehow rudimentary. Most writers, nonetheless, use the terms interchangeably. Panzer, who introduced the term *blindes Motiv* (note 359, p. 115), speaks of "motifs that are brought in but not developed." What is generally referred to by the term is not an actual motif, but part of a motif, an individual feature, a figure, so the cover term should be *blind* or *blunted narrative element. See* pp. 64–67. See also motif.

**blunted motif** *(stumpfes Motiv)*. See blind motif.

**book fairytale** *(Buchmärchen)*. A fairytale edited for printing (e.g., those of Perrault, the Brothers Grimm, and Bechstein) and to be distinguished from the so-called literary fairytales *(Kunstmärchen)*, like those of Brentano or Andersen, which have been freely invented or drastically altered by a particular author. At times the term is used in another, even contradictory, sense for a fairytale which has gone over into the oral tradition from a printed source, e.g., one from Musäus (see Ranke 1955, p. 205).

**completely different** *(Ganz Anderes)*. See numinous.

**contrary irony** *(Konträrironie)*. A variety of irony typical of the fairytale, where things are actually better than they appear to be. See pp. 129ff.

**constellation** *(Miteinander)*. A typical cooccurrence of features or figures. See p. 7.

**contamination.** The combining or mixing of tale or genre types. See pp. 112ff.

**emphasis on final element** *(Achtergewicht)*. Narrative principle where the last member of a series of elements is the most significant (the most difficult task, the most beautiful princess, success after twice failing). See Olrik (note 228, p. 7): "The emphasis of the epic is always placed on the final element," and

"Emphasis on the final element in conjunction with tripling is the most prominent feature of folk literature." Cf. emphasis on initial element.

**emphasis on initial element** *(Toppgewicht)*. Where the first member of a series or group is singled out for emphasis, e.g., where the robber chieftain, oldest dwarf, or oldest "black maiden" is protagonist, or in the unusual case where the eldest son is fairytale hero. Cf. emphasis on final element.

**end forms** *(Zielformen)*. The result of the development of potentialities implicit in the narrative kernel. See pp. 74f. Cf. self-generation.

**esthetics.** The study of the beautiful, in the broader sense of art, style, and the means of artistic expression; alternatively, the study of what is implied by Greek *aisthesis*, sensory perception, specifically the perceptions of eye and ear.

**etiology.** The explanation of causes, in the animal fairytale especially the explanation of the origin of the characteristics of and the relationships between particular animals.

**factoring** *(Ausfaltung)*. The breaking down of potential feature complexes into their component elements and the juxtaposing of these. See p. 24 and 29. Cf. juxtaposition.

**fairytale of magic** *(Zaubermärchen)*. Fairytale containing significant supernatural elements (AT 300–749). For many scholars and for the nonprofessional it is the "fairytale proper." An attempt at a definition encompassing the fairytale of magic, the novella fairytale, and the farce fairytale can be found in Lüthi 1982, pp. 82f.

**farce fairytale** *(Schwankmärchen)*. Fairytale containing pithy farce elements and having a farcical tone. In contrast to the realistic farce *(Schwank)*, the farce fairytale takes delight in what would be impossible in reality. Examples: AT 1383–84, KHM 34 ("Clever Elsie") and 59 ("Frederick and Catherine").

**feature** *(Zug)*. See motif.

**formula.** Conventional expression or device tending to recur under similar circumstances, as in the case of conventional openings and closings in the fairytale and in the use of devices like tripling. See pp. 44ff.

**function.** In the context of the theories of Vladimir Propp, one of the "functions of the dramatis personae," basic plot segments which can appear in similar form in all fairytales. Alan Dundes has suggested the term *motifeme* for Propp's "function." See "From Etic to Emic Units in the Structural Study of Folktales," *Journal of American Folklore* 75 (1962): 101.

**Galland, Antoine** (1646–1715). Publisher of the most influential of the European renditions of the Arabian Nights. His *Mille et une nuits: Contes arabes*, based on a fourteenth-century manuscript and a collection of oral tales obtained from a Syrian narrator, appeared in ten small volumes between 1704 and 1712, with two additional volumes appearing posthumously in 1717. See Arabian Nights.

**Grimm, Jacob** (1785–1863) **and Wilhelm** (1786–1859). Editors of the two-volume Grimms' Fairytales *(Kinder- und Hausmärchen*, 1812 and 1815 respectively). In later editions they made partial substitutions of texts as well as of individual episodes and elements and lightly altered the style of narration. To date there have been countless new editions, both complete and partial (almost always without the Grimms' notes), and translations into many languages, but no critical edition. See the edition of the Grimms' final text (1857) by Heinz Rölleke (Stuttgart, 1980). English translations include *German Folk Tales*, trans. Francis P. Magoun, Jr. and Alexander H. Krappe (Carbondale, Ill., 1969), and *The Complete Grimm's Fairytales*, ed. James Stern (New York, 1976).

**Griselda** *(Griseldis)*. The name of the farmer's daughter who married a marquis in the last novella of Boccaccio's *Decamerone* (ca. 1350, printed 1470). Obedient, patient, and humble, she is the prototype of the long-suffering wife (AT 887). On the question of whether the story originates in oral tradition, see W. E.

Bettridge and Francis Lee Utley, "New Light on the Origin of the Griselda Story," *Texas Studies in Language and Literature* 12 (1971): 153–208.

**hero(ine).** The main figure in a narrative. The fairytale hero has little in common with the heroes of the heroic epic.

**Hodscha Nasreddin** (or Nasr-eddin Chodja). A well-known Turkish farce hero— an "Osmanli Eulenspiegel"—who is supposed to have lived in Anatolia in the fourteenth century. See note 254.

**individual literature** *(Individualdichtung)*. Literature associated with a particular author, as opposed to folk literature.

**just barely** *(Gerade noch)*. The principle that tasks in the fairytale should be accomplished just in the nick of time and with nothing to spare. See pp. 58ff.

**juxtaposition** *(Nebeneinander)*. The placing of figures or features side by side, generally for the purpose of contrast; the linking of elements paratactically (words, sentences, or episodes). See pp. 29 and 41 respectively. Cf. subordination.

**local legend fairytale** *(Sagenmärchen)*. Fairytale displaying local legend *(Sage)* features. In contrast to the terms *novella fairytale* and *farce fairytale*, a questionable designation, since the fairytale and the local legend contrast so sharply as genres. Example: KHM 28 ("The Singing Bone"). See pp. 114f.

**magical flight.** Flight from a demonic pursuer (witch or monster). The fugitives (the fairytale hero and the magically talented daughter of the pursuer) save themselves by casting magical hindrances behind them or going through various transformations. See also paradigmatic.

**motif.** A plot kernel, a concrete pattern of events, in contrast to a *theme*, where a conception is involved (an idea, principle, or belief; a hope, a fear, an illusion, etc.). When a monster is so manipulated that it falls victim to its own plot (e.g., the witch in "Hansel and Gretel"), that is a motif. It can be the carrier of various themes: involuntary self-destruction, self-injury in general (the actor as his own enemy), or manipulability; in the case of "Hansel and Gretel" and in numerous other instances, it is also the carrier of the theme of defeat of the big/strong by the small/weak (cleverness triumphs over strength, intellect over power). A subordinate motif segment or detail (e.g., pretending not to know how to place one's head on the chopping block [see pp. 131f.]) is a feature *(Zug)*. Figures, plants, things and parts of things, animals, persons, etc. are neither motifs nor features but simply content elements (element taken in the strict sense of simple, elementary building block), but they can function as important carriers of the action. See pp. 115 and 124f.

**Musäus, Johann Karl August** (1735–1787). Editor of *Volksmärchen der Deutschen* (1782–86), a collection of tales partially reflecting oral tradition but arbitrarily expanded, embellished, and ironized. New edition (Munich, 1961).

**novella fairytale** *(Novellenmärchen)*. Fairytale in which the supernatural, magical elements are lacking or largely pushed into the background (AT 850–999). Example: AT 851 *(The princess who cannot solve the riddle)*, KHM 22 ("The Riddle"). See also pp. 92f.

**numinous.** Referring to a fascinating and terrifying mysterious power taken to be otherworldly (completely different, transcendent). See note 107.

**Ölenberg Manuscript.** Manuscript containing the earliest versions of forty-six of the Grimms' fairytales, named for Ölenberg Monastery in Alsace, where it was earlier deposited along with the other papers of Clemens Brentano, to whom the Brothers Grimm had entrusted their fair copies. It is now in the Bibliotheca Bodmeriana. Critical edition: Heinz Rölleke, ed., *Die älteste Märchensammlung der Brüder Grimm: Synopse der handschriftlichen Urfassung von 1810 und der Erstdrucke von 1812* (Cologny-Geneva, 1975).

**paradigmatic.** Referring to a relationship between elements, features, motifs, etc., based upon their being substitutable for one another in the same frame; e.g., the motifs obstacle flight and transformation flight stand in a relationship of mutual substitutability in the context of the magical flight. Cf. syntagmatic.

**Pauli, Johannes** (ca. 1450–ca. 1530). Alsatian Franciscan friar who in 1522 published a collection of farces entitled *Schimpf und Ernst*. See note 254.

**performance.** Technical designation for the act of narration seen as a totality, i.e., including consideration of the behavior of the listeners and the actual conditions involved, the social and cultural "context," as well as, of course, the gestures, facial expressions, and rhythms used by the narrator. See Dan Ben-Amos and Kenneth S. Goldstein, eds., *Folklore: Performance and Communication* (The Hague, 1975).

**Perrault, Charles** (1628–1703). Publisher of a famous collection of French fairytales, two in verse (1693, 1694) and eight in prose (1696, 1697), most of which clearly go back to folktales. In the French area they play a role comparable to that of the Grimms' Fairytales in Germany.

**polarity.** The use of binary (plus/minus) juxtaposition for the purpose of clear contrast or organizational emphasis. See pp. 54ff.

**polygenesis.** The independent development of similar narrative motifs or whole narratives at different places and different times.

**premitation** *(Vorahmung).* Narrative principle involved when earlier narrative sequences turn out to be rehearsals of what is to come later (pre-imitation). See pp. 103f. and note 257.

**quantity contrast.** A contrast pointed up by differences in amount. See pp. 105f. and note 259.

**religious fairytale** *(Legendenmärchen).* Fairytale containing religious figures, motifs, or themes (AT 750–849). Example: AT 812 *(The devil's riddle),* KHM 125 ("The Devil and his Grandmother"). See the collection of Schier and Karlinger (note 120).

**self-generation** *(Sichvonselbermachen).* The principle that certain characteristics and features of folk literature can develop naturally in and of themselves, virtually of their own accord, as a result of requirements and potentialities inherent in narrative structures or techniques. See also end forms.

**sequencing** *(Nacheinander).* Juxtaposition transposed onto the time axis. See pp. 29, 133. See also juxtaposition.

**subordination.** The linking of elements (grammatical entities, episodes, etc.) hypotactically, including the use of embeddings (e.g., narrative within the narrative) and subordination contrasts. Cf. juxtaposition.

**subordination contrast.** The appearance of a secondary contrastive element in the narrative, e.g., of an anti-fairytale in the fairytale, of a realistic element amid the wondrous, or of the magical amid the everyday. See p. 54.

**syntagmatic.** Referring to a relationship between elements, features, motifs, etc. based on cooccurrence and contiguity. Cf. paradigmatic.

**theme.** See motif.

**tiny flaw** *(kleiner Fehl).* A small imperfection providing a quantity contrast in the normally perfectionistic context of the fairytale. See pp. 59.

**tripling** *(Dreizahl).* The use of patterns of three as a formulaic principle. See also emphasis on final element.

**troll.** Common designation for monster (ogre, giant, or dragon) in Scandinavian fairytales.

**type.** A constant basic pattern associated with a larger or smaller group of closely related fairytales, e.g., AT 300 *(The dragon-slayer),* AT 709 *(Snow-White).*

# NOTES

*Abbreviations*

**AT**   Aarne, Antti, and Thompson, Stith. *The Types of the Folktale.* 2d rev. FFC no. 184. Helsinki, 1973.

**Bolte-Polívka**   Bolte, Johannes, and Polívka, Georg. *Anmerkungen zu den Kinder- und Hausmärchen der Brüder Grimm.* 5 vols. Leipzig, 1913–32. Reprint. Hildesheim, 1963.

**Delarue-Tenèze**   Delarue, Paul, and Tenèze, Marie-Louise. *Le Conte populaire français.* 3 vols. to date. Paris, 1957, 1964, 1976.

**Eberhard-Boratav**   Eberhard, Wolfram, and Boratav, Pertev Naili. *Typen türkischer Volksmärchen.* Wiesbaden, 1953.

**EM**   Ranke, Kurt et al., eds. *Enzyklopädie des Märchens.* Berlin/New York, 1977–.

**FFC**   Folklore Fellows Communications

**Gonzenbach**   Gonzenbach, Laura. *Sizilianische Märchen.* 2 pts. Leipzig, 1870.

**Hahn**   Hahn, Johann Georg v. *Griechische und albanesische Märchen.* 2 vols. Leipzig, 1864. 2d ed., Munich, 1918.

**HDA**   Bächtold-Stäubli, Hanns. *Handwörterbuch des deutschen Aberglaubens.* 10 vols. Berlin/Leipzig, 1927–42.

**HDM**   Mackensen, Lutz, ed. *Handwörterbuch des deutschen Märchens.* 2 vols. Berlin/Leipzig, 1930–40.

**KHM**   *Kinder- und Hausmärchen der Brüder Grimm*

**Littmann**   Littmann, Enno. *Die Erzählungen aus den Tausendundein Nächten.* 6 vols. Leipzig, 1923–28.

**Lüthi**

**1943**   "Die Gabe im Märchen und in der Sage." Dissertation, Bern, 1943.

**1951**   *Europäische Volksmärchen.* Zürich, 1951.

**1970**   *Volksliteratur und Hochliteratur: Menschenbild, Thematik, Formstreben.* Bern/Munich, 1970.

**1975**   *Volksmärchen und Volkssage: Zwei Grundformen erzählender Dichtung.* Bern/Munich, 1961. 3d ed., 1975.

**1976**   *So leben sie noch heute: Betrachtungen zum Volksmärchen.* Göttingen, 1969. 2d ed., 1976.

**1976a**   *Once upon a time: On the Nature of Fairy Tales.* Translated from the German *Es war einmal . . . : Vom Wesen des Volksmärchens* (Göttingen, 1962; 6th ed., 1983) by Lee Chadeayne and Paul Gottwald. With additions by the author and an introduction by Francis Lee Utley. Bloomington, Ind., 1976.

**1979**   *Märchen.* Sammlung Metzler, no. 16. Stuttgart, 1962. 7th ed., 1979.

**1982**   *The European Folktale: Form and Nature.* Translated from the German *Das europäische Volksmärchen: Form und Wesen* (Bern, 1947. 7th ed., 1981) by John D. Niles. Philadelphia, 1982.

**MdW**   Leyen, Friedrich v. der, founding ed. (later eds. Kurt Schier and Felix Karlinger). *Märchen der Weltliteratur.* Jena, 1912–; Düsseldorf/Cologne, 1952–

**Megas**   Megas, Georgios A., ed. *Griechenland—Deutschland.* Begegnung der Völker im Märchen, vol. 3. Münster, 1968.

**Propp**   Propp, Vladimir. *Morphology of the Folktale.* 2d ed., rev. and ed. by
Louis A. Wagner with a new introduction by Alan Dundes. Austin/London,
1968.
**Ranke**   Ranke, Kurt. *Schleswig-Holsteinische Volksmärchen (AT 300–960).* 3
vols. Kiel, 1955, 1958, 1962.
**Röhrich**   Röhrich, Lutz. *Märchen und Wirklichkeit.* Wiesbaden, 1956. 3d print-
ing, 1974.
**Schmitz**   Schmitz, Nancy. *La Mensongère (conte-type 710).* Les Archives de
Folklore, no. 14. Quebec, 1972.
**Taikon**   Tillhagen, C. H. *Taikon erzählt Zigeunermärchen.* Zürich, 1948. 2d ed.,
1973.
**Uffer**   Uffer, Leza. *Las Tarablas da Guarda.* Basel, 1970.

KHM numbering is according to Bolte-Polívka. Motif numbers refer to Stith
Thompson, *Motif-Index of Folk-Literature,* rev. and enl. 6 vols. (Copenhagen/
Bloomington, Ind., 1955–1958).

## INTRODUCTION

1. Petr Bogatyrev and Roman Jakobson, "Die Folklore als eine besondere Art
des Schaffens," in *Donum Natalicium Schrijnen* (Nijmegen/Utrecht, 1929); reprinted in Roman Jakobson, *Selected Writings,* vol. 4 (The Hague, 1966), pp. 1–
15, and in Heinz Blumensath, ed., *Strukturalismus in der Literaturwissenschaft*
(Cologne, 1972), pp. 13–24.
2. See especially *The European Folktale: Form and Nature* (Philadelphia,
1982), trans. John D. Niles from the German *Das europäische Volksmärchen:
Form und Wesen* (Bern, 1947; 7th ed., Munich, 1981); *Volksmärchen und
Volkssage: Zwei Grundformen erzählender Dichtung* (Bern/Munich, 1961; 3d ed.,
1975); *Volksliteratur und Hochliteratur: Menschenbild, Thematik, Formstreben*
(Bern/Munich, 1970); and *So leben sie noch heute: Betrachtungen zum
Volksmärchen* (Göttingen, 1969; 2d ed., 1976); see also pp. 40–44.
3. Vladimir Propp, *Morphology of the Folktale,* 2d ed., rev. and ed. Louis A.
Wagner with a new introduction by Alan Dundes (Austin/London, 1968), trans.
from the Russian *Morfologija skazki* (Leningrad, 1928; 2d ed., Moscow, 1969).
The Italian edition, *Morfologia della fiaba,* 2d ed. (Turin, 1966), has appended to
it a discussion of Propp by Claude Lévi-Strauss, "La struttura e la forma" (original
title "L'Analyse morphologique des contes russes," *International Journal of Slavic
Linguistics and Poetics* 3 [1960]: 122–49), and a reply by Propp, "Struttura e storia
nello studio della favola," pp. 203–27. The French edition, *Morphologie du conte,*
2d ed. (Paris, 1970), and the German, *Morphologie des Märchens* (Munich, 1972),
include an article by Propp on transformations in the fairytale (from 1928): in the
German, "Transformationen von Zaubermärchen," pp. 155–80; and a discussion of
the structural and typological study of the fairytale by Eleasar M. Meletinsky
(Mélétinski/Meletinskij): in the German, "Zur strukturell-typologischen Er-
forschung des Volksmärchens," pp. 241–76, which first appeared in the Moscow
edition. The German edition also contains a German translation of the Lévi-
Strauss discussion and of Propp's reply.

## 1. BEAUTY AND ITS SHOCK EFFECT

4. See Joseph Courtès, "De la description à la spécificité du conte populaire
merveilleux français," *Ethnologie Française* 2 (1972): 9–42, particularly pp. 27f.
5. Nancy Schmitz, *La Mensongère (conte-type 710),* Les Archives de Folklore,

no. 14 (Québec, 1972), pp. 218–36. "Le Beau Magicien d'Afrique" was told by Mrs. André Blanchard on 6 July 1954 in Gloucester, New Brunswick; she had heard the fairytale more than fifty years before in Saint-Léolin.

6. Traute Scharf, *Koreanische Märchen* (Frankfurt am Main, 1963), p. 114.

7. Schmitz, p. 253; See also pp. 120, 127, 128, 149, 166, 172, 191, 194, 212, 241, 245, 260, 261, 263, 264, 270, 275, and 277. Eberhard-Boratav, pp. 167f., Type 154, *Der Geduldstein;* cf. AT 894, *The ghoulish schoolmaster and the stone of pity* (related to AT 710, *Our Lady's child*), and Georgios A. Megas, "Die Novelle vom menschenfressenden Lehrer," in I. Baumer et al., eds., *Demologia e Folklore: Studi in memoria di Guiseppe Cocchiara* (Palermo, 1974), pp. 199–208.

8. Georgios A. Megas, ed., *Griechische Volksmärchen,* MdW (1965), no. 29 (a *Rapunzel* version).

9. Karl Haiding, *Österreichs Märchenschatz: Ein Hausbuch für Jung und Alt* (Vienna, 1953), no. 11.

10. Hahn, no. 54.

11. Johann Wilhelm Wolf, *Deutsche Hausmärchen* (Göttingen/Leipzig, 1851; reprint, Hildesheim, 1972), pp. 286ff.; see also Josef Haltrich, *Deutsche Volksmärchen aus dem Sachsenlande in Siebenbürgen* (Berlin, 1856; reprint, Munich, 1956; Bucharest, 1972), no. 27. Many more examples could easily be found. In all such cases one should first consult AT (here AT 313 and 313 A, B, C) and the references there to Bolte-Polívka.

12. Ulrich Kratz, ed., *Indonesische Volksmärchen,* MdW (1973), no. 42.

13. See Paul Kretschmer, ed., *Neugriechische Märchen,* MdW (1917), pp. xf.

14. Hahn, no. 97.

15. Georgios A. Megas, ed., *Griechenland-Deutschland,* Begegnung der Völker im Märchen, vol. 3 (Münster, 1968), no. 9.

16. *Griechische Volksmärchen* (note 8 above), no. 41.

17. Ibid., no. 31; Greek with German translation in Georg Hüllen, ed., *Von Prinzen, Trollen, und Herrn Fro,* Märchen der europäischer Völker, vol. 2 (Schloß Bentlage near Rheine in Westphalia, 1957), pp. 7ff., 21ff.

18. August Leskien, ed., *Balkanmärchen,* MdW (1915), no. 53.

19. Erich Rösch, *Der getreue Johannes,* FFC no. 77 (Helsinki, 1928), p. 80 (a Finnish variant).

20. August von Löwis of Menar, ed., *Russische Volksmärchen,* MdW (1914; reprint, 1955), no. 55 (a broadside fairytale from 1786!); available in English as *Russian Folktales,* trans. E. C. Elstob and Richard Barber (London, 1971).

21. See my article "Rapunzel" in Lüthi 1975, pp. 62–96.

22. For the fairytale type *Faithful John,* see the analysis of Rösch (note 19 above) and my article "Von der Freiheit der Erzähler: Anmerkungen zu einigen Versionen des 'Treuen Johannes'," in W. van Nespen, ed., *Miscellanea Prof. Em. Dr. K. C. Peeters* (Antwerp, 1975), pp. 458–72. A Pomeranian variant can be found in Ulrich Jahn, *Volksmärchen aus Pommern und Rügen,* vol. 1 (Norden/Leipzig, 1891), no. 7.

23. See also Lüthi 1975, pp. 15f., 29–33.

24. The Transylvanian variant is to be found in *Archiv des Vereins für Siebenbürgische Landeskunde,* n.s. 33 (1905): 46off.; the Rhaeto-romance (with German translation) in Leza Uffer, *Las Tarablas da Guarda* (Basel, 1970), pp. 62ff.; the Danish in E. T. Kristensen, *Aeventyr fra Jylland,* vol. 2 (Copenhagen, 1884), pp. 43ff. ("Den tro Stalbroder"); the Bulgarian-Macedonian in Rösch (note 19), p. 64. With respect to the Slovakian versions, see Rösch, p. 52; for the *grateful dead,* see Bolte-Polívka, vol. 3, pp. 501–506.

25. The ancient Egyptian text has been translated and commented on a num-

ber of times; see, for example, Emma Brunner-Traut, ed., *Altägyptische Märchen*, MdW (1963), no. 5.

26. The tale of the *Two Brothers*. See Leo Reinisch, *Texte*, Die Somalisprache, vol. 1 (Vienna, 1900), pp. 259–77, and David Heinrich Müller, *Texte*, Die Mehriund Soqotrisprache, vol. 1 (Vienna, 1902), pp. 193–203 (both texts the result of expeditions to southern Arabia by members of the Vienna Academy of Sciences).

27. See Karel Horálek, "Le conte des deux frères (Anoubis et Bata), un coup d'oeil rétrospectif et la revue des varientes orientales," *Man and Culture* 2 (Prague, 1968): 80–98, and "Les relations entre l'Europe et l'Orient," *Folklorica Pragensia* 1 (1969): 7–74 (the second is an expansion of the first, with the inclusion of European material). By the same author, "Ein Beitrag zur volkskundlichen Balkanologie," *Fabula* 7 (1964): 1–32.

28. *Archiv des Vereins für siebenbürgische Landeskunde*, n.s. 33 (1905): 387. The occurrence of this picture motif in other fairytale types is noted by Yolando Pino-Saavedra in "Das verschlafene Stelldichein: Ein kleiner Beitrag zum Märchentyp AT 861" in Fritz Harkort, Karel C. Peeters, and Robert Wildhaber, eds., *Volksüberlieferung: Festschrift für Kurt Ranke* (Göttingen, 1968), pp. 313–20. He speaks of the "structural instability of our fairytale group"; only the motif of falling in love with a person one has but seen in a picture (Motif T 11.2, not T 12, as mistakenly appears in the article) occurs with any frequency—evidence of the fascination of this motif (cf. also AT 900, *King Thrushbeard*).

29. Felix Karlinger and Ovidiu Birlea, eds., *Rumänische Volksmärchen*, MdW (1969), pp. 214, 225.

30. Peter von Matt, "Die gemalte Geliebte," chap. 2 of *Die Augen der Automaten: E. T. A. Hoffmanns Imaginationslehre als Prinzip seiner Erzählkunst* (Tübingen, 1971), pp. 38–75. See in particular pp. 50, 52, 57f., 62, 64, 66f., 72, and 74.

31. See Hedwig von Beit, *Symbolik des Märchens: Versuch einer Deutung*, vol. 1 (Bern, 1952; 4th ed., 1971), pp. 762–70.

32. This interpretation is according to the "Vienna Mythological School"; see Lüthi 1979, pp. 64f.

33. *Antony and Cleopatra*, II.ii.194–226. See Lüthi, "Die Macht des Nichtwirklichen in Shakespeares Spielen," in Karl L. Klein, ed., *Wege der Shakespeareforschung* (Darmstadt, 1971), pp. 138–59, particularly pp. 142f.

34. See my article "Altern" in EM.

35. See the Kurt Ranke article "Abtragen der Schuhe" in EM. The tale of "Mr. Marzipan" is to be found in Irene Naumann-Mavrogordato, *Es war einmal: Neugriechische Märchen* (Istanbul, 1942), pp. 5ff.; cf. *Griechische Volksmärchen* (note 8 above), no. 48. In this regard, see the observations of Georgios A. Megas in *Das Märchen von Amor und Psyche in der griechischen Volksüberlieferung* (Athens, 1971), pp. 129–36, and my own comments in Lüthi 1970, pp. 54–65.

36. Eberhard-Boratav, p. 218, Type 188.

37. Ibid., pp. 221, 488, Type 190.

38. Rösch (note 19 above), pp. 25, 44 (French and Rumanian); Megas, no. 8.

39. Ibid., no. 19.

40. Otto Huth, "Märchen und Megalithreligion," *Paideuma* 5 (1950): 12: "The royal element in the fairytale marks out sacred spheres; beauty in the fairytale is always divine beauty. Ecstatic experiences stand behind the telling of fairytales." The shamanistic theory appears, for example, in Karl Meuli, "Scythica," *Hermes* 70 (1935): 121–76; in Reidar Th. Christiansen, "Ecstasy and Arctic Religion," *Studia Septentrionalia* 4 (1953): 19–92; and in Luise Resatz, "Das Märchen als Ausdruck elementarer Wirklichkeit," *Die Freundesgabe: Jahrbuch der Gesellschaft zur Pflege des Märchengutes der europäischer Völker*, vol. 2 (1959): 35–

41—following Mircea Eliade, *Shamanism: Archaic Techniques of Ecstasy,* trans. W. R. Trask (London, 1964; German, Zürich/Stuttgart, 1956/57); Friedrich von der Leyen, *Das Märchen: Ein Versuch,* 4th ed. in cooperation with Kurt Schier (Heidelberg, 1958), pp. 65f., 74, 76–80, likewise makes reference to Eliade. See Lüthi 1975, pp. 169f. and note 150 below.

41. Bolte-Polívka, vol. 1, p. 50.

42. This description appears in the edition of 1819; later simplified by Wilhelm Grimm to *blinkendes Wasser* ("flashing water").

43. Marc Soriano, *Les Contes de Perrault* (Paris, 1968), pp. 41f., 144f. Delarue-Tenèze, vol. 1, p. 382: "Quel chemin prends-tu? Celui des Epingles ou celui des Aiguilles?" Thus the folktale (example from Nivernais on p. 373) is completely different from Perrault; it is absurdly playful, moving into the much-loved domain of the nonreal and artificial and in our example at the same time even reaching into the metallic, so appropriate to the fairytale; while in Perrault, dryly rational, the Wolf takes one way *(ce chemin-icy)* and Little Red Riding Hood the other *(ce chemin-là).*

44. *Griechische Volksmärchen* (note 8 above), pp. 42, 64, 96, 209; see also Megas, pp. 192f.

45. Gonzenbach, no. 33 [ = Felix Karlinger, ed., *Italienische Volksmärchen,* MdW (1973), no. 44].

46. *Griechische Volksmärchen* (note 8 above), p. 71; Uffer, p. 63.

47. E. Róna-Sklarek, *Ungarische Volksmärchen,* n.s. (Leipzig, 1909), p. 87; *Rumänische Volksmärchen* (note 29 above), pp. 162, 271, 233, 225.

48. Róna-Sklarek, p. 90 [ = Lüthi 1951, p. 461]; cf. Hahn, no. 28 ("Vom Mädchen, das Rosen lacht und Perlen weint"); see also Bolte-Polívka, vol. 1, p. 100, n. 1, and Samuel Singer, *Schweizer Märchen: Anfang eines Kommentars zu der veröffentlichten Märchenliteratur,* vol. 1 (Bern, 1903; reprint, Munich-Pullach, 1971), p. 38.

49. Littmann, vol. 4, pp. 241f, 254, 256 (Nights 566–78: "Die Geschichte von der Messingstadt"); vol. 3, p. 197.

50. Enno Littmann, *Arabische Märchen: Aus mündlicher Überlieferung gesammelt und übertragen von Enno Littmann* (Leipzig, n.d. [1935]), p. 79.

51. C. H. Tillhagen, *Taikon erzählt Zigeunermärchen* (Zürich, 1948; 2d ed., 1973), p. 134.

52. Dov Noy, *Jefet Schwili erzählt: Hundertsechzig Volkserzählungen, aufgezeichnet in Israel 1957–1960* (Berlin, 1963), p. 91.

53. For a discussion of the degree to which the fairytale is a timeless or ahistorical phenomenon and of whether it contains ahistorical elements, see the Gottfried Korff article "Ahistorisch" in EM, and my comments on pp. 159–160 above, which place the emphasis slightly differently.

54. Felix Karlinger and Gertrude Gréciano, eds., *Provenzalische Märchen,* MdW (1974), pp. 132, 177.

55. Max Weisweiler, ed., *Arabische Märchen,* vol. 1, MdW (1965), pp. 84, 97; Felix Tauer, *Erzählungen aus den Tausendundein Nächten* (Frankfurt am Main, 1966), p. 35.

56. Tauer, pp. 29, 49, 220; Weisweiler, p. 23.

57. Weisweiler, p. 107; cf. p. 119.

58. Tauer, pp. 208, 241, 289; cf. p. 216.

59. Agnes Kovács, ed., *Ungarische Volksmärchen,* MdW (1966), p. 294.

60. Kurt Schier and Felix Karlinger, eds., *Bulgarische Volksmärchen,* MdW (1971), pp. 42, 122.

61. Oldrich Sirovátka, ed., *Tschechische Volksmärchen,* MdW (1969), p. 39.

62. Taikon, p. 135.

63. Ibid., pp. 137, 170, 175f.

64. *Griechische Volksmärchen* (note 8 above), pp. 232, 186.

65. Scharf (note 6 above), p. 88; cf. pp. 34 above.

66. Walther Aichele and Martin Block, eds., *Zigeunermärchen*, MdW (1926; reprint, 1962), no. 24.

67. Kretschmer (note 13 above), p. xi, n. 7.

68. Taikon, pp. 147, 97.

69. Weisweiler (note 55 above), p. 111.

70. Toshio Ozawa, *Japanische Märchen* (Frankfurt am Main, 1974), p. 57.

71. Scharf (note 6 above), pp. 81, 108, 44, 16, 18, 74, 82.

72. *Summa Theologiae*, bk. 2, pt. 1, question 27, subdiv. 1, as cited in Rosario Assunto, *Die Theorie des Schönen im Mittelalter* (Cologne, 1963), p. 178.

73. Sidney Oldall Addy, *Household Tales* (London, 1895), no. 1; German translation in Lüthi 1951, pp. 107ff.

74. Felix Karlinger, *Das Feigenkörbchen: Volksmärchen aus Sardinien* (Kassel, 1973), pp. 86f., 187. The power of music comes through impressively in the Hungarian fairytale of the painted room. See Gyula Ortutay, *Ungarische Volksmärchen* (Berlin, 1957), no. 15; see also note 234 below.

75. *Summa Theologiae*, bk. 1, question 5, subdiv. 4, as cited in Assunto (note 72 above); for art as an organ of knowledge, see pp. 78 above. Cf. Herder: "Sight [is] the richest, finest, and clearest sense . . . : consequently the philosophy of sensual objects must get practice on it for all the other senses" (from the introduction to *Über Bild, Dichtung, und Fabel*, Zerstreute Blätter, vol. 3 [1787]; Bernhard Suphan, ed., *Werke*, vol. 15 [Berlin, 1888], p. 525).

76. Uffer, pp. 62ff.

77. August von Löwis of Menar, ed., *Finnische und estnische Volksmärchen*, MdW (1922; reprint, 1962), no. 42 [ = Lüthi 1951, pp. 379ff.].

78. See Dietz-Rüdiger Moser, "Märchensingverse in mündlicher Überlieferung," *Jahrbuch für Volksliedforschung* 13 (1968): 85–122, especially pp. 101–108. One of the long-playing recordings of Johannes Künzig and Waltraud Werner has a version with sung verses: "Von der Hollerdudel," *Die "Blinden Madel" aus Gant im Schildgebirge*, no. 1, *Ungarndeutsche Märchenerzähler*, vol. 2 (Freiburg, 1971); on pp. 70–74 of the accompanying text, there is a commentary by Moser.

79. Latin text with German translation in Adolf Reinle, *Die Heilige Verena von Zurzach* (Basel, 1948), p. 61.

80. Leopold Schmidt, *Die Volkserzählung* (Berlin, 1963), p. 48 ("Der singende Knochen," pp. 48–54).

81. Felix Karlinger, *Die Funktion des Liedes im Märchen der Romania* (Salzburg/Munich, 1968), p. 6.

82. Cf. Karlinger, p. 9: "Singing and talking are . . . two different levels." Talking belongs to "everyday life," whereas singing is associated with "extraordinary situations and circumstances."

83. Theodor W. Adorno, *Ästhetische Theorie* (Frankfurt am Main, 1973), p. 81. On the subject of the "esthetic of the ugly," see several of the contributions in the collection edited by H. R. Jauß, *Die nicht mehr schönen Künste: Grenzphänomene des Ästhetischen* (Munich, 1968). On pp. 180f. Jacob Taubes quotes from the oration delivered by the crucified Peter in the apocryphal *Acts of Peter* ("to look upon what is not beautiful as beautiful and what seems good to the senses as bad") and from that "of the enemy" (i.e., the devil) in the apocryphal *Acts of Thomas* (Christ "tricked . . . us with his completely ugly appearance"). On p. 157, Jauß calls attention to Augustine's speaking of the *deformitas Christi*, to the ugliness of the crucified figure, and to Luther's translation of Isaiah 53.2: "weil seine Gestalt häßlicher ist als anderer Leute" ("Because his form is uglier than that of other people"); cf. I Corinthians 1.28: "God has chosen things low in the eyes of

the world and contemptible." See also Paul Michel, *Formosa deformitas: Bewältigungsformen des Häßlichen in mittelalterlicher Literatur* (Bonn, 1976), and my article "Ästhetik im Märchen" in EM.

84. Delarue-Tenèze, vol. 2, p. 189 (AT 408).

85. Hahn, no. 49 (AT 408).

86. Kurt Schier and Felix Karlinger, eds., *Mazedonische Volksmärchen*, MdW (1972), no. 31 (AT 408).

87. *Italienische Volksmärchen* (note 45 above), p. 198.

88. Siegfried Neumann, *Mecklenburgische Volksmärchen* (Berlin, 1971), nos. 70, 71.

89. Elfriede Moser-Rath, ed., *Deutsche Volksmärchen*, MdW (1966), p. 155.

90. Alfred Cammann, *Westpreussische Märchen* (Berlin, 1961), p. 72.

91. *Tschechische Volksmärchen* (note 61 above), p. 81.

92. Hahn, no. 98.

93. Emmanuel Cosquin, *Contes populaires de Lorraine*, vol 1 (Paris, 1886), no. 3; German translation in Lüthi 1951, pp. 155ff.

94. Hahn, nos. 25, 65 (Variant 2).

95. *Tschechische Volksmärchen* (note 61 above), pp. 66, 76.

96. Megas, no. 19; Hahn, no. 100. Cf. Jan-Öjvind Swahn, *The Tale of Cupid and Psyche* (AT 425 and 428), pp. 30, 261; Megas (note 35 above), pp. 8, 118; and Milko Matičetov, "Godovčičaci: Zur Deutung slovenischer Varianten vom Typ AT 480," in Helge Gerndt and George R. Schroubek, eds., *Dona Ethnologica: Beiträge zur vergleichenden Volkskunde, Leopold Kretzenbacher zum 60. Geburtstag*, p. 310: "Either following the advice of her grandmother or on her own initiative . . . Lena answers the godovčičaci (mythical creatures encountered in the woods, each corresponding to one of the twelve months—see W. E. Roberts, *The Tale of the Kind and Unkind Girls* [Berlin, 1958]) to the effect that they have beautiful, clean heads. The truth is that they are covered with wounds and scurf, and not only with lice but also with other vermin—snakes, lizards, newts, frogs, spiders, and the like. The godovčičaci reward the kind girl [with marvelous firewood and place a star on her forehead]." This story is an especially clear example of elevation through praise—which must not be equated with false flattery—of the ugly to the beautiful, of the unpleasant to the pleasant, of the negative to the positive; cf. note 83 above and, in a nonesthetic framework, the notion of addressing a witch or monster as "Mother" or "Father" (see pp. 48 above).

97. Addy (note 73 above), pp. 109f.; cf. pp. 26 above.

98. Claude Lévi-Strauss, *Structural Anthropology*, vol. 1 (Harmondsworth: Penguin, 1972), pp. 225f. ("The Structural Study of Myth," pp. 206–31).

99. Bruno Jöckel, "Das Reifungserlebnis im Märchen," *Psyche* 1 (1948): 382–95; abridged in Wilhelm Laiblin, ed., *Märchenforschung und Tiefenpsychologie* (Darmstadt, 1969; 2d ed., 1975), pp. 195–211 (quotation from p. 197).

100. Gonzenbach, no. 33 [ = *Italienische Volksmärchen* (note 45 above), no. 44, p. 199]; cf. Clemens Brentano, "Das Märchen von dem Baron von Hüpfenstich," after Basile, tale 5 of day 1: "The Flea" ("Lo polece"), AT 621.

101. Gonzenbach, no. 27 [ = *Italienische Volksmärchen*, no. 38, pp. 164ff.].

102. Rösch (note 19 above), pp. 80, 101.

103. Leza Uffer, ed., *Rätoromanische Märchen*, MdW (1973), no. 22; the Italian dialect text and German translation in Uffer, ed., *Schweiz-Deutschland, Begegnung der Völker im Märchen*, vol. 5 (Münster, 1972), pp. 102ff. ("beleztga mata—tutas, tutas sorts caluers!" on p. 111, the colors being a special sign of beauty).

104. Megas, p. 62; cf. Rösch (note 19 above), pp. 97, 100.

105. Scharf (note 6 above), p. 88; cf. pp. 24f. above.

106. Cf. pp. 20 above and note 53.

107. For the notion *numinous* ("mysterium tremendum et fascinosum"), see Rudolf Otto, *Das Heilige* (Breslau, 1918); translated into English as *The Idea of the Holy* by John W. Harvey (London, 1923). For the place of the numinous in the fairytale and in the local legend, see Lüthi 1943, pp. 60, 79, 96, 119, 122f., 139; Lüthi 1982, passim (consult index); Lüthi 1979, pp. 6–12, 109; Heda Jason, "Aspects of the Fabulous in Oral Literature," *Fabula* 19 (1978): 14–31 (cf. Lüthi 1979, p. 7).

108. Adolf Dirr, ed., *Kaukasische Märchen*, MdW (1920), no. 30 (Armenian), no. 9 (Georgian), both included in *Das Feuerpferd*, Diederichs *Löwenbuch* series for children, vol. 9 (Düsseldorf/Cologne, 1974), pp. 42, 9.

109. In an unpublished essay on the beautiful in fairytales (Zürich, 1975), Käthi Knüsel-Hagmann speaks of "the beautiful as an absolute concept" with "absolute power" (pp. 2, 18) and of its function as *movens* (p. 5).

## 2. STYLE AND COMPOSITION

110. See notes 2 and 105.

111. See Delarue-Tenèze, vol. 1, p. 264.

112. In her article on Egypt in EM ("Ägypten"), cols. 180f., Emma Brunner-Traut does not wish to accept the characteristics sublimation, abstraction, clearcut contours, juxtaposition, and others as features of style, since these "criteria . . . do not belong to 'style' proper but are the expression of a level of mentality"; they are "more or less characteristic of *all* of Egypt's literature"; they "characterize 'pre-Greek' literature as well as the European fairytale, for which a similar claim as to 'style' is made. But strictly speaking, it is not only the European 'fairytale' which is characterized by this style, but every genuine folktale, for sociolect and early language, just like the language of children, reflect a similar cognitive level. Therefore, one should not say that the fairytale 'sublimes', 'abstracts', or 'stylizes'. . . . Behind it is an initial, childlike experiencing of the world which allows this sort of presentation and no other" (sec. 1.2). In opposition, one can say that for the folk narrator other techniques of presentation are certainly possible: The local legend focuses more strongly on individuals, isolating and abstracting considerably less than the fairytale. It integrates its actors into a landscape, a village or city, into the group (the neighborhood); it emphasizes certain physiognomic features ("a girl with eyebrows that grow together," for example). The folksong prefers certain intermediate colors, like brown and green, which are noticeably avoided in the fairytale, with its tendency toward extremes and thus to extremes in color (see, for example, Lüthi 1982, pp. 27f., 153, note 47). The fact that the illiterate narrator is also capable of departing from his usual narrative style where he thinks it appropriate is demonstrable (see pp. 24 and 110 above). It does not seem defensible to me virtually to throw together works of higher Egyptian culture, children's language, "folk speech," and early languages, as the "reflection of a similar cognitive level." At each "cognitive level" (unconcernedly identified by Brunner-Traut with "mental attitude" [*Geisteshaltung*]) there are manifold possibilities of expression, just as there are the manifold needs of the recipient and a variety of genre styles, each of which has a specific reason for existence, its special meaning, its particular "place in life."

113. Ranke, vol. 1, p. 226.

114. Ranke, vol. 3, p. 188.

115. Charlotte Bühler and Josephine Bilz, *Das Märchen und die Phantasie des Kindes*, 3d ed. (Munich, 1971); see also the summary in Lüthi 1979, p. 106.

116. Lutz Mackensen in his article "Das deutsche Volksmärchen," in *Hand-*

*buch der deutschen Volkskunde,* vol. 2, ed. W. Peßler (Potsdam, 1938), pp. 308f., calls the pattern of threes *(Dreizahl)* a "structural formula" *(Bauformel),* in contrast to a pattern of twelves *(Zwölfzahl),* which is only a "stylistic formula" *(Stilformel).*

117. Cammann (note 90 above), pp. 39, 43, 47, 50, 54, 61f., etc.

118. *Rumänische Volksmärchen* (note 29 above), pp. 135, 137, 141, 144f., 241, 243–46, 248.

119. Schmitz, p. 145.

120. Kurt Schier and Felix Karlinger, eds., *Legendenmärchen aus Europa,* MdW (1967), p. 50; cf. p. 135; Angelika Merkelbach-Pinck *Lothringer erzählen,* vol. 1 (Saarbrücken, n.d. [1936]), p. 230; Robert Wildhaber and Leza Uffer, eds., *Schweizer Volksmärchen,* MdW (1971), p. 228; Felix Karlinger and Ulrike Ehrgott, eds., *Märchen aus Mallorca,* MdW (1968), p. 265; Ulrich Kratz, ed., *Indonesische Märchen,* MdW (1973), p. 162; Littmann, vol. 2, p. 880 (in an "Ali Baba" version), similarly, pp. 847, 854, 856, 867, 874, 879, 887, 891, 896, and 907. At the corresponding points in Galland, this formula is almost always missing; only once does one find: "Sire, laissons Ali Baba jouir des commencements de sa bonne fortune, et parlons des quarante voleurs" (at the beginning of Night 368); in other places the formula is only vaguely hinted at: "Ali Baba, cependant . . . ," "Le capitaine des voleurs, cependant. . . ."

121. In the summer of 1966, during a discussion with me in Bischofswiesen, Alfred Karasek-Langer vigorously argued this point of view.

122. Further examples are to be found in Bolte-Polívka, vol. 4, pp. 21f., in Lüthi 1982, p. 141, n. 38, and in the MdW volumes *Griechische Volksmärchen* (note 8 above), p. 235, *Rumänische Volksmärchen* (note 29 above), p. 217, and Otto Spiess, ed., *Türkische Märchen* (1967), p. 308, etc.

123. *Griechische Volksmärchen* (note 8 above), p. 268; cf. p. 274; Katherine M. Briggs, "Folk Narratives," *A Dictionary of British Folk Tales in the English Language,* vol. 1, part A (London/Bloomington, Ind., 1970), p. 318; cf. p. 332, as well as Briggs and Ruth Michaelis-Jena, eds., *Englische Volksmärchen,* MdW (1970), p. 55; Hildegard Klein, ed., *Märchen der Kabylen,* MdW (1967), p. 59.

124. *Ungarische Volksmärchen* (note 59 above), p. 147; *Rumänische Volksmärchen* (note 29 above), p. 87; cf. pp. 93, 114, 139, and 142; *Legendenmärchen* (note 120 above), p. 53; *Zigeunermärchen* (note 66 above), p. 258; cf. pp. 78, 95, 165, 228, 255, 278, and 364; Megas, pp. 60, 71; Felix Karlinger and Geraldo de Freitas, eds., *Brasilianische Märchen,* MdW (1972), p. 39 (cf. p. 40: "I slept well." "You didn't sleep at all! The fighting fox ate you up."). See Theodor Koch-Grünberg, ed., *Indianermärchen aus Südamerika,* MdW (1920), p. 330: "The words . . . 'I slept well' can be found . . . in numerous legends of this kind all through the Americas." The *jahu* is a huge fish.

125. *Ungarische Volksmärchen* (note 59 above), p. 36; cf. p. 128. Threatening to tear someone to pieces is a motif which frequently appears in legends about witches and demons.

126. *Märchen der Kabylen* (note 123 above), pp. 73, 87. See the Kurt Ranke article "Adoption" in EM. Ranke speaks of Islamic, perhaps even pre-Islamic, legal forms (Koran: "He who drinks the milk of a woman becomes her child"). Cf. also note 96.

127. Megas, pp. 122, 131; *Greichische Volksmärchen* (note 8 above), pp. 220f.

128. *Provenzalische Märchen* (note 54 above), pp. 57f. [ = Ré Soupault, ed., *Französische Märchen,* MdW (1963), p. 216]; *Griechische Volksmärchen* (note 8 above), pp. 85f.

129. Taikon, p. 97 (cf. pp. 98, 100, 133, 135, 137, 170, and 176) and p. 143.

130. "What was said was done." *Provenzalische Märchen* (note 54 above), p. 70

[ = Lüthi 1951, pp. 192, 198]; the French in Jean-François Bladé, *Contes populaires de la Gascogne*, vol. 2 (Paris, 1887), pp. 28, 36.

131. *Griechische Volksmärchen* (note 8 above), pp. 77, 117; similarly Megas, pp. 191, 193 ("We don't want to waste too many words"); Hannah Aitken and Ruth Michaelis-Jena, eds., *Schottische Volksmärchen*, MdW (1965), pp. 49f.; Georg Fausch, "Testi dialettali e tradizioni popolari della Garfagnana," Dissertation, Zürich, 1962, p. 76 (two similar instances on the same page).

132. Käte Hamburger, *The Logic of Literature*, trans. Marilynn J. Rose (Bloomington, Ind., 1973).

133. In his lecture "Sinnverknüpfung und Ironie im Roman," presented 15 January 1975 in Zürich, Hans-Jost Frey brought this last point of view again into the foreground.

134. *Russische Volksmärchen* (note 20 above), no. 26.

135. Mihai Pop, "Die Funktion der Anfangs- und Schlußformeln im rumänischen Märchen," in *Festschrift Ranke* (note 28 above), pp. 321–26. Cf. Isidor Levin in Hans F. Foltin, Ina-Maria Greverus, and Joachim Schwebe, eds., *Kontakte und Grenzen: Probleme der Volks-, Kultur-, und Sozialforschung, Festschrift für Gerhard Heilfurth zum 60. Geburtstag* (Göttingen, 1969), p. 105: "This very general observation is not at all new" ("Tiermärchen im Tadschikischen," pp. 93–113). References to Bolte-Polívka, vol. 4, pp. 17ff., 26f. and HDM, vol. 2, pp. 196–99, follow, and then he remarks: "But no researcher of the narrative before Pop had dared to bring everything together under a system resembling communication theory." And on p. 106 he observes that by no means does each opening formula correspond to a complementary closing formula.

136. Roman Jakobson, *Selected Writings*, vol. 4 (The Hague, 1966), pp. 94f. ("On Russian Fairy Tales," pp. 82–100); cf. Bolte-Polívka, vol. 4, pp. 35f.

137. *Griechische Volksmärchen* (note 8 above), pp. 216, 219; cf. Megas, pp. 220, 222, and Hahn, no. 26.

138. *Griechische Volksmärchen*, p. 238.

139. In a letter dated 12 January 1975.

140. Hahn, no 49.

141. Gonzenbach, nos. 56, 33, 54, 49. Out of a total number of ninety-two, fifty-seven, or more than half, have precisely corresponding closing formulas, beginning with no. 1: "Iddi ristaru felici e cuntenti"/"E nui ristammu senza nenti." On the other hand, two religious fairytales close as follows: "He . . . lived a holy life, and when he died he entered into paradise. And may this also be the case with us" (no. 86) and ". . . and when they died, they also went to heaven. And so may this also happen to us." (no. 87).

142. *Provenzalische Märchen* (note 54 above), pp. 16, 63.

143. Ozawa, (note 70 above), pp. 10f.

144. Levin (note 135 above), p. 102 (a little more than thirteen percent of all formulaic closings of the Tadzhik animal fairytales examined).

145. Germain Lemieux, *Placide-Eustache: Source et parallèles du conte-type 938*, Les Archives de Folklore, no. 10 (Québec, 1970), p. 194: "Pis si i's sont pas morts, i's viv' encore. C'est tout." ("That's all."); cf. Bolte-Polívka, vol. 4, pp. 30f.

146. *Griechische Volksmärchen* (note 8 above), p. 39.

147. Christian Schneller, *Märchen und Sagen aus Wälschtirol* (Innsbruck, 1867), p. 162. This is the closing of a *Rumpelstiltskin* variant and thus pointedly appropriate. Cf. Robert Petsch, *Formelhafte Schlüsse im Volksmärchen* (Berlin, 1900), p. 43.

148. See "Freiheit und Bindung im Märchen" in Lüthi 1970, pp. 170–80.

149. *Rätoromanische Märchen* (note 103 above), p. 19.

150. See Bolte-Polívka, vol. 4, p. 28 (French); Angelika Merkelbach-Pinck,

ed., *Lothringer Volksmärchen*, MdW (1961), p. 55. Being brought back to reality so roughly, no matter how playful, is reminiscent of the slap, the box on the ear (*Chlapf* in Swiss-German), which wakes someone from a trance or a state of hypnosis; cf. note 40 above (on the subject of ecstasy and shamanism). According to Sergius Golowin, who sees fairytales as reports of transformations, of "wonderous travels of the soul, often made possible with the aid of plant drugs" (dream journeys), a number of closing formulas give us a "sense of transition, of awakening from a common journey of fantastic reality back into the everyday. . . ." ("Psychedelische Volkskunde," *Antaios* 12 [1971]: 590–604). "Once, telling fairytales was one of the high points in life" (*Die Magie der verbotenen Märchen: Von Hexenkräutern und Feendrogen* [Hamburg, 1974], pp. 59f.).

151. *Rätoromanische Märchen* (note 103 above), pp. 242, 248.

152. Hahn, no. 64 (Variant 3).

153. Taikon, pp. 192, 234, 282; cf. pp. 40, 158, 167, 183: "Sas pe, haj nas pe" ("It was, and it wasn't"); cf. Tadzhik "bud na bud" ("It was or not"), which accounts for more than ninety-six percent of the formulaic openings in the material examined by Levin (see notes 135 and 144 above).

154. Ortutay (note 74 above), p. 73.

155. Linda Dégh, *Märchen, Erzähler und Erzählgemeinschaft* (Berlin, 1962), p. 342.

156. *Türkische Märchen* (note 122 above), no. 28.

157. See Bladé (note 130 above), vol. 1 (1886), p. xlii.

158. In the Italian edition of Propp (see note 3 above), p. 222: "leggi formali (della composizione) . . . ferree."

159. For the term *Antimärchen* ("anti-fairytale"), coined by André Jolles, see the Elfriede Moser-Rath article "Antimärchen" in EM. Peter Dienstbier, who emphasizes the "libertarian character" of the fairytale, unlike Jolles, does not wish to call the "tragic fairytales" anti-fairytales, but rather narratives constructed like fairytales which stand in "contradiction to the international typology of the fairytale" and which represent an "ideological transformation of it into its opposite" ("Carlo Gozzi, Jean Cocteau und die Identität des Märchens: Ursachen und Zustände typologischer Deformation beim Märchen in seiner Entwichlung bis zur Gegenwart," Dissertation, Salzburg, 1975, pp. 3, 49: *"Der Sarotti-Mohr macht Märchen wahr* ("The Sarotti Moor turns fairytale into reality") runs the ad of a German chocolate firm: That is the essence of the anti-fairytale summarized in one sentence."). For the present writer, the term applies both to "fairytales with unhappy ending," in the sense of Röhrich (pp. 46–62) and of André Jolles (*Einfache Formen* [Tübingen, 1930; reprint, 1974], p. 202), and to narratives of the *Lucky Hans* type (see pp. 137f.) and negative contrastive episodes within the normal fairytale (Lüthi 1981, p. 81).

160. Röhrich, pp. 48f.

161. Alan Dundes, *The Morphology of North American Indian Folktales*, FFC no. 195 (Helsinki, 1964), pp. 61–64.

162. Propp, pp. 35f. (Function VIIIa).

163. The "Erdtkülin," "Ein schön History von einer Frawen mit zweien Kindlin" [The little earth cow: A beautiful story of a woman and her two children], is the earliest relatively faithful German-language record of a fairytale—by Martin Montanus in *Ander theyl der Gartengesellschaft* (Strasbourg, ca. 1560); see Albert Wesselski, *Deutsche Märchen vor Grimm* (Leipzig, 1938), pp. 1–10, 304–14, and Lüthi 1976a, pp. 71–81.

164. See Propp, pp. 30ff. (Function VIII).

165. See Lüthi 1982, pp. 130f., where some basic structural and nonstructural differences between the myth and the fairytale have been assembled, partially

based on Meletinsky: In the myth the most important goals are contact with guardian spirits and the acquisition of natural objects and cultural artifacts, which in the fairytale are only a means to an end or intermediate goals; tests play an important role in the fairytale, but a rather unimportant one in the myth; in the fairytale the "lack of something" mainly affects a single person, in the myth, a group; the myth can do without bringing in human beings, but in the fairytale of magic, man is the central carrier of the action. Cf. note 351 below.

166. Propp, pp. 26f.

167. Donatus: "Inter tragoediam autem et comoediam cum multa tum inprimis hoc distat . . . : illic prima turbulenta, tranquilla ultima, in tradoedia contrario ordine res aguntur" (comedy: "laeti . . . sunt exitus actionum"; tragedy: "exitus funesti habentur"). See Paul Wessner's edition of the *Commentum Terenti* of Donatus, p. 20 (praef. 4, par. 2). Diomedes: "Comoedia a tragoedia differt . . . , quod in illa frequenter et paene semper laetis rebus exitus tristes et leberorum fortunarumque priorum in peius adgnitio. . . ." (the sentence has come down to us incomplete). See Heinrich Keil's edition of the *Ars grammatica* of Diomedes, p. 488 (bk. 3, sec. "De poematibus") in *Grammatici Latini*, vol. 1 (Leipzig, 1857). The documentation of these quotations I owe to my colleague Hermann Tränkle.

168. Karl Haiding, *Märchen und Schwänke aus Oberösterreich* (Berlin, 1969), p. 11 (AT 570 combined with 314): In addition, the rabbit-herd has to be success-ful in jousts; the magic helper brings him "snow-white armor; . . . it fit like a glove—because this is a story, and in a story everything has to fit."

169. Paul Zaunert, ed., *Deutsche Märchen seit Grimm*, MdW (1912; rev. ed. 1964, Elfriede Moser-Rath), no. 1.

170. Cf. my article "Goal-Orientation in Storytelling," in Linda Dégh, Henry Glassie, and Felix Oinas, eds., *Folklore Today: Festschrift for Richard M. Dorson* (Bloomington, Ind., 1976), pp. 357–68.

171. Megas, (note 35 above), pp. 157–66; Eberhard-Boratav, pp. 212ff.; *Griechische Volksmärchen* (note 8 above), no. 32; R. M. Dawkins, *Modern Greek Folktales* (Oxford, 1953), no. 32; *More Greek Folktales* (1955), no. 5; Gonzenbach, no. 11. See also Megas (note 7 above).

172. See Leopold Schmidt, *Die Volkserzählung* (Berlin, 1963), pp. 145–55 ("Pelops und die Haselhexe").

173. For example, Josef Müller, *Sagen aus Uri* (Basel, 1929; reprint, 1969), no. 917; Johannes Jegerlehner, *Sagen aus dem Unterwallis* (Basel, 1909), pp. 107ff.

174. Basile, tale 5 of day 5: "Sole, Luna e Talia," Perrault: "La Belle au bois dormant"; cf. Fritz Ernst, *Dornröschen in drei Sprachen* (Bern, 1949). In his article "Die 'Stockhessischen' Märchen der 'Alten Marie': Das Ende eines Mythos um die frühesten KHM-Aufzeichnungen der Brüder Grimm," *Germanisch-Romanische Monatsschrift* 25 (1975): 74–86, Heinz Rölleke argues that it is young Marie Hassenpflug (1788–1856) and not, as had been believed, the aged Marie Müller (1747–1826), housekeeper in the family of the apothecary Wild, who must be regarded as the source of numerous Grimms' fairytales.

175. See HDA, vol. 2, pp. 92–95; cf. p. 58 above (note 169).

176. HDA, vol. 2, p. 99. The Karl Spiess article "Abschlagen der Ferse" (pp. 92–104) offers a number of examples of the "tiny loss."

177. See Megas (note 7 above).

178. Geneviève Massignon, *Contes corses* (Aix-en-Provence, 1969), no. 76.

179. Haltrich (note 11 above), no. 24.

180. Cosquin (note 93 above); cf. p. 31 above.

181. See *Archivio per lo Studio delle Tradizioni Popolari*, vol. 1 (1882), pp. 525ff.; cf. Lüthi 1975, pp. 81f. ("Il bacio").

182. *Kaukasische Märchen* (note 108 above), no. 30 [ = *Das Feuerpferd* (note 108 above), pp. 43ff.].

183. Massignon (note 178 above), no. 77.

184. *Rätoromanische Märchen* (note 103 above), no. 29.

185. Delarue-Tenèze, vol. 2, pp. 77–81.

186. *Zigeunermärchen* (note 66 above), no. 8.

187. *Rätoromanische Märchen* (note 103 above), no. 28.

188. Hahn, no. 66 (from Syra); Dawkins 1953 (note 171 above), no. 33; Eberhard-Boratav, Type 154; Schmitz, pp. 99–102; cf. Megas (note 35 above).

189. Schmitz, p. 259.

190. Ibid., p. 260 (Irish).

191. *Provenzalische Märchen* (note 54 above), p. 41.

192. Ibid., p. 28.

193. Littmann, vol. 2, p. 853 (Night 270).

194. Ranke, vol. 3, p. 22.

195. See Lüthi 1982, pp. 62ff.

196. Ibid.

197. Volker Roloff, *Reden und Schweigen* (Munich, 1973), p. 119: "The harsh, unexplained interdiction, one apparently not understood by Enide, shows clearly . . . the characteristics of taboo"; p. 171: ". . . the irrational taboo requirement of the fairytale theme."

198. Ibid., p. 189.

199. Gyula Ortutay, "Principles of Oral Transmission in Folklore," *Acta Ethnographica* 8 (1959): 175–221. The Bogatyrev-Jakobson notion of the "absolute domination of the correcting influence of the group" (see p. x above) already points in this direction.

200. According to Vilma Mönckeberg, *Das Märchen und unsere Welt* (Düsseldorf/Cologne, 1972), p. 188.

201. On the balance between constraint and freedom in general, see Lüthi 1970, pp. 170–80.

202. See "Aspects of the *Märchen* and the Legend," *Genre* 2 (1966): 162–78 (reprinted in German in Felix Karlinger, ed., *Wege der Märchenforschung* [Darmstadt, 1973], pp. 408–27); "Urform und Zielform in Sage und Märchen," in Lüthi 1970, pp. 198–210 (a Hungarian translation with a few additions is to be found in *Ethnographica* 85 [Budapest, 1974]: 1–17); "Europäische Volksliteratur—Themen, Motive, Zielkräfte," in Albert Schaefer, ed., *Weltliteratur und Volksliteratur* (Munich, 1972), pp. 55–79; and "Goal-Orientation in Storytelling," in *Festschrift Dorson* (note 170 above). Here is also a connection with Roman Jakobson, who uses the terms *goal-orientation, end-directedness, purposiveness, anticipation, teleology, teleonomy,* and *finality* in his *Main Trends in the Science of Language* (New York, 1974), pp. 55–57; for him, goal-orientation is "a manifest, perhaps even decisive, difference" between "living systems" and "objects of inorganic nature"; see also the section entitled "Teleonomy" in Elmar Holenstein, *Roman Jakobson's Approach to Language: Phenomenological Structuralism,* trans. Catherine Schelbert and Tarcisius Schelbert (Bloomington, Ind./ London, 1976), pp. 118–21. For the relationship to Sganzini's notion of "anticipation" *(Vorwegnahme),* see note 231.

203. See Ernst Böklen, *Sneewittchenstudien,* vol. 1 (Leipzig, 1910; reprint, 1974), p. 95.

204. Hahn, no. 19.

205. Róna-Sklarek (note 47 above), no. 8 [ = Lüthi 1951, pp. 455ff.]. Evidently the asymmetry does not bother the narrator who makes use of isolation any more

than it does the audience taking in each scene as isolated—presumably it is not even noticed.

206. The formulation from Peter Dienstbier (note 159 above), pp. 161f.

207. See *Zeitschrift des Historischen Vereins für Steiermark* 55 (1964): 132f. ("Ländliche Erzähltypen," pp. 117–33).

208. *Jahrbuch für ostdeutsche Volkskunde* 10 (1966/67): 123 ("Porträt eines ungarndeutschen Märchenerzählers," pp. 120–41).

209. Karlinger (note 74 above).

210. *Italienische Volksmärchen* (note 45 above), pp. 265f.

211. Cammann (note 90 above), p. 47.

212. This shift of tenses can be observed in many tales which have been taken down faithfully; the shift from third person to first person, though, of course, less frequent, is also well documented. See, for example, Gottfried Henßen, *Überlieferung und Persönlichkeit* (Münster, 1951), p. 25; Taikon, pp. 173ff., 260, 288f.

213. Maja Bošković-Stulli, ed., *Kroatische Volksmärchen*, MdW (1975), p. 295.

214. Ibid., pp. 288f.

215. See notes 202 and 170 above.

216. See "Die Lügenbrücke" in Edith Ennen and Günter Wiegelmann, eds., *Festschrift Matthias Zender: Studien zu Volkskultur, Sprache, und Landesgeschichte*, vol. 1 (Bonn, 1972), pp. 868–74 (quotation from p. 873). Jaromír Jech has concerned himself with the phenomenon of stability and variability in mode of narration (of one and the same narrator, but also examining different narrative types). See "Variabilität und Stabilität in den einzelnen Kategorien der Volksprosa," *Fabula* 9 (1967): 55–62, and "Relativitätsaspekte bei der Beurteilung der Variabilität und Stabilität," in *Festschrift Ranke* (note 28 above), pp. 115–31.

217. Cf. Courtès (note 4 above), pp. 28, 36.

## 3. Technical Means and Artistic Effects

218. *Novalis: Gesammelte Werke*, ed. Carl Seeling (Zürich, 1946), vol 4, p. 301, no. 3053; see also Lüthi 1975, p. 154. On the subject of art as organ of knowledge, see St. Thomas Aquinas, pp. 26. above (esthetics as the study of αἴσθησις, sensory perception).

219. Klara Stroebe, ed., *Nordische Volksmärchen*, vol. 2, MdW (1915); omitted in the reprinting of 1967 (Stroebe and Reidar Th. Christiansen), but reprinted in Lüthi 1951, pp. 102ff.

220. Erna Pomeranzewa, *Russische Volksmärchen* (Berlin, 1964), no. 17 (Afanás'ev, vol. 1, no. 36).

221. HDM, vol. 2, pp. 165–91 (quotation from p. 170); cf. p. 179.

222. See Lüthi 1976, pp. 101–10 (p. 101: "High spirits and creature comforts— these are the poles of the farce").

223. Roman Jakobson, *Child Language, Aphasia, and Phonological Universals* (The Hague, 1968), pp. 20–31.

224. "Die Metamorphose der Pflanze," written in 1798 and in 1817 incorporated into the first fascicle of *Zur Morphologie* (as part of the essay "Verfolg"; cf. *Versuch, die Metamorphose der Pflanze zu erklären* from 1790). On p. 29, Jakobson points out that "a short period may sometimes intervene between the stage of spontaneous babbling and that of true language development, in which children are completely mute" (an observation made by E. Meumann in *Die Sprache des Kindes* [Zürich, 1903]). Goethe notes something similar in the transition from leaf to blossom:

Blattlos aber und schnell erhebt sich der zärtere Stengel,
Und ein Wundergebild zieht den Betrachtenden an.

But leafless and quick the more delicate shoot rises,
And a wondrous creation catches the eye of the beholder.

225. HDM, vol. 2, p. 166.

226. *Russische Volksmärchen* (note 20 above), no. 29.

227. *Deutsche Volksmärchen* (note 89 above), nos. 15, 17 (in Ranke, vol. 2, pp. 201f., 23f.).

228. Axel Olrik, "Epische Gesetze der Volksdichtung," *Zeitschrift für deutsches Altertum* 51 (1909): 1–12 (emphasis on the final element [*Achtergewicht*], p. 7). Other "laws" are repetition *(Wiederholung)*, p. 3; contrast *(Gegensatz)*, p. 6; and single-strandedness *(Einsträngigkeit)*, p. 8. English translation "The Epic Laws of Folk Narrative," in Alan Dundes, ed., *The Study of Folklore* (Englewood Cliffs, N.J., 1965), pp. 129–41.

229. Uffer, pp. 69–71.

230. Bennison Gray, "Repetition in Oral Literature," *Journal of American Folklore* 84 (1971): 288–303. Gray's prime example is tale no. 4 of Linda Dégh's *Folktales of Hungary* (Chicago, 1965): "Pretty Maid Ilonka" (AT 407 B). The tale contains the well-known denial of having seen a "tremendum" from the *Our Lady's child* story (cf. the model narrative, pp. 2–5 above).

231. As early as his lectures from the 1920s and '30s at the University of Bern. In the collection of essays published by Hans Ryffel and Gottfried Frankhauser, *Carlo Sganzini (1881–1948): Ursprung und Wirklichkeit* (Bern, 1951), see principally the essay "Vom grundsätzlichen Gebrauche des Gesichtspunkts 'Vorwegnahme' (Antizipation)," first published in 1940: "Anticipation . . . [is] in a fundamental and universal sense the essence of the mind *(des Seelischen)*" (p. 130); see also "Zur Biogenese des Erkennens," first published in 1928: "What happens in life [is] (unmediated or mediated) always the actualization of situational anticipations built up in advance" (p. 273). Anticipation is the keystone of Sganzini's philosophical theories, as well as of his theories of psychology and pedagogy. In Bloch, the phenomenon of anticipation stands at the center of his theories of utopia and change. "Das antizipierende Bewußtsein" is the title of the second part of his major work *Das Prinzip Hoffnung* (first published in Berlin, 1954; paperback, Frankfurt am Main, 1973, pp. 49–391). The final sentence, "Krummes will gerade werden, Halbes voll" ("What is crooked wishes to be straight; what is half full, to be full"), can be brought together with the Jakobsonian notion of teleonomy and with the striving toward end forms which we have attributed to "folk narrators" (see note 202 above). For the history of the term (first attested in Epicurus: πρόληψις and in Latin in the writings of Cicero), see Joachim Ritter, ed., *Historisches Wörterbuch der Philosophie* (Basel, 1971), vol. 1, cols. 419–25 (H. Ebling and F. Weinert); cf. pp. 79 and 92 above on the subject of remembering as the complement of anticipation.

232. For example, Karlinger (note 74 above), p. 39.

233. This well-known motif (H 13 *Recognition by overheard conversation,* "using a trick to escape an oath," "confessing to a stove") is already attested in ancient times: Chelidonis tells a water pitcher that she was raped by Aëdon's husband and that on pain of death she has been sworn to silence. Aëdon is listening. See the Kurt Ranke article "Aëdon" in EM. On "confessing to a stove," in particular, see HDA, vol. 4, cols. 1192f.

234. *Tschechische Volksmärchen* (note 61 above), no. 2. In the Hungarian

fairytale "Das gemalte Zimmer" [The painted room], no. 15 in Ortutay (note 74 above), the painting is particularly rich; the story, divided into more than twenty scenes, is almost completely repeated, and on the walls there are painted dialogs (!): "That was all painted there," as the eighty-four-year-old farmer put it in 1915. (H 11.1.3 *Life story painted on wall*, AT 506, IVb.)

235. Lüthi 1951, pp. 170ff; the French in F. M. Luzel, *Contes populaires de Basse Bretagne*, vol. 3 (Paris, 1887), p. 337 (AT 853).

236. Marie-Louise Tenèze, *Approches de nos traditions orales* (Paris, 1970), pp. 20–24, with reference to AT 853 ("Du conte merveilleux comme genre," pp. 11–65).

237. In a lecture, which has unfortunately remained in manuscript, delivered at a conference of Swiss high school teachers in the fall of 1956.

238. Pino-Saavedra (note 28 above), pp. 319f. The story was recorded on tape in 1965, the narrator a seventy-one-year-old Chilean farmer.

239. For example, Ranke, vol. 2., p. 276.

240. Cf. p. 44 above, note 116.

241. See Lüthi in *Festschrift Dorson* (note 170 above).

242. Goethe, 1810: "Jedes ausgesprochene Wort erregt den Gegensinn" ("Each word uttered evokes its opposite"), *Wahlverwandtschaften*, pt. 2, chapt. 4; see Lüthi in *Festschrift Dorson* (note 170 above), note 3.

243. Cf. "the moment of final tension" before the catastrophe in Gustaf Freitag's *Technik des Dramas*, 11th printing (Leipzig, 1908), pp. 118ff. (chap. 2, sec. 4). While in the literary tragedy a last flickering of hope can precede the catastrophe, the fairytale prefers the reverse subordination contrast, a last negative interlude before the final radiant triumph of the positive.

244. *Griechische Volksmärchen* (note 8 above), no. 48; cf. Megas (note 35 above), pp. 129f., 133f., and Lüthi 1976a, pp. 87–94.

245. AT 531, *Bulgarische Volksmärchen* (note 60 above), no. 16; as contrast, cf. the medieval Tristan romances.

246. See Sándor Solymossy, "Elements orientaux dans les contes populaires hongrois," *Revue des Études Hongrois* 6 (Paris, 1928): 311–36, in particular pp. 314–25. Solymossy believes the motif to be part of the inheritance of the Hungarians from a time when they were still living on the Sarmatian Plain (p. 325).

247. Gonzenbach, no. 28 [ = Lüthi 1951, pp. 231ff.].

248. *Bulgarische Volksmärchen* (note 60 above), no. 24, Eberhard-Boratav Type 91.

249. Bolte-Polívka, vol. 2, p. 162 (on KHM 81 "Bruder Lustig"), HDM, vol. 1, p. 87.

250. See Hannjost Lixfeld, *Gott und Teufel als Weltschöpfer* (Munich, 1971), passim.

251. Cf. Alan Dundes, "The Binary Structure of 'Unsuccessful Repetition' in Lithuanian Folktales," *Western Folklore* 11 (1962): 165–74, especially p. 170.

252. Haiding (note 9 above), no. 62; cf. *Brasilianische Märchen* (note 124 above), no. 86 (a Malazarte story; Malazarte is the malicious Brazilian "Eulenspiegel"). For the Austrian farce fairytale, see my article "Regisseure und Marionetten im Raum der Volkserzählung," in *Festschrift Zender* (note 216 above), pp. 857–67 (quotation from p. 863); other forms of long-distance manipulation *(Fernregie)* are to be found on pp. 859–61.

253. Text and German translation in Karl Langosch,*Waltharius, Ruodlieb: Märchenepen* (Basel/Stuttgart, 1956), pp. 251–305 (quotation from pp. 204f.). Langosch believes that the writer has extended "the fairytale and elevated it from oral into written tradition" (p. 380).

254. For the *Hodscha Nasredin*, see the two-volume edition of Albert Wesselski (Weimar, 1911); for Johannes Pauli's *Schimpf und Ernst*, the edition of Johannes Bolte (Berlin, 1924; reprint, Hildesheim, 1972)—both containing rich commentary. For Aesop, see Walter Wienert, *Die Typen der griechischrömischen Fabel* (Narrative Type 45: *Der Esel will wie das Hündchen seinen Herrn liebkosen* [The donkey, like the little dog, wants to fawn on its master]), the Greek in Carl Halm, ed., *Fabulae Aesopicae Collectae* (Leipzig, 1901).

255. See Bolte-Polívka, vol. 2, pp. 468ff.; Mia I. Gerhardt, *Two Wayfarers* (Utrecht, 1964), pp. 9–13; and my article "Dichterische Ökonomie in der Volkserzählung," in Walter Escher, Theo Gantner, and Hans Trümpy, eds., *Festschrift für Robert Wildhaber zum 70. Geburtstag* [ = *Schweizerisches Archiv für Volkskunde*, vol. 68/69] (Basel, 1973), pp. 388–98, in particular p. 390 with respect to KHM 107.

256. Johannes Bolte, 1930: "The Simeli Mountain fairytale . . . has come down directly from Ali Baba" (Bolte-Polívka, vol. 4, p. 405; similarly, vol. 3., pp. 138f.); von der Leyen, 1964: "It is a predecessor of the Arabian original" (*Das deutsche Märchen und die Brüder Grimm* [Düsseldorf/Cologne], p. 327). This vast difference of opinion between two of the most prominent folktale scholars of our century illustrates the difficulty and uncertainty in determining origins. It seems to me that the evidence here favors Bolte's hypothesis.

257. Martin Luserke, "Shakespeare und das heutige deutsche Laienspiel," *Shakespeare-Jahrbuch* 69 (1933): 117ff. The neologism *premitation* was coined by Christine Trautvetter as a translation for Luserke's term *Vorahmung*. See Lüthi, "Imitation and Anticipation in Folktales," in Nikolai Burlakoff and Carl Lindahl, eds., *Folklore on Two Continents: Essays in Honor of Linda Dégh* (Bloomington, Ind., 1980), pp. 3–13, especially p. 4.

258. Dundes (note 251 above), p. 173.

259. See Johannes Itten, *Kunst der Farbe* (Ravensburg, 1961), pp. 104–109: "The quantity contrast . . . is a proportion contrast. . . . That color which is in the minority, endangered, so to speak, offers resistance and appears more luminous, . . . more intensive and stimulating" (p. 107).

260. See Röhrich, passim.

261. *Deutsche Märchen seit Grimm* (note 169 above), pp. 402–12 ("Bruder und Schwester").

262. Similarly, *Deutsche Volksmärchen* (note 89 above), no. 75, and *Märchen aus Mallorca* (note 120 above), no. 14.

263. Ewa Bukowska-Grosse and Erwin Koschmieder, eds., *Polnische Volksmärchen*, MdW (1967), no. 32; cf. Jaromír Jech, *Tschechische Volksmärchen* (Berlin, 1961), no. 23.

264. *Bulgarische Volksmärchen* (note 60 above), no. 12; similarly, *Kaukasische Märchen*, no. 30 [ = *Das Feuerpferd* (note 108 above), pp. 43ff.].

265. Hahn, no. 70; Felix Karlinger, ed., *Inselmärchen des Mittelmeeres*, MdW (1960), no. 16 (from Syra).

266. *Tschechische Volksmärchen* (note 61 above), no. 8.

267. Wilhelm Wisser, ed., *Plattdeutsche Volksmärchen*, MdW (1914), p. 163; Wisser (rev. ed., 1970), no. 46; similarly, Gonzenbach, no. 64.

268. *Balkanmärchen* (note 18 above), no. 23 (Serbian); for still other methods, see the compilation in Bolte-Polívka, vol. 1, p. 514.

269. Karlinger (note 74 above), no. 9. For the answering spittle, see Bolte-Polívka, vol. 1, p. 501; vol. 2, pp. 526f.; and Motif D 1001 and 1611.5 (AT 313). The drying out of the spittle is also mentioned expressly in other places, e.g., in Gonzenbach, no. 14.

270. Karlinger (note 74 above), no. 7.

271. Megas, pp. 81f; correspondingly in Paul Zaunert, ed., *Deutsche Märchen aus dem Donaulande*, MdW (1926), p. 86 (in the 2d ed. of 1958, pp. 90f.). On the subject, see Haiding (note 9 above), p. 54, differing from Lüthi 1975, p. 147.

272. Heinz Barüske, *Skandinavische Märchen* (Frankfurt am Main, 1972), p. 100 (a Norwegian *two brothers* tale).

273. A number of examples can be found in my article on poetic economy in *Festschrift Wildhaber* (note 255 above).

274. *Deutsche Volksmärchen* (note 89 above), no. 42 (Sudeten German).

275. *Schweizer Volksmärchen* (note 120 above), p. 185.

276. *Provenzalische Märchen* (note 54 above), p. 185.

277. *Rumänische Volksmärchen* (note 29 above), p. 178.

278. *Provenzalische Märchen*, p. 74.

279. *Schweizer Volksmärchen*, p. 184.

280. *Rumänische Volksmärchen*, p. 53.

281. Ibid., p. 67.

282. *Schweizer Volksmärchen*, p. 150.

283. *Rumänische Volksmärchen*, p. 48.

284. Ibid., p. 59.

285. *Provenzalische Märchen*, p. 140.

286. *Tschechische Volksmärchen* (note 61 above), p. 39.

287. Ibid., p. 255.

288. Ibid., p. 256.

289. *Rumänische Volksmärchen* (note 29 above), pp. 216f., 231.

290. Cammann (note 90 above), p. 82.

291. Ibid., p. 84.

292. Ibid., p. 68.

293. *Kroatische Volksmärchen* (note 213 above), pp. 293f.

294. *Tschechische Volksmärchen* (note 61 above), p. 167.

295. Lutz Röhrich, "Rumpelstilzchen: Vom Methodenpluralismus in der Erzählforschung," in *Festschrift Wildhaber* (note 255 above), pp. 567–96 (quotation from p. 595); reprinted in Röhrich, *Sage und Märchen: Erzählforschung heute* (Freiburg/Basel/Vienna, 1976), pp. 272–91.

296. Werner (note 208 above), p. 138.

297. Ranke, vol. 1, p. 44.

298. Uffer, pp. 22f.

299. Ranke, vol. 1, p. 55.

## 4. Interaction of Motifs and Themes

300. Cf. Eleasar M. Meletinsky, "Typological Analysis of the Paleo-Asiatic Raven Myths," *Acta Ethnographica* 22 (Budapest, 1973): 110: "Man is not distinct from the universe surrounding him . . . . Metamorphosis is, in this context, just as simple as, say, changing clothing or masks."

301. Cf. Röhrich, pp. 64f. and note 269 above.

302. Cf. p. 64 above, note 181.

303. Bertha Ilg, *Maltesische Märchen und Schwänke*, vol. 1, (Hanover, 1901), no. 51.

304. Such is the case in the following episode of our Maltese fairytale (quoted in Lüthi 1975, pp. 80f.). There are numerous examples in Antti Aarne, *Schwänke über schwerhörige Menschen*, FFC no. 20 (Hamina, 1914).

305. Delarue-Tenèze, vol. 1, pp. 177f.

306. Ilg (note 303 above), vol. 1, no. 2; cf. Lüthi 1975, p. 81.

307. Gonzenbach, no. 55. Motif D 2006.1.1 and 1413.15, 1413.16; cf. AT 313 Vb, 425 N, Swahn (note 94 above), pp. 35, 344, and Bolte-Polívka, vol. 2, pp. 231, 234, 517, 527; cf. also *Provenzalische Märchen* (note 54 above), no. 2, and Ranke, vol. 1, p. 156, no. 2.

308. J. R. Bünker, *Schwänke, Sagen und Märchen in heanzischer Mundart* (Leipzig, 1906), no. 78.

309. Róna-Sklarek (note 47 above), no. 13 (here the forgetful bridegroom himself becomes the duped suitor!); Ortutay (note 154 above), no. 16.

310. Eileen O'Faoláin, *Children of the Salmon and Other Irish Folktales* (London, 1965), p. 265.

311. Richard Wossidlo and Gottfried Henßen, *Mecklenburger erzählen* (Berlin, 1957), no. 31.

312. KHM, 1st ed. (1812), no. 54 (Bolte-Polívka, vol. 1, pp. 485ff.).

313. Uffer, pp. 26f.

314. Roloff (note 197 above), p. 21.

315. Motif C 400–499 *Speaking tabu* (cf. 944 *Dumbness as punishment for breaking tabu*).

316. *Rumänische Volksmärchen* (note 29 above), no. 23 (told in 1956).

317. *Rätoromanische Märchen* (note 103 above), no. 21; the Rhaeto-romance text with literal German translation in Uffer (note 103 above), pp. 41–55.

318. Uffer (note 24 above), pp. 62f.

319. Bünker (note 308 above), p. 99.

320. *Balkanmärchen* (note 18 above), no. 46.

321. Felix Karlinger, *Einführung in die romanische Volksliteratur*, vol. 1 (Munich, 1969), pp. 148f. St. Brandan was a sixth-century Irish saint. The tenth-century life narrates his journey into the otherworld and is permeated with features from visionary literature (discussed by the late Ernst Mudrak in a manuscript concerned with the interrelations between literature and popular tradition, pp. 105f.), but, according to Karlinger, the structure of the frame is similar to that of the fairytale.

322. For example, in the Rhaeto-romance fairytale about the princess from days of yore (AT 516). See *Schweizer Volksmärchen* (note 120 above), no. 55.

323. Cammann (note 90 above), pp. 43f.

324. *Italienische Volksmärchen* (note 45 above), no. 20. AT 408 *The three oranges*, but here one finds a walnut, a hazelnut, and a chestnut; cf. *Mazedonische Märchen* (note 86 above), a twig.

325. Adorno (note 83 above), p. 84.

326. Andreas Briner, "Kommet, eilet, laufet," *Neue Züricher Zeitung*, 29/30 March 1975 (no. 73), p. 53, on Johann Sebastian Bach's Easter Oratorio.

327. According to Meletinsky in the German edition of Propp (see note 3 above), p. 214.

328. Stith Thompson, *The Folktale*, 2d ed. (New York, 1951; reprint, Berkeley/Los Angeles/London, 1977), pp. 415–16.

329. Cf. Gaston Paris, "Die undankbare Gattin," *Zeitschrift für Volkskunde* 13 (1903): 1–24, 129–50; on this matter, see Georg Polívka, "Die treulose Gattin," ibid., pp. 399–412; Karel Horálek, "Ein Beitrag zu dem Studium der afrikanischen Märchen," *Archiv Orientální* 32 (1964): 501–21, particularly pp. 515–19; and Horálek, "Zur Neuauflage des internationalen Märchenkatalogs," *Zeitschrift für Slawistik* 9 (1964): 439–49, particularly pp. 445–47.

330. Cf. Knüsel-Hagmann (note 109 above), p. 10: "There is only absolute beauty; anything less is of no interest. . . . Snow White's mother, who, because of her daughter, is demoted from most beautiful to second most beautiful, is thus also wicked."

331. Tadzhik *bud na bud;* see Levin (note 135 above), pp. 101, 103, and cf. note 153 above.

332. Ortutay (note 74 above), p. 73.

333. Pop (note 135 above), p. 323, and note 28 above for the Rumanian.

334. Taikon, p. 282.

335. Ibid., p. 284.

336. Pop (note 135 above), p. 325.

337. Cf. p. 49 above and note 135.

338. See Oskar Dähnhardt, *Natursagen,* vol. 4 (Leipzig/Berlin, 1912), pp. 46–97.

339. Cf. Lüthi, "Rumpelstilzchen," *Antaios* 12 (1971): 419–36.

340. See my lecture "Ironien in der Volkserzählung," printed in Juha Pentikäinen and Tuula Juurikka, eds., *Folk Narrative Research: Some Papers Presented at the VI Congress of the International Society for Folk Narrative Research,* Studia Fennica no. 20 (Helsinki, 1976), pp. 62–74.

341. Cf. also Lüthi 1976, pp. 63, 65, 68, 72f., and 76.

342. On the significance of anger and other changes of disposition, see my article "Affekte" in EM.

343. Investigating the incidence of contrary irony in literature (for example, in that of the ancient Greeks) would, in my opinion, be a rewarding task. I hope to have the opportunity to look more closely at the contrary irony in Goethe's *Iphigenie.*

344. Laurits Bødker, ed., *Dänische Volksmärchen,* MdW (1964), no. 6 [ = Lüthi 1951, pp. 12ff.]; cf. P. Asbjörnsen and Jörgen Moe, *Norwegische Volksmärchen* (Berlin, n.d. [1908]), pp. 1ff. (male Cinderella, see note 359 below) and pp. 237ff. ("Schmierbock"). Both tales are full of irony and displays of cleverness in manipulation similar to what is found in the Ederland tale, but are not as typical. On the difference between eating humans and cannibalism, see Jacques Geninasca, "Conte populaire et identité du cannibalisme," *Nouvelle Revue de Psychanalyse* 6 (1972): 215–20 (cf. Lüthi 1979, pp. 130f.).

345. Motif K 1611 *Substituted caps* can be found as early as the classical Greek Aëdon legend (see note 233 above). Jealous of Niobe, Aëdon kills not Niobe's son but her own, since the boys' nightcaps have been switched. Motif G 61 *Relative's flesh eaten unwillingly* also appears: Aëdon kills and cooks her husband's son and serves him up to the father to eat *(Thyestean feast).* See Ranke, "Aëdon" in EM.

346. For example, *Italienische Volksmärchen* (note 45 above), no. 1 (AT 311, Motif G 561).

347. At 774, 785, "Wer aß das Herz des Lammes?" ("Who ate the lamb's heart?"). Available on recording with written commentary: Johannes Künzig, Waltraud Werner, and Hannjost Lixfeld, *Schwänke aus mündlicher Überlieferung* (Frieburg, 1973).

348. See my Athens lecture, "Parallele Themen in der Volkserzählung und in der Hochliteratur," in Lüthi 1970, pp. 90–99, in particular pp. 90 and 99, and "Themen und Motive im Werke Shakespeares," ibid., pp. 114–24, in particular p. 121.

## 5. PORTRAIT OF MAN

349. Lüthi 1979, pp. 88f; as contrast, see p. 27. above: A narrator who is himself a minstrel does not necessarily make his heroes minstrels, not even where that would obviously fit.

350. On the differentiation of male and female roles (the frequency of the Griselda and stepmother/witch types), see p. 156.

351. Karl Justus Obenauer, *Das Märchen: Dichtung und Deutung* (Frankfurt am Main, 1959), p. 35: "The fairytale's way of thinking is more human [than the myth's] . . . it is clearly interested in what is characteristically human." In my dissertation (Lüthi 1943, p. 113), I contrast the myth, the fairytale, and the local legend as follows: "All three forms have their own laws and characteristics. . . . The myth is a poetic view of a nonhuman world. The fairytale delineates in an abstractly stylized manner human destinies full of interactions with the other-worldly. In the local legend, it is specifically the experiencing of such interactions which constitutes the focus of the narrative and determines its form." Cf. note 165 above.

352. See Walter Scherf, "Ablösungskonflikte in Zaubermärchen und Kinder-spiel," *Medien und Sexualpädagogik* 2, no. 4 (1974): 4–24: Fairytales are told "because the accumulated family conflicts of the listeners demand it. . . . Fairy-tales are psychodramas about family conflicts which have to be worked out" (p. 21). "The function of the fairytale of magic and of certain children's games is precisely release and self-discovery" (p. 23). See also my article "Familie und Natur im Märchen" in Lüthi 1970, pp. 63–78.

353. See especially Arnold Gehlen, "Grundzüge einer Gesamttheorie des Menschen: Mängelwesen und Prometheus" (1942), reprinted in the Gehlen col-lection, *Anthropologische Forschung*, rowohlts deutsche enzyklopädie (Reinbek, 1961), p. 46. Cf. Herder: "The human child enters the world weaker than none of the animals. . . . The weak child is . . . an invalid because of its superior abilities." (*Ideen zur Philosophie der Geschichte der Menschheit*, pt. 1, bk. 4, chap. 4 [1784]).

354. "Das Märchen als Weltordnung," *Neue Rundschau* (1970), p. 78.

355. Ernst Bloch (note 231 above), p. 54: "The conscious human being . . . is—in the pursuit of the satisfaction of his wishes—an animal that makes detours."

356. For the "disenchantment fairytale" (*Erlösungsmärchen*) as a tale of mat-uration and development, see Laiblin (note 99 above), passim (for example, Jöckel, pp. 195–211). *Lebensläufe nach aufsteigender Linie* (Biographies advanc-ing progressively upward) is the title of a once widely read series of novels by Theodor Gottlieb von Hippel, which appeared between 1778 and 1781.

357. On the theme of transgressing boundaries, cf. the unpublished licentiate thesis of Käthi Knüsel-Hagmann, "Das Motif der verbotenen Türen: Versuch einer psychologischen Deutung" (Zürich, 1975); see also p. 151. According to Katalin Horn in *Der aktive und der passive Märchenheld* (Basel, 1983), the fairytale hero generally disregards a prohibition only then—but then almost regu-larly—when it leads him into adventure, bringing him into contact with the magical world (pp. 10, 48f).

358. *Rätoromanische Märchen* (note 103 above), p. 181; cf. the Kurt Ranke article "Abtragen der Schuhe" in EM.

359. See Singer (note 48 above), vol. 2 (1906; reprint, Munich-Pullach, 1971), pp. 28ff., his article "Aschenputtel" in HDM, and Marian Roalf Cox, *Cinderella* (London, 1893), pp. 437–62. Especially well-known is the Norwegian ash-peter, ash-sitter, or male Cinderella. (See Klara Stroebe and Reidar Th. Christiansen, eds., *Norwegische Volksmärchen*, MdW [1967], no. 35; cf. note 344 above.) But this figure can be found in numerous other places, as well, e.g., the Georgian ash-poker (*Kaukasische Märchen* [note 108 above], no. 2 [ = *Das Feuerpferd*, p. 69]). The expression *Goldenermärchen* ("tales of the golden one") was coined by Friederich Panzer. See his *Hilde-Gudrun: Eine Sagen- und literaturgeschichtliche Untersuchung* (Halle an der Saale, 1901), p. 251.

360. Hahn, no. 12; cf. p. 92. above and note 233.

361. Hahn, no. 19.

362. See "Rapunzel" in Lüthi 1975, pp. 62–96.

363. *Kroatische Märchen* (note 213 above), no. 1. In this Croatian fairytale, recorded in 1957, the radiant beauty of the girl is unmistakably set in relation to the years she endured in the form of an animal. Cf. p. 3. above for the motif of being "frozen in one's tracks" by the power of beauty.

364. *Provenzalische Märchen* (note 54 above), pp. 57f.

365. Christianity seems suspicious to more than one contemporary school of folktale research, to the followers of Jung because it simply rejects evil, instead of trying to integrate it; to the social critics because it functions as the "opium of the people" (Marx in the introduction to his *Kritik der Hegelschen Rechtsphilosophie* [1843/44], Karl Marx, Friedrich Engels, *Werke*, vol. 1 [Berlin, 1970], p. 178; cf. Klotz [note 390 below]). The latter is the basis on which Christa Bürger criticizes Lutz Röhrich, who calls it a "profound truth" that "real wealth can only be attained by overcoming initial poverty" ("Deutschunterricht und Volkskunde," *Der Deutschunterricht* 13, no. 1 [1961]: 94), and Lüthi, "who attributes 'Christian views' to the fairytale." (See Bürger, "Die soziale Funktion volkstümlicher Erzählformen: Sage und Märchen," in Heinz Ide, ed., *Projekt Deutschunterricht*, vol. 1 [Stuttgart, 1971], pp. 26f., 53; cf. Lüthi 1976, p. 88.) Even giving due regard to criticism of the propertied classes—who are pleased when the underprivileged cling to the idea that "true riches" are not material—it must be said that it is not really possible to relegate the function of religion and Christianity to that of "assuaging the poor," no more, or even less, than one can do so with the fairytale. On the surface the fairytale of magic shows very little that is specifically Christian. Mercy and grace play a small role, just as do Christian figures and institutions. Wealth and power are not in the least despised, but rather aspired to, the final goal being not something in another world but happiness in this one. Magic is delighted in, with help rarely coming from God but rather from anonymous powers. The fairytale is thus scarcely a creation of the Christian church. But in many respects it reflects something approximating Christian ideas and those of religion in general: Man is in need of help and salvation; there is a great gulf between appearance and reality; anything can change into its opposite, the last becoming first, the humble being raised up; he who is ready to sacrifice himself can as a result find himself; he who takes suffering onto himself can help himself and others (cf. note 83 above). Moreover, the abstractly stylizing fairytale has wealth and kingdom as closing apotheosis; it causes marriage to the princess to appear not as something fundamentally material but as a sign of achievement in life, thus as "true wealth." That the material, the satisfaction of purely sensual desires, is not the highest goal is a notion that—like anything else—can be abused, but it is nevertheless something essentially human—i.e., a notion belonging to man as man.

366. Not only in the old story from Apuleius, but also in fairytales recorded in the nineteenth and twentieth centuries. See Megas (note 35 above), pp. 8, 111–16; Megas emphasizes that this sort of help fits in better with the whole in oral variants than in Apuleius.

367. The term *dark figure (Dunkelgestalt)* is a coinage of the "Viennese Mythological School." "Bearskin" *(der Bärenhäuter)*, for example (AT 361, KHM 101), becomes "for a certain time a 'dark figure'" (Edmund Mudrak, *Hundert Volksmärchen* [Vienna, 1947], p. 528).

368. *Norwegische Volksmärchen* (note 359 above), no. 27 [ = Lüthi 1951, pp. 69ff.].

369. Carl Spitteler, "Das Kriterium der epischen Veranlagung," in *Lachende Wahrheiten*, 3d ed. (Jena, 1908), pp. 216ff. [ = *Gesammelte Werke*, vol. 7 (Zürich, 1947), pp. 18off.]: "the principal law of epic art [is] . . . to turn psychological states

into visible representations." Axel Olrik, 1909 (note 228 above), p. 8: "Each attribute of persons and things must be expressed in action; otherwise it is nothing." Thus writer and folklorist almost simultaneously (1908 and 1909) make similar pronouncements, apparently without knowing of one another—the first two editions of the *Lachende Wahrheiten* (1898, 1905) did not contain the article cited.

370. For the separate life of individual folktale elements (figures, props, and motifs) and the balance between their individual significance and their function within the whole, their structural roles, see p. 122.

371. See the Carolingian version of the so-called "Hoftagefabel" (AT 50 *The sick lion*) in Ernestus Duemmler, *Poetae Latini Aevi Carolini*, vol. 1 (Berlin, 1881), pp. 62ff.; German translation in Paul von Winterfeld, *Deutsche Dichter des lateinischen Mittelalters*, 4th ed. (Munich, 1922), pp. 140ff. Cf. the Kurt Ranke article "Abtragen der Schuhe" in EM.

372. See, for example, Cosquin (note 93 above).

373. *Balkanmärchen* (note 18 above), no. 46 (Serbo-Croatian).

374. Naumann-Mavrogordato (note 35 above), no. 4 (AT 303 and 302).

375. Geneviève Massignon, *Contes traditionnels des Teilleurs de lin du Trégor (Basse Bretagne)* (Paris, 1965), no. 3.

376. Uffer, pp. 63–81.

377. I am grateful to my colleague Ulrich Moser for the reference to Searles.

378. Schmitz, pp. 102, 259.

379. In conversation with me on 12 March 1975 in Stuttgart.

380. See Hermann Bausinger, "Volkssage und Geschichte," *Zeitschrift des Historischen Vereins für das württembergische Franken* 41 (1957): 1–23: "Man suffers more by acting than he achieves through it . . . the special value of these legends is that they simultaneously bring out the pathological side of historical events . . . therein also lies their truth" (p. 22). And in his *Formen der "Volkspoesie"* (Berlin, 1968), p. 182: "The local legend does not so much tell of great deeds as of great suffering . . . ; [it projects] a kind of counterhistory (*Gegengeschichte*)." On the portrait of man in the local legend, see also my two collections of articles, Lüthi 1975 and especially Lüthi 1970.

381. Ernst Bloch, *Verfremdungen*, vol. 1 (Frankfurt am Main, 1962), p. 159: "the spell (*Bann*) which, in contrast to the fairytale, emanates from the local legend." Christa Bürger (note 365 above), p. 51: "the local legend's fascination with the spell of fate (*Schicksalsbann*)"; p. 40: the narrators "held in the spell of their own ideology"; p. 43: "the spell-like (*bannhaft*) rigidity of the action in local legends"; p. 29: "the spell-like shock effect of the local legend"; p. 38: "Ignorance about society and nature takes on a spell-like form in the local legend."

382. Bürger, p. 26. The following quote appears on p. 37.

383. Friedrich Ranke, "Sage," in John Meier, ed., *Deutsche Volkskunde* (Berlin, 1926), p. 198: "narratives demonstrating the primitive science, history, and state of belief of the people." Cf. Bausinger's views in note 380 above.

384. See Lüthi 1970, pp. 19ff.

385. Examples can be found in Inez Diller-Sellschopp, ed., *Die Hexe von Patmos: Märchen von den griechischen Inseln*, Diederichs Löwenbuch series for children, vol. 8 (Düsseldorf/Cologne, 1974).

386. Ottokar Graf Wittgenstein, *Märchen, Träume, Schicksale* (Düsseldorf/Cologne, 1965). When Klaus F. Geiger, in opposition to this sort of argumentation, declares that it is more important to try to conquer anxiety by going into its real causes in children than "to compensate for anxiety by reading fairytales," this assertion is basically true, only the "real causes" can neither be fully done away with nor even completely determined; and the fairytale does not merely "compensate," it can be an impetus to and an aid in the "conquest" of anxiety on the level of

fantasy. Cf. the Geiger article "Angst" in EM with its references to Dieter Richter and Johannes Merkel, *Märchen, Phantasie und soziales Lernen* (Berlin, 1974), where it is suggested that childhood anxiety deriving from a feeling of powerlessness with respect to adults should be worked out by strengthening the child's independence, ability to make judgments, and ability to act, by dismantling the "super-ego structures" resulting from authoritarian upbringing, and by aiding the efforts of the child "to bring his needs and experiences into harmony" (see especially pp. 106–13). The difficulty of even determining the causes of anxiety is demonstrated by the fact that Freud in the last instance traces it back to the shock of being born, Heidegger makes it an aspect of the basic condition *(Grundbefindlichkeit)* of man—anxiety at "being in the world" *(In-der-Welt-Sein)*—and for Bloch it is the basic, partially historically and partially socially determined "feeling of negative expectation" *(negativer Erwartungsaffekt)*; see Bloch (note 231 above), pp. 121–26.

387. Novalis (note 218 above), vol. 4, p. 141, no. 2320.

388. Bürger (note 381 above), pp. 39ff.

389. Bürger, p. 51; Bloch (note 381 above), p. 159 and "Vier Reden" (text accompanying the recording *Es spricht Ernst Bloch*), p. 10. Paul Ludwig Sauer criticizes the position of Bloch and Bürger in "Märchen und Sage," *Wirkendes Wort* 23 (1973): 228–46.

390. Bloch (note 231 above), p. 412. While Christa Bürger, following Bloch, proclaims that "local legends portray social relationships as eternally unchangeable, something to which the individual must accomodate himself" (p. 34: "Local legends do not wish to change anything; much more, they support existing conditions"), other social critics complain of the same thing in the farce and the fairytale, the farce, to be sure, delighting in showing the intellectual superiority of the hired hand over the farmer or of the sexton over the vicar, and the fairytale even making the underprivileged king, but the hierarchy as such, "the class character of . . . the society," is left untouched. (Siegfried Neumann, *Der mecklenburgische Volksschwank* [Berlin, 1964], p. 63.) Here it is the fairytale that is "the opium of the people," a "pleasant, apparently harmless narcotic"; it "awakens no need at all to alter existing conditions" (Klotz, note 354 above, p. 82; cf. Marx, note 365 above). These interpretations are thus diametrically opposed. Both local legends (tyrant legends!), on the one hand, and farces and fairytales, on the other, contain elements of social criticism, but none of these genres comes across as strongly sociopolitical. Possibly they inhibit change to the degree that they contribute to the well-being of the individual, but calling them a narcotic for that reason seems misguided. Literature is at all levels an aid to living *(Lebenshilfe)*—for a long time this notion was unrightly rejected—and an aid to living always has stabilizing, sometimes dynamizing, but seldom revolutionary effects. This is no reason to run it down. Along with the ability to criticize and the will to change, it has been necessary for man, in all periods and under every political system, to display an appreciable amount of psychological balance and adaptability. It is not just the Gypsy who narrates for the "happiness and well-being" of his listeners (p. 52 above); kings also once took pleasure in being told fairytales. Fairytales are representations of good fortune in life (see p. 13 above and note 365). An individual's success in life, however, is not to be equated with individual or family egoism—and that is also true in the fairytale.

391. *Schweizer Volksmärchen* (note 120 above), no. 1.

392. In the opinion of Hermann Pongs, those (Grimms') fairytales which have heroines reflect more strongly the creative power and the depth of the unconscious, while the "masculine adventure tales" *(männliche Abenteuermärchen)* do

not lead "into the depths . . . where there are 'mother' archetypes." ("Lüthi's conception of the fairytale gets at the essence of the male hero: 'The fairytale is a world-encompassing adventure story with . . . a sublimating style.'") (Pongs, *Symbolik der einfachen Formen,* Das Bild in der Dichtung, vol. 4 [Marburg, 1973], pp. 66f., 84, 92, 106.) In my view, Cinderella's encounters with the prince; those of the Maid Maleen with the tower prison, with the false bride, and with the bridegroom she has chosen for herself; and those of Snow White with the dwarfs and with the dangerous peddler woman are certainly also "adventures," and one can find symbolic meaning in the masculine adventure tales of a depth comparable to that in tales having heroines. See my article "Abenteuer" in EM.

393. See Obenauer (note 351 above), p. 230: Things that had originally been believed could "only very slowly, through the fading . . . of the old belief . . . , become symbols." Leopold Schmidt, *Heiliges Blei* (Vienna, 1958), pp. 14f.: "The special attention, particularly the cult recognition, given to the 'holiness' of some material, form, or sign [is] often [related to] . . . the fact that it belonged to the everyday life of an epoch long since past." Richter and Merkel (note 386 above) take the opposite view: "The foreign nature of the historical representational material with which fairytales work makes it scarcely possible to connect these symbols with our own experience in any conscious way."

394. In the magazine *Eltern,* 1972 and 1973; collected as *Gmelin-Märchen,* Fibel, vol. 2 (Bad Homburg, n.d. [1973]).

395. Haiding (note 168 above), no. 13 ("Pechkappenhans").

396. Bloch (note 381 above), p. 159.

397. See Lüthi 1979, pp. 90ff., 107.

398. Friedrich Dürrenmat, *Friedrich Schiller* (Zürich, 1959), pp. 46f.

399. Such concern about the portrait of man is expressed, for example, in the Gottfried Korff article "Ahistorisch" in EM, and in Richter and Merkel (note 386 above); but where the latter maintain that the Jungian School "believes eternally valid archetypes [are] to be found in the fairytale" (p. 57), the assertion is true only to a limited degree (see p. 161f.).

400. Mircea Eliade, "Les savants et les contes de fées," *Nouvelle Revue Française* 4 (1956): 884–91; German translation "Wissenschaft und Märchen" in Karlinger (note 202 above), pp. 311–19.

401. First mentioned in *Instinkt und Unbewußtes* (Zürich, 1919). Jolande Jacobi *(Die Psychologie von C. G. Jung,* 4th ed. [Zürich, 1959], p. 57) states: "Jung took the term *archetype* from the *Corpus Hermeticum* (II. 140, 22; ed. Scott) [Walter Scott, ed., *Hermetica,* vol. 1 (Oxford, 1924), p. 140] and from Dionysius Areopagita's work *De divinis nominibus,* chap. 2, par. 6. . . . But above all it was the 'ideae principales' of St. Augustine that brought him to choose the term" (Aurelius Augustinus, *De diversis quaestionibus octoginta tribus,* question 46, par. 2); cf. the Gotthilf Isler article "Archetypus" in EM. Against Jung's (allegedly "backward captivated") conception of the archetype, Bloch (note 231 above, pp. 67–71, 181–87) sets his conception of archetypes which open up to the future, "emblems of the future with true utopian function" *(Embleme der Zukunft, in echter utopischer Funktion),* p. 185. For the history of the concept, see Ritter (note 231 above), cols. 497–500 (J. Hüllen). The expression appears frequently in Plotinus, who had already "argued that all souls finally merge and exist undifferentiated in a collective soul" (according to Hans Rudolf Schwyzer, "Archetyp und absoluter Geist: C. G. Jung und Plotin," *Neue Züricher Zeitung,* 26/27 July 1975 [no. 171], p. 38); see as well Schwyzer's article "The Intellect in Plotinus and the Archetypes of C. G. Jung," in J. Mansfeld and L. M. Rijk, eds., *Kephalaion: Studies in Greek Philosophy offered to Prof. C. J. de Vogel* (Assen, 1975), pp. 214–

22, where on p. 220 it is shown that in St. Augustine it is not "ideae principales" but "formae principales" that can perhaps be considered the translation of the Greek ἀρχέτυπα.

402. Without having recourse to the unconscious, Katalin Horn (note 357 above, p. 98) proposes a plausible explanation: "The peculiar morality of the fairytale admits of only one sensible way of using miracles. It is for that reason that the hero . . . is allowed to get possession of the magic objects by tricking their owners: The hero needs them for his task."

403. Hedwig von Beit (note 31 above), vol. 2 (1956; 2d ed., 1965), p. 417. See my review of von Beit in *Fabula* 2 (1959): 182–89 [ = Laiblin (note 99 above), pp. 391–403]; see particularly p. 400 in Laiblin.

404. Von Beit, vol. 1, p. 677.

405. See, for example, von Beit, vol. 2, p. 470.

406. Von Beit, vol. 2, p. 412. For a critique of the interpretation of the fairytale jointly authored by von Beit and Marie-Louise von Franz, see Hermann Bausinger, "Aschenputtel: Zum Problem der Märchensymbolik," *Zeitschrift für Volkskunde* 52 (1955): 144–55 [= Laiblin (note 99 above), pp. 284–98].

407. *Provenzalische Märchen* (note 54 above), no. 8 (Languedoc).

408. Ibid., no. 7 (Limousin); cf. "Ringerzählungen" in Lüthi 1975, pp. 118–44.

409. Kant, *Grundlegung zur Metaphysik der Sitten* (1785), sec. 2, par. 46.

410. C. G. Jung, *Seelenprobleme der Gegenwart* (Zürich, 1931), pp. 11f., as quoted in von Beit (note 31 above), vol. 1, p. 192. Cf. Marie Louise von Franz, "Das Problem des Bösen im Märchen," in *Das Böse: Studien aus dem C. G. Jung Institut* (Zürich/Stuttgart, 1961), pp. 91–126; Karl Schmid, "Aspekte des Bösen im Schöpferischen," ibid., pp. 237–60; and Friedrich Seifert, "Gut und Böse als Antinomie und als Polarität," in Adolf Guggenbühl-Craig, ed., *Der Archetyp: Verhandlungen des internationalen Kongresses für analytische Psychologie*, vol. 2 (Basel/New York, 1964), pp. 63–80.

411. With respect to the relationship real/nonreal in the fairytale, see the remarkable presentation by Bernd Wollenweber, "Märchenhaftes als sozial-kritische Literatur und Mitteilung von Erkenntnissen," in Heinz Ide and Bodo Lecke, eds., *Projekt Deutschunterricht*, vol. 6 (Stuttgart, 1974), pp. 13–64. Wollenweber's article, written with an eye to "the fairytale in the schools," emphasizes the "realism" of the fairytale narration: a simplified, condensed (literarily compressed and graphic) presentation of real (private and social) tensions, conflicts, and aims.

# INDEX OF TALE TYPES AND TALES

The first listing indexes references in the text to the Aarne-Thompson tale types (AT), both where the AT number is mentioned directly and where the tale type is mentioned but without number. The second listing indexes references to tales from the Grimms' *Kinder- und Hausmärchen* (KHM), again both where the Bolte-Polívka number is mentioned directly and where the Grimms' tale is referred to without number. The KHM listing is cross-referenced with the AT.

# GENERAL INDEX

Key words which have particular significance in the book are printed in italics. Common German technical terms are cross-referenced to their translations.